W9-AYZ-630

Pensions in the U.S. Economy

A National Bureau
of Economic Research
Project Report

Pensions in the U.S. Economy

Edited by Zvi Bodie
John B. Shoven, and
David A. Wise

The University of Chicago Press

Chicago and London

ZVI BODIE is professor of finance and economics at the School of
Management, Boston University, and a research associate of the
National Bureau of Economic Research.
JOHN B. SHOVEN is professor of economics at Stanford University
and a research associate of the National Bureau of Economic
Research.
DAVID A. WISE is the John F. Stambaugh Professor of Political
Economy at the John F. Kennedy School of Government, Harvard
University, and a research associate of the National Bureau of
Economic Research.

The University of Chicago Press, Chicago 60637
The University of Chicago Press, Ltd., London

Library of Congress Cataloging-in-Publication Data

Pensions in the U.S. economy / edited by Zvi Bodie,
    John B. Shoven, and David A. Wise.
        p.   cm. — (A National Bureau of Economic Research
    project report)
        Bibliography: p.
        Includes index.
        ISBN 0-226-06285-6
        1. Pension trusts—United States—Congresses. 2. Individual
    retirement accounts—United States—Congresses. I. Bodie, Zvi.
    II. Shoven, John B.   III. Wise, David A.   IV. Title: Pensions in
    the US economy.   V. Series.
    HD7105.45.U6P46   1988
    331.25'2'0973—dc19   87-19987
                                                                    CIP

Contents

Acknowledgments

This volume consists of papers presented at a conference held on 21–22 March 1985. It is part of NBER's ongoing project on the economics of the U.S. pension system. Most of the work reported here was sponsored by the U.S. Department of Health and Human Services. Additional work on the project has been supported by the following organizations: American Telephone and Telegraph Company, the Boeing Company, E. I. du Pont de Nemours & Company, Exxon Corporation, Ford Motor Company, IBM Corporation, the Lilly Endowment, the Proctor & Gamble Fund, and the Sarah Scaife Foundation, Inc.

Any opinions expressed in this volume are those of the respective authors and do not necessarily reflect the views of the National Bureau of Economic Research or any of the sponsoring organizations.

Introduction

Zvi Bodie, John B. Shoven, and David A. Wise

This is the fourth in a series of National Bureau of Economic Research (NBER) conference volumes on pensions in the United States. The first was *Financial Aspects of the United States Pension System,* the second, *Pensions, Labor, and Individual Choice,* and the third, *Issues in Pension Economics.*

This volume begins with a series of four papers on retirement saving of individuals and the saving which results from corporate funding of their pension plans. The first paper discusses individual retirement accounts (IRAs). The second considers reasons why more individual retirement saving is not used to purchase annuities. The third examines the reasons for recent reductions in saving through private pension plans. The fourth deals with poverty among retirees, whose saving preparation for retirement may have been inadequate. Following are two papers that address particular aspects of pension plans themselves: The first considers the relative merits of defined benefit versus defined contribution plans from the perspective of the employee wishing to avoid retirement income uncertainty. The second is an empirical investigation of the relationship between pension plan provisions and job turnover.

Individual and Corporate Retirement Saving Behavior

Individual Saving for Retirement: IRAs and Annuities

While increasingly large numbers of employees are covered by pension plans, many are not. In recognition of this fact, individual retire-

Zvi Bodie is a professor of finance and economics at the School of Management, Boston University, and a research associate of the National Bureau of Economic Research. John B. Shoven is a professor of economics at Stanford University and a research

ment accounts (IRAs) were established as part of the Employee Retirement Income Security Act (ERISA) to encourage employees without private plans to save for retirement. The Economic Recovery Tax Act of 1981, emphasizing the need to increase national saving as well as the need to prepare for retirement, extended the availability of IRAs to all employees. The principal incentive of IRAs for saving is that federal taxes on contributions and accrued interest are paid only when funds are withdrawn from the accounts. In particular, if the rate of return on saving is r $(1 - t)$, where t is the marginal tax rate, the return on IRAs is r. There is a penalty, however, for withdrawal of funds before age 59½, presumably to discourage using these tax-deferred saving vehicles for nonretirement purposes. Any employee can now contribute $2000 to an IRA each year; an employee and a nonworking spouse can contribute $2250. Recent tax proposals have suggested substantial increases in these limits.

"The Determinants of IRA Contributions and the Effect of Limit Changes" are analyzed by David A. Wise and Steven F. Venti. They find that IRAs are no more likely to be used by those without than by those with private pension plans, after controlling for income and other individual attributes. Thus, they do not, in general, serve as a substitute for private pension plans. Nonetheless, many persons with or without private plans who contribute to IRAs may save more than they otherwise would. An annual contribution of $2000 to an IRA represents much more in future retirement income than most private pension plans. The extent to which IRAs represent actual increases in individual saving, versus a substitute for other forms of saving, is not addressed in this paper, but this will be addressed in subsequent work by the authors.

About 72 percent of all contributors have incomes between $10,000 and $40,000, although only about 20 percent of persons in this income interval have an IRA. Only about 5 percent of employees with incomes less than $10,000 have IRAs, while approximately 60 percent of those with incomes greater than $100,000 do.

Although they are not typically substitutes for private pensions and are uncommon among low- income employees, IRA limit increases like those currently under consideration would lead to substantial increases in tax-deferred saving according to the estimates in the paper. For example, if both employee and spousal limits were raised to $2500, their estimates indicate that total IRA contributions would increase by about 30 percent.

associate of the National Bureau of Economic Research. David A. Wise is the John F. Stambaugh Professor of Political Economy at the John F. Kennedy School of Government, Harvard University, and a research associate of the National Bureau of Economic Research.

Model estimates based on Canadian Registered Retirement Savings Plan (RRSP) data, the counterpart of IRA and Keogh plans in the United States, are very similar to the U.S. estimates, even though the Canadian plan has been in effect since 1957 and the contribution limits are very different from those in the United States. Thus, similar parameter estimates in the two countries tend to lend support to the behavioral implications of the model specifications.

If saving for retirement is a major motivation for saving, it is puzzling that more of it does not take the form of the accumulation of annuities. Annuities have the advantage of insuring the individual against a very long life, thus tending to reduce the cost of financing a particular standard of living in retirement. They do have some disadvantages, of course. First, they leave no bequeathable wealth. Second, in the real world, annuities are not indexed for inflation, and, therefore, they are less adequate in providing long life insurance than indexed annuities would be. Third, the private voluntary annuity market suffers from adverse selection. Those who purchase them tend to live longer than the general population, so there is less risk pooling than with universal participation.

Friedman and Warshawsky provide an interesting examination of why the market for individual annuities is so thin. In the first section of their paper, they provide the first careful computation of the "load factor" charged by insurance companies on annuity policies. That is, they compare the cost of the annuity with the expected present value of the benefits evaluated at two market interest rates. When they do this calculation using general population mortality assumptions, they find that the load factor ranges from 20 percent to 55 percent, depending on the issuing company and the interest rate assumption. When they take account of the better mortality experience of annuity purchasers (the adverse selection problem, from the point of view of the insurance company), the load factor ranges from 6 percent to 40 percent. The average load factor is in the 25 percent range. This is not above the load factor for other types of insurance policies.

Friedman and Warshawsky develop an extended version of the life-cycle saving and portfolio behavior model which incorporates a bequest motive, uncertain lifetimes, and the presence of Social Security. They find, for reasonable parameterizations of their model, that the load factor would have to be much larger than they calculate it to be in order to account for observed behavior in the absence of a bequest motive. However, they find that a modest weight on bequests in lifetime utility can lead to model behavior consistent with observations. Their paper, thus, indicates that it is the structure of preferences at least as much as the load factor which is responsible for the predominance of saving in forms other than annuities.

Corporate Saving for Retirement

Bernheim and Shoven's paper, "Pension Funding and Saving," first documents a series of facts regarding the funding of corporate and government pensions as a source of loanable funds saving in the economy. They find that despite the fact that 70 percent of pension plans are defined contribution, 70 percent of assets and participants are covered by defined benefit plans. Clearly, defined benefit plans are much larger on average. They also note that the net contributions (net of payouts) to pensions are a major and growing part of personal saving in the economy. In the 1950s, pension accumulations amounted to roughly a quarter of personal saving; in the second half of the 1970s, pensions accounted for more than half of personal saving; and in the first four years of the 1980s, pensions accounted for 92 percent of personal saving.

The main point of the Bernheim-Shoven paper, however, is that pension saving may be the answer to why personal saving has not increased in spite of the several saving and investment incentives enacted by the Reagan administration. Defined benefit pensions, by their very nature, have negative contribution elasticities with respect to the rate of return on financial securities. That is, the higher the earnings on the pension fund assets, the lower are new contributions. To see this, one simply needs to look at a defined benefit pension plan from the perspective of the firm. The firm has pension obligations based on its employees' salaries and years of service. In order to compute the adequacy of its funding of those promises, the firm typically projects the future obligations and then discounts them to obtain their present value using an assumed interest rate (which amounts to the assumed rate of return on assets funding the plan). It then compares this derived expected present value of liabilities to the pension fund's assets to compute the unfunded liability and to determine the appropriate level of contributions. Clearly, this is the classic example of target saving, and a higher rate of return permits meeting the target with lower contribution levels.

Bernheim and Shoven estimate the magnitude of the negative elasticity both econometrically and with a simple analytic model. The two approaches lead to consistent conclusions. Namely, they find that the negative elasticity is large and significant for net pension contributions. A 1 percentage point increase in real interest rates, for instance, is predicted to decrease net pension contributions in the long run by between 20 and 30 percent. Such sensitivity is consistent with the recent weakness in pension funding and in personal saving in general in the United States.

Inadequacies in Saving of Current Retirees

In their paper "Poverty among the Elderly: Where Are the Holes in the Safety Net?" Michael J. Boskin and John B. Shoven supplement previous research, which has concentrated on the elderly as a whole or on representative elderly, with an in-depth examination of those who end up poor in retirement. First, they find that a nontrivial fraction of the elderly in the Retirement History Survey (those where the household head was born between 1905 and 1911) either remained poor, became poor, or had a much lower standard of living in retirement than earlier in their life. This occurred despite the enormous general improvement of the economic status of the elderly, part of which was made possible by very large increases in real Social Security benefits.

Examination of the characteristics of those who fell through the safety net reveals that women, especially widows, were the most likely candidates for economic difficulty in this cohort in this stage of their lives.

A variety of other variables seem to be related to the probability of low incomes and/or low replacement rates. For example, those who retired relatively early tended to be more likely to be poor and/or to have low replacement rates. This partly reflects particular institutional features surrounding Social Security and its double indexing for a brief period, but it also reflects in part factors influencing retirement in the first place.

A variety of other intriguing findings are mentioned, including the sharp differences in realizations of retirement income expectations among those who were poor and/or had low replacement rates relative to those who did well. Perhaps much of this seems self-evident in retrospect, but it is important to attempt to get behind these numbers to the reasons why these events occurred. Undoubtedly, many of them had case-specific causes. The results of this study suggest a need for further research on the structure and nature of the survivorship and annuity features of pensions; the coverage and marital status provisions of Social Security; as well as a more detailed study of the relationships between actual retirement income outcomes and expectations.

Corporate Pension Financing and Employee Pension Effects

Corporate Funding and Investment Policy

In "Defined Benefit versus Defined Contribution Pension Plans: What Are the Real Trade-offs?" Zvi Bodie, Alan J. Marcus, and Robert C. Merton concentrate on the differences between defined benefit and defined contribution plans from the point of view of the employee. Their emphasis is on the risk aspects of the two types of plans.

Defined benefit (DB) and defined contribution (DC) pension plans have significantly different characteristics with respect to the risks faced by employers and employees, the sensitivity of benefits to inflation, the flexibility of funding, and the importance of governmental supervision. Bodie, Marcus, and Merton examine some of the main trade-offs involved in the choice between DB and DC plans. Their most general conclusion is that neither type of plan can be said to wholly dominate the other from the perspective of employee welfare.

The major advantage of DB plans is their potential for providing a stable replacement rate of final income to workers. The pegging of benefits in DB plans to final average wage would appear to provide employees with a type of income maintenance insurance not available in DC plans. This conclusion is, however, not robust. If wage paths are unpredictable at the start of a career, then individuals may view it as very risky to have their retirement benefits depend so heavily on final salary. Indeed, employees might prefer a retirement benefit tied to inflation-adjusted career average earnings to eliminate excessive dependence on the realized wage in the final years of employment. This time-averaging feature is achieved by a DC plan because benefits will depend on the contribution in each year of service, rather than on a final wage formula. Although inflation-adjusted career average DB plans would achieve the same goal, in practice these plans are quite rare. In fact, the only major DB plan that pays a benefit computed in such a fashion is the Social Security system.

It is often asserted that a DC plan subjects an employee to the investment risk associated with the performance of the fund's assets, whereas in a DB plan such risk is absent. However, it is always feasible for a DC plan to select an investment strategy which has low risk even in *real* terms. There are, however, no strong *a priori* reasons to believe that most individuals would choose to invest accumulated DC funds in the lowest risk asset. DC plans typically offer employees sufficient flexibility to select a risk-return strategy suited to their individual preferences and circumstances. In contrast, DB plans force individuals to accumulate the pension portion of their retirement savings in the form of nominal deferred life annuities and thus limit their risk-return choice.

DB plans have accrual patterns which are inherently backloaded. DC plans can be backloaded too by choosing a contribution rate that rises with a worker's age and tenure. Therefore, the salient inherent differences in accrual patterns between the two plan designs is that DB backloading is stochastic in the sense that real benefit accruals depend upon the rate of wage inflation. This seems to be an avoidable source of uncertainty which both parties (employer and employee) might benefit by shedding.

It is commonly assumed that considerations of portability favor DC plans. The typical justification is that the worker in a DB plan who leaves his job for reasons beyond his control forfeits future indexation of benefits already accrued. It is further asserted that there are implicit contracts between employees and firms which require larger total compensation (wage plus pension accrual) for more highly tenured workers. Hence, termination of employment causes a forfeiture of the ability to work for advantageous total compensation rates in particular, indexation of total pension accruals). Under this line of reasoning, DC plans are more portable. Clearly this advantage of DC plans is most apparent during periods of inflation.

The authors conclude that neither type of plan can be said to wholly dominate the other from the point of view of the employee. Whether one is better than the other depends both on employee preferences and on uncertainty about inflation and interest rates.

Individual Benefits and Incentive Effects

To find out what the incentive effects of pension plans are, Edward P. Lazear and Robert L. Moore in "Pensions and Turnover" analyze the relationship between pension plan versions and worker turnover. There are two primary innovations in this empirical work: First, they use data from six different firms that include information on the precise provisions of the firms' pension plans. There is considerable variation in the individual plans' provisions. Second, instead of considering the relationship between accrued pension wealth and the probability of leaving the firm at a particular age, the authors consider the option value of retirement now versus working for an additional year. The option of working an additional year allows the employee the chance to choose the best of subsequent retirement years. For example, an employee who enters the plan with a ten-year vesting period has no accrued pension wealth during the first ten years. Nonetheless, working during the third year, for example, instead of retiring at the end of the second year, brings the worker nearer to the year in which he will be vested. The option of working until the vesting year is not foreclosed if the person remains with the firm. The authors argue that at any age the option value of continuing work is the appropriate variable to include in a regression framework.

The authors' initial results show that a 10 percent increase in the option value reduces the probability of turnover for older workers by 1 percent. They predict turnover rates to be twice as high for workers without pensions as for those with average pensions. The actual change in turnover is predicted to be 4 percent instead of 9 percent for workers without pension plans. The paper also investigates empirically the difference in the implications for turnover of the two measures of pension value, that is, the more commonly used accrued pension wealth versus the pension option value as defined by the authors.

1   The Determinants of IRA Contributions and the Effect of Limit Changes

Steven F. Venti and David A. Wise

To encourage employees not covered by private pension plans to save for retirement, individual retirement accounts (IRAs) were established in 1974 as part of the Employee Retirement Income Security Act (ERISA). Emphasizing the need to enhance economic well-being of future retirees and the need to increase national saving, the Economic Recovery Tax Act of 1981 extended the availability of IRAs to all employees and raised the contribution limit. Now (1985) any employee with earnings in excess of $2000 can contribute up to $2000 to an IRA account each year, with tax deferred on the principle and interest until money is withdrawn from the account. The combined contribution of an employee and a nonworking spouse can be as high as $2250. A married couple who are both working can contribute $2000 each. A proposed change in the law contemplates raising the individual IRA limit to $2500 and the (nonworking) spousal IRA limit from $2250 to $2500.

Tax-deferred saving is potentially an important component of saving for retirement and could represent a very substantial increase in tax-free saving for many employees. Indeed, a $2000 contribution to a retirement account represents a future pension benefit greater than many employer-provided private pension plans. The availability of IRAs may also have a substantial effect on national saving. According to IRS data, total IRA contributions in 1982 were over $29 billion.

Steven F. Venti is an assistant professor of economics at Dartmouth College and a faculty research fellow of the National Bureau of Economic Research. David A. Wise is the John F. Stambaugh Professor of Political Economy at the John F. Kennedy School of Government, Harvard University, and a research associate of the National Bureau of Economic Research.

The final version of this paper has benefited from the comments of Gary Burtless. The research was funded in part by the Department of Health and Human Services (HHS) grant #67A-83 and in part by HHS grant #84ASPE130A.

Despite the program's size and potential significance, surprisingly little is known about the determinants of IRA contributions. Thus the goals of this paper are: (1) to analyze the effect of individual attributes on whether a person contributes to IRAs, (2) to determine the effect of individual attributes on how much is contributed, and (3) to simulate the effect of potential changes in contribution limits on the amount contributed to IRAs. The results can be used to judge whether the goals that justified introducing the program are being realized. Obviously, persons who do not contribute to IRA accounts will not benefit from them. With national concern about the federal deficit, the short-run tax cost of the program is of substantial interest. The simulations suggest what this cost is and what the cost of proposed changes in the program would be. A fourth issue, the effect of tax-deferred saving on net individual saving, is not addressed in this paper but will be analyzed in future work.

This analysis is based on data obtained through a special supplement of the May 1983 Current Population Survey (CPS). Subsequent analysis will be based on the 1983 Survey of Consumer Finances and a special Carnegie Commission Survey of college and university employees.

Descriptive statistics on contributions to IRA accounts are presented in section 1.1. The statistical model used in the analysis is described in section 1.2. The results are presented in section 1.3, and in section 1.4, results of a similar analysis based on Canadian data (Wise 1985) are compared with results for the United States. The Registered Retirement Savings Plan (RRSP) in Canada is a tax-deferred program that incorporates the characteristics of both IRA and Keogh-like plans in the United States, although the contribution limits are quite different in the two countries. The same statistical model has been estimated on data from both countries.

The major empirical findings may be summarized briefly: tax-deferred saving plans are unlikely to be used by low-income persons. Thus they do not in general substitute for private pension plans, since higher-income persons are more likely than those with lower incomes to be covered by private plans. Given income and other individual characteristics, persons with private pension plans are no less likely than those without such plans to contribute to an IRA. The findings for Canada are very similar to those for the United States. Since the contribution limits are very different, the similar findings support the statistical specification.

Simulations based on the parameter estimates for the United States indicate that if the limits were increased in accordance with the recently proposed Treasury Department changes to the tax system, contributions would increase by about 30 percent.

1.1 Descriptive Statistics

Since model parameter estimates for the United States will ultimately be compared with those for Canada, descriptive statistics for both countries are presented in this section. For several reasons the data for the two countries are not strictly comparable, but they allow rough comparisons.

Most contributions are made by middle-income employees. Although nearly 32 percent of employed persons in the United States have incomes below $10,000, this group is responsible for only about 10 percent of total IRA contributions. Approximately 80 percent of contributions are made by persons with incomes between $10,000 and $50,000. Persons with incomes greater than $50,000 contribute only about 10 percent of total contributions. In Canada, about 82 percent of contributions are made by individuals with incomes between $10,000 and $50,000, and about 15 percent by persons with incomes above $50,000. Only 3 percent of contributions are made by those with incomes below $10,000, compared with 10 percent in the United States (see table 1.1).

As shown in table 1.2, only 5 percent of persons with incomes less than $10,000 made an IRA contribution in 1982 in the United States, and only about 2 percent in Canada. The proportions of higher-income groups making contributions are similar in the United States and Canada, although in general the proportions are lower in the United States than in Canada. Whereas the IRA program is new for most people in the United States, the Canadian RRSP plan was started in 1957.

Only 11 percent of all contributors in the United States have incomes less than $10,000, 80 percent have incomes between $10,000 and $50,000, and about 9 percent have incomes greater than $50,000. Again, the percentages in Canada are very similar to those in the United States. Over 6 percent of contributors have incomes less than $10,000, about 87.5 percent have incomes between $10,000 and $50,000, and 7 percent have incomes greater than $50,000.

Proportions of individuals that contribute to the contribution limits in the two countries are shown in table 1.3. Because the contribution limits vary substantially between the two countries, the numbers must be viewed accordingly.[1] In neither country does the proportion contributing to the limit in any income group exceed 60 percent. In addition, women are apparently more likely than men to contribute to the limit in the United States, whereas in Canada the difference seems less apparent, although at least for persons with incomes below $50,000 the proportion for women is greater than for men, with the exception of the $0–$10,000 income group.

Table 1.1   **Percent Distribution of Individuals and of Contributions, by Income Interval[a]**

Income Interval[b]	United States		Canada	
	Percent of Employed Individuals	Percent of IRA Contributions[c]	Percent of Tax Filers	Percent of RRSP Contributions
0–10	31.7	9.9	46.3	2.9
10–20	35.8	26.1	31.0	21.8
20–30	19.8	26.5	15.4	32.0
30–40	7.7	18.1	4.3	18.2
40–50	2.6	9.1	1.5	9.9
50–60			0.6	5.3
50–70	1.6	6.5	—	—
60–70	—	—	0.3	3.0
70–80			0.2	2.0
70+	0.8	3.8	—	—
80–90	—	—	0.1	1.2
90–100	—	—	0.1	0.8
100+	—	—	0.3	3.0

[a]The Canadian data pertain to 1980 and the U.S. data to 1982. Tabulations for the United States are in U.S. dollars and those for Canada in Canadian dollars. Data for the United States are from the May 1983 CPS and supplemental Survey of Pension and Retirement Plan Coverage. The data are weighted to represent the employed population, ages 18–65, excluding the self-employed. The Canadian data are based on a random sample of tax filers and are weighted to represent all tax filers.

[b]In thousands.

[c]Calculations are based on midpoints of reported IRA contribution intervals (see appendix B).

Average contributions in the United States range from $75 for the lowest income group to $1116 for those with incomes greater than $70,000; while the average contribution of contributors ranges from $1517 to $1883 (see table 1.4). This suggests that among those who contribute, a large proportion in each income group contributes at the limit. Unreported tabulations indicate that at very high income levels 85–90 percent of all contributions are at the limit. The percentage of employees with contributions at the limit ranges from about 3 percent for low-income to about 50 percent for high-income employees. The figures for Canada are comparable, but the average contribution levels are considerably higher, reflecting the higher limits. In addition, the Canadian data pertain to both employees and self-employed persons,

Table 1.2   **Percent with Contributions Greater than Zero and Percent of Total Contributors, by Income Interval[a]**

Income Interval[b]	Percent with Contribution > 0		Percent of Total Contributors	
	United States	Canada	United States	Canada
0–10	5.0	1.9	10.9	6.6
10–20	11.3	13.4	28.0	31.8
20–30	19.2	28.0	26.5	33.1
30–40	32.4	45.1	17.2	14.9
40–50	44.9	56.9	8.2	7.7
50–60	—	59.5	—	2.9
50–70	53.5	—	5.8	—
60–70	—	58.5	—	1.4
70–80	—	63.0	—	0.8
70+	59.3	—	3.4	—
80–90	—	63.0	—	0.5
90–100	—	62.6	—	0.4
100+	—	53.6	—	1.0

[a]The Canadian data pertain to 1980 and the U.S. data to 1982. Tabulations for the United States are in U.S. dollars and those for Canada in Canadian dollars. Data for the United States are from the May 1983 CPS and supplemental Survey of Pension and Retirement Plan Coverage. The data are weighted to represent the employed population, ages 18–65, excluding the self-employed. The Canadian data are based on a random sample of tax filers and are weighted to represent all tax filers.

[b]In thousands.

[c]Calculations are based on midpoints of reported IRA contribution intervals (see appendix B).

while the U.S. data pertain only to employees and thus exclude contributions to Keogh plans.

Individuals covered by private pension plans in the United States tend to make somewhat larger contributions than those who are not, and they are also somewhat more likely to make contributions at the limit, as shown in table 1.5. In Canada, the limit on RRSP contributions increases with income and the maximum is higher for persons without than for those with a private plan. Thus for high-income persons, contributions are higher for those without private plans. Nonetheless, for most income intervals those *with* a private pension plan are more likely to contribute at the limit.

In summary, the descriptive data indicate that IRAs are typically not used by low-income employees, and that they do not in general serve as a substitute for private pension plans.

Table 1.3   **Percent with Contributions at the Limit, by Income Interval and Sex[a]**

Income Interval[b]	United States		Canada	
	Men	Women	Men	Women
0–10	1.0	3.7	0.7	0.6
10–20	3.8	9.2	2.8	4.1
20–30	10.5	19.5	6.3	12.9
30–40	21.8	33.4	17.3	25.1
40–50	35.5	41.0	34.0	36.7
50–60	—	—	38.8	33.3
50–70	44.4	58.1	—	—
60–70	—	—	45.6	29.9
70–80	—	—	49.4	31.0
70+	51.0	30.7	—	—
80–90	—	—	51.9	30.5
90–100	—	—	51.3	24.7
100+	—	—	45.7	19.0

[a]The Canadian data pertain to 1980 and the U.S. data to 1982. Tabulations for the United States are in U.S. dollars and those for Canada in Canadian dollars. Data for the United States are from the May 1983 CPS and supplemental Survey of Pension and Retirement Plan Coverage. The data are weighted to represent the employed population, ages 18–65, excluding the self-employed. The Canadian data are based on a random sample of tax filers and are weighted to represent all tax filers.

[b]In thousands.

1.2 The Statistical Model

The results suggest that relatively unambiguous answers can be provided to the three questions addressed in this paper. On the other hand, an analysis of the effect of tax-deferred accounts on net saving will require related but new and somewhat more complicated statistical procedures, and it seems apparent that this question will be answered with more ambiguity and less confidence than the first three. Thus it is important to set forth the analysis so that questions that can be answered relatively precisely can be distinguished from those that inherently leave room for doubt. To put the analysis conducted in this paper in perspective, it may be useful to illustrate how it is related to a more general analysis designed to estimate the net effect of tax-deferred accounts on individual saving. With this goal in mind, a simple but general illustrative model is described first. It serves to motivate statistical analysis of each of the three questions discussed in this paper, while providing a framework within which the fourth question can be

Table 1.4   **Average Contribution, by Income Interval[a]**

	United States			Canada		
Income Interval[b]	Average[c]	Average, Given Contribution > 0[c]	Percent with Contribution at Limit	Average	Average, Given Contribution > 0	Percent with Contribution at Limit[d]
0–10	$ 75	$1517	2.8	$ 16	$ 834	0.7
10–20	176	1564	6.5	176	1315	3.3
20–30	324	1685	12.9	520	1858	7.6
30–40	571	1762	23.3	1059	2346	18.0
40–50	838	1865	35.8	1637	2877	34.3
50–60	—	—	—	2078	3493	38.2
50–70	1010	1887	45.4	—	—	—
60–70	—	—	—	2489	4181	43.5
70+	1116	1883	49.6	—	—	—
70–80	—	—	—	2899	4604	47.4
80–90	—	—	—	2951	4687	49.2
90–100	—	—	—	2960	4731	48.4
100+	—	—	—	2843	5306	41.8

NOTE: The figures for the United States are *not* comparable becuase the contribution limits are different in the two countries.

[a]The Canadian data pertain to 1980 and the U.S. data to 1982. Tabulations for the United States are in U.S. dollars and those for Canada in Canadian dollars. Data for the United States are from the May 1983 CPS and supplemental Survey of Pension and Retirement Plan Coverage. The data are weighted to represent the employed population, ages 18–65, excluding the self-employed. The Canadian data are based on a random sample of tax filers and are weighted to represent all tax filers.

[b]In thousands.

[c]Calculations are based on midpoints of reported IRA contribution intervals (see appendix B).

[d]Taken to be greater than or equal to 95 percent of actual limit.

addressed. It demonstrates succinctly how the first three questions are related to the fourth. The illustrative model also provides motivation for treating the first three separately from the fourth, although in principle, one general model could be used to address all four questions jointly. Estimation procedures designed to answer the first three questions are then considered, with particular attention given to whether a correctly specified, single behavioral equation can be used to describe both zero and positive levels of tax-deferred saving, or whether two behavioral relationships—one describing whether a person is a potential contributor and the other the desired IRA contribution—are required.

Table 1.5   **Average Contributions and Percent with Contribution at the Limit, by Income Interval and Private Pension Coverage[a]**

Income Interval[b]	United States				Canada			
	Employees with Private Pension		Employees without Private Pension		Employees with RPP Contribution[d]		Employees without RPP Contribution[e]	
	$[c]	% at L	$[c]	% at L	$	% at L	$	% at L
0–10	138	5.3	61	2.2	54	1.9	17	0.7
10–20	190	7.2	161	5.7	188	3.5	161	3.0
20–30	342	13.7	275	10.7	494	9.1	568	5.1
30–40	588	24.1	516	20.9	830	22.8	1305	12.4
40–50	883	38.2	650	25.9	983	39.3	2429	30.2
50–60	—	—	—	—	1199	45.0	2654	31.9
50–70	1073	48.5	809	35.7	—	—	—	—
60–70	—	—	—	—	1381	47.9	2968	38.1
70 +	1170	51.7	978	44.0	—	—	—	—
70–80	—	—	—	—	1355	40.0	3655	50.0
80–90	—	—	—	—	1724	44.6	3396	50.1
90–100	—	—	—	—	1397	41.7	3646	51.3
100 +	—	—	—	—	1503	37.8	3641	47.1

[a]The Canadian data pertain to 1980 and the U.S. data to 1982. Tabulations for the United States are in U.S. dollars and those for Canada in Canadian dollars. Data for the United States are from the May 1983 CPS and supplemental Survey of Pension and Retirement Plan Coverage. The data are weighted to represent the employed population, ages 18–65, excluding the self-employed. The Canadian data are based on a random sample of tax filers and are weighted to represent all tax filers.

[b]In thousands.

[c]Calculations are based on midpoints of reported IRA contribution intervals (see appendix B).

[d]Contributes to a Registered Pension Plan (RPP).

[e]The vast majority of this group do not have a pension plan.

1.2.1   A General Illustrative Model

Decisions about the amount to save in various forms are undoubtedly made jointly so that one decision cannot be considered fixed while the other is made. In addition, unmeasured individual attributes are likely to affect decisions about saving in each of two or more different forms. Thus persons who are observed to save more in one form are also likely to save more in another, not because saving in one form induces them to save more in another but rather because they are more inclined to save in any form. This means that one must disentangle the effects of individual-specific attributes from the effect that saving in one form has on saving in another.

The procedure outlined here addresses these problems by considering an individual's preferred allocation of current income to current consumption, tax-deferred saving, and other forms of saving, and then by considering how observed choices are affected by the limit on the tax-deferred saving alternative. Based on such a model, it would be possible to simulate, for example, how total saving would be changed if the limit on tax-deferred saving were raised or lowered. The procedure relies heavily on the fact that the optimal saving behavior of individuals who are not constrained by the limit differs from the behavior of those who are, with a statistical correction for the fact that persons who are at the limit, everything else equal, are likely to have a greater preference for saving than those who are not constrained; they are likely to save more in any form. In practice, the idea is to estimate the parameters of a "preference" function whose primary arguments are IRA contributions, at least one other form of saving, and current consumption. Associated with the preference function are optimal IRA contributions and optimal saving in other forms. In practice, it is necessary to choose these "demand" functions to fit the observable data and then to choose the preference function consistent with them. The procedure can be illustrated by a simple preference function.

Suppose that preferences for consumption and saving out of current income may be described by the simple form:

(1) $$V = (Y - S_1 - S_2)^{1-\beta_1-\beta_2} S_1^{\beta_1} S_2^{\beta_2},$$

where Y is income, S_1 and S_2 are tax-deferred saving and other saving, respectively, and β_1 and β_2 are parameters to be estimated. This function is intended to represent preferences over possible allocations of current income conditional on individual attributes like income and age, and on individual perceptions of the riskiness of different forms of saving.[2] This approach allows inferences about the relationship of income allocation to age without constraining the functional form to correspond to a particular life-cycle hypothesis. In practice, the parameters would depend upon measured individual attributes and would be allowed to vary randomly among individuals to capture unmeasured variation in individual preferences for current versus future consumption as well as different perceptions of risk, and so forth. In this simple case, the unconstrained optimal saving choices are

(2) $$S_1 = \beta_1 Y, \text{ and}$$

$$S_2 = \beta_2 Y.$$

But in fact, the optimal choice is subject to a constraint; S_1 contributions cannot be greater than the IRA limit L. Until this limit is reached, contributions obey the equations above. But more generally the S_1 and S_2 functions are of the form:

(3)
$$S_1 = \begin{cases} \beta_1 Y & \text{if } \beta_1 Y < L, \\ L & \text{if } \beta_1 Y \geq L, \end{cases}$$

$$S_2 = \begin{cases} \beta_2 Y & \text{if } \beta_1 Y < L, \\ \dfrac{\beta_2}{1-\beta_1}(Y - L) & \text{if } \beta_1 Y \geq L. \end{cases}$$

Thus there are two S_2 saving functions. As long as the IRA limit has not been reached, saving obeys the optimizing rule $\beta_2 Y$. But after the limit is reached, the saving function is of the form $[\beta_2/(1-\beta_1)](Y-L)$. This illustration ignores the tax deferment that makes IRAs more attractive than alternative forms of retirement saving. Introducing the tax rate in the example changes the utility function to

(4) $V = [Y(1 - t) - S_1(1 - t) - S_2]^{1-\beta_1-\beta_2} S_1^{\beta_1} S_2^{\beta_2},$

where, assuming that saving is small relative to income, t is the marginal tax rate. The optimal saving choices then become

$$S_1 = \begin{cases} \beta_1 Y & \text{if } \beta_1 Y < L, \\ L & \text{if } \beta_1 Y \geq L, \end{cases}$$

$$S_2 = \begin{cases} \beta_2 Y(1 - t) & \text{if } \beta_1 Y < L, \\ \dfrac{\beta_2}{1 - \beta_1}(Y - L)(1 - t) & \text{if } \beta_1 Y \geq L. \end{cases}$$

In this formulation, the marginal tax rate does not affect S_1 (IRA) saving, unless it affects preferences for current versus future consumption through the parameters β_1 and β_2. The empirical findings reported below suggest an uncertain effect of the marginal tax rate independent of income, even though the rate of return on IRAs does depend on the marginal tax rate.

In practice, the parameters β_1 and β_2 would be made functions of individual characteristics like age, occupation, possibly income itself, the tax rate, and other conditioning variables that would likely determine individual preferences of possible allocations of current income. To estimate the model, it is also necessary to choose a stochastic specification for the βs. One also needs to choose a specification that allows optimal, or "desired", values S_1 and S_2 to be negative, since many individuals will not save in any form and indeed will borrow.[3]

As emphasized above, this particular functional form is only for illustrative purposes; the form that is ultimately chosen must be determined by the data. But this simple example demonstrates how changes in the limit may affect behavior. In particular, explicit reference to a preference function assures a specification of saving S_2 after the limit L on S_1 is reached that is internally consistent with the function that applies before the limit is reached. And, in a fully specified model, estimates of the βs could be used to simulate the effects of changes in the limit L on total saving, not just the effect on tax-deferred saving.[4] Estimation of only the S_1 function is treated in this paper.[5]

1.2.2   Independent Analysis of Contributions to Tax-Deferred Saving Accounts

Within the general framework described above, one can treat the tax-deferred saving equation separately. At least two important issues must be addressed in order to analyze determinants of IRA contributions. The first is simply that in addition to the upper limit on contributions, many individuals, indeed the majority, do not contribute anything at all to IRA (or Keogh) accounts. The standard way to conduct an analysis in this situation would be to use a Tobit model with a lower truncation point at zero and an upper truncation point at the contribution limit. The second issue, however, is that the determinants of whether one contributes at all may be different from the determinants of how much one contributes once an account is established. While it is true that the short-run effect of changes in contribution limits on total contributions is determined only by initial contributors, there may be considerably more room to change total contributions through increasing the number of persons who contribute than by increasing the contributions of current contributors. It is important, therefore, to understand the determinants of the contributor status decision.

Key Issues

To provide accurate predictions of the determinants of IRA contributions and of the effect on contributions of changes in the existing contribution limits, the most important consideration in estimation is to account for the existing limit on observed contributions. Thus, an intuitive discussion of the effect of the limit on estimation, together with procedures that can be used to correct for it, helps to put the important ideas in perspective, although part of the discussion will be familiar to many readers. Mathematical details of the estimation procedure are presented in appendix A.

Consider first figure 1.1. Suppose that the relationship between income and IRA contributions if there were no contribution limits would be represented by the solid line $a + bY$. That is, given Y the average (expected) contribution would be $a + bY$. Of course, for any level of income Y there would be a distribution of contribution levels, represented by the vertical lines; not everyone with income level Y would contribute the same amount. Now suppose that everyone in the sample faced a contribution limit L. We would now observe no contributions above L, and presumably individuals who otherwise would contribute

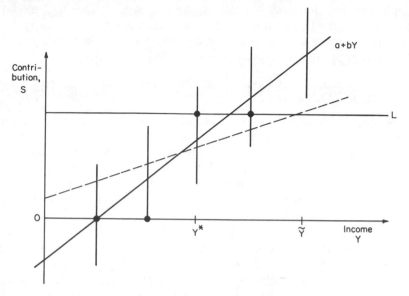

Fig. 1.1   Effect of contribution limits on estimation.

above this limit would in the face of the limit contribute at the limit. This would give rise to a concentration of contributions at the limit, indicated by the heavy dots at that level. In addition, it is not possible to contribute less than zero; we would observe a concentration of points at zero, indicated by the heavy dots along the horizontal axis. If we think of fitting a line, say by least squares, to the data points that are actually observed, we would obtain a fitted line something like the dashed line in the figure.

Suppose that from this fitted line we attempted to predict the relationship between income and contributions S. It is easy to see that this estimate would be a very substantial underprediction. Thus it is clear that standard estimation procedures will not lead to plausible conclusions in this case. And it should also be clear from the figure that the reason is that observed contributions do not represent the contributions that individuals would like to make were they not constrained by the limit.

It is also useful to consider the distribution of contributions for persons with a particular level of income, say Y^*. An illustration of such a distribution is show in figure 1.2. If it were not for the limit at L and the limit at zero, the distribution of contributions S would look something like a bell-shaped curve. But as demonstrated in figure 1.1, we know that we will not observe contributions greater than L, and we will observe no contributions less than zero. The distribution of observed contributions between zero and L would look just like the underlying curve. But instead of a distribution tapering off smoothly to the right and to the left, there would be concentrations of contributions at L and at zero.

The standard Tobit maximum likelihood estimation procedure that takes account of this truncation effect is based on an assumed underlying relationship like $a + bY$, as show in figure 1.1, together with a distribution of contributions around this relationship. In this case there are three possible outcomes: the contribution is zero, it is between zero and L, or it is at L. The values of a, b, and σ that maximize the likelihood of observing the sample values yield estimates of the relationship labeled $a + bY$ in figure 1.1, as well as the dispersion of underlying observations around this expected value. Thus the estimates that are obtained need to be interpreted as pertaining to this underlying relationship. For example, b indicates the relationship between Y and S if there were no limit on contributions. Or, it tells us how an increase in income would affect contributions as long as the contribution limit was not reached; after that, contributions would be observed at the limit L but desired contributions would be above L.

It is also important to realize that only persons who are constrained by the current limit will be affected by a new higher limit. (If the limit is lowered, of course, increasingly large numbers of people will be constrained by it.) With the help of figure 1.2, it is easy to determine the effect of small changes in L on contributions. Consider first an individual whose observed contribution is less than L. Such an individual could contribute more but chooses not to; he is not constrained by the limit. His desired contribution level is less than L, so raising the limit would not increase his contribution level. Consider, on the other hand, a person who is observed to contribute at the limit L. If L were raised, this person would likely contribute more. Thus the effect

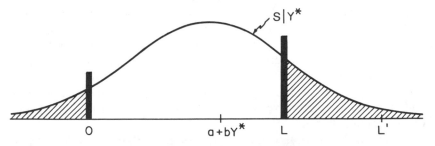

Fig. 1.2   Distribution of contributions, given income level Y^*.

of raising the limit by 1 is just 1 times the probability that the individual is constrained by the limit. Somewhat more formally, we can write the derivative as

(5)
$$\frac{dC}{dL} = \begin{cases} 0 \text{ if } C < L \\ 1 \text{ if } C > L \end{cases}$$
$$= 0 \cdot \Pr[C < L] + 1 \cdot \Pr[C > L]$$
$$= \Pr[C > L].$$

Thus for any individual the expected change in the contribution level is equal to the probability that the underlying desired contribution is greater than L.

It is also important to realize that this derivative depends upon the level of L. Suppose that L were farther to the right than is shown in figure 1.2, say at L'. The effect on contributions of an increase in the limit from L' would be much smaller than the effect of an increase from L because the likelihood that an individual with income Y^* would like to contribute more than L' is much lower than the likelihood that he would like to contribute more than L. While all people, or almost all people, with observed contributions at L would increase their contributions if the limit were raised, very few would increase their contributions to the level L'. Thus to infer the effect of an increase in the limit on contributions, it is necessary to have an estimate of the underlying distribution of desired contribution levels. With an estimate of the distribution of S given Y^*, it is possible to predict the expected contribution given Y^* for any level of L.

Estimation Possibilities

In practice, estimates that address the issues discussed above can be developed in several ways, depending on the hypothesized underlying process that leads to observed contributions. There are two basic possibilities. The first possibility assumes, as in the discussion above, that zero contributions can be thought of simply as a special case of a single underlying preferred contribution behavioral relationship. That is, one could think of a preferred contribution level that declines continuously with decreases in income until the zero contribution level is reached. The second general possibility is that there are two underlying behavioral relationships that determine observed contributions: one relationship describes the likelihood that a person will be a contributor and the second relationship describes the desired contribution, should one be a contributor.

If only one behavioral relationship is assumed, there are at least three ways to obtain estimates. The alternative procedures allow a test of the underlying assumption itself. One procedure uses all observations including those with zero contributions; the second uses only observations with positive contributions; and the third uses only the information on whether a person contributes without using the amount of a positive contribution.[6] If there is, in fact, only one underlying relationship that determines observed contributions, then each of these methods yields consistent estimates of the parameters of this single relationship (except for the third which yields estimates up to a variance scaling factor). If the estimates based on the different groups of observations lead to different estimates, then it is likely that the underlying process should be described by two relationships.

If the goal of the analysis were only to predict the effect of changes in the limits, it is reasonable to concentrate on those who contribute and to allow the parameter estimates to be determined by this group, since noncontributors are not initially affected by changes in the limit. It is at least as important, however, to understand the factors that determine whether a person is a contributor. As emphasized above, changes in the number of contributors at any limit could have a much greater effect on national saving than changes in the limit. To the extent that the determinants of whether one is a contributor are different from the determinants of the amount of the contribution, it is important to consider both of these relationships. The formal details of a two-equation model, together with details of the single-equation estimation possibilities and related tests of behavioral assumptions, are presented in appendix A.

1.2.3   The Empirical Specification

In the illustrative specification in section 1.2.1, desired contributions to tax-deferred saving are of the form $S = \beta Y$. A direct statistical counterpart of this specification is

$$(6) \qquad S = \beta Y e^{\epsilon} = a Y^b \cdot Y \cdot e^{\epsilon} = \alpha_0 X_1^{\alpha_1} X_2^{\alpha_2} \ldots Y^b \cdot Y \cdot e^{\epsilon}.$$

Based on estimates for Canada, this specification fits the observations on positive contributions extremely well. Note that the specification implies that given Y (and the other variables X) the variance of S increases with Y; the disturbance term is heteroscedastic. The specification also leads to a constant income elasticity and is conveniently log-linear. However, this specification is not appropriate if we incorporate contributions at zero and, in the abstract, the possibility of desired contributions less than zero. To consider whether the determinants of contributor status are different from the determinants of the amount of positive contributions, a specification that in principle allows negative as well as positive values and that also fits the observations on positive contributions must be used. Such a specification, and one that in practice fits the observed data well, is of the form

(7) $S = a + (Y^b + \eta)Y + \epsilon$

$\quad = \alpha_0 + \alpha_1 X_1 + \alpha_2 X_2 + \ldots + Y^{1+b} + \eta Y + \epsilon,$

where η and ϵ are disturbance terms and the variance of $\eta Y + \epsilon$ is given by

(8) $$V(\eta Y + \epsilon) = \sigma_\eta^2 Y^2 + \sigma_\epsilon^2 = \sigma^2$$

Thus the specification incorporates the property that the variance of S increases with income, and it also allows for "desired" contributions less than zero. The elasticity of desired contributions with respect to income is given by $(1 + b)/[1 + (a/Y^{1+b})]$ and thus approaches $1 + b$ as income increases.[7]

For simplification, appendix A, which describes the details of the alternative estimation procedures, is written in terms of the specification $S = X\beta + \epsilon$, where $V(\epsilon) = \sigma^2$. Development in terms of the above specification may be obtained by replacing $X\beta$ by $a + Y^{1+b}$ and σ^2 by $(\sigma_\eta^2 Y^2 + \sigma_\epsilon^2)$. Recall that the three single-equation approaches use: (a) all observations including those with zero contributions (two-limit Tobit); (b) only observations with positive contributions (one-limit Tobit); and (c) only information on contributor status (probit). A two-equation model that jointly estimates contribu*tor* and contribu*tion* outcomes is also described in appendix A. This model permits the determinants of whether a person contributes to differ from the determinants of the desired level of a positive contribution and allows the stochastic components of the two choices to be correlated.

In addition, the CPS data on IRA contributions are reported only by intervals—$0, $0–$100, $100–$500, $500–$1000, $1000–$2000. Thus the probabilities of positive contributions are of the form

(9) $$\Phi[(u - X\beta)/\sigma] - \Phi[(l - X\beta)/\sigma],$$

where u and l are the upper and lower bounds of an interval, and $\Phi[\cdot]$ denotes the standard normal distribution function. Thus the likelihood function in this case includes no density function terms; it is composed only of normal cumulative distribution functions. This may be contrasted with the Canadian data that record exact positive contributions.

1.3   Results

1.3.1   Data

The data were obtained through a special supplement to the May 1983 Current Population Survey (CPS). The data on IRA contributions pertain to the 1982 tax year. No information is provided on 1982 contributions to Keogh plans, thus self-employed persons have been excluded from this analysis. In addition, the raw data pertain to individuals, not families. Some of the estimates reported below are based on the individual data, with indicator variables for marital status and sex. Since it is not known from the individual data whether an individual's spouse works, the actual upper limit on family contributions cannot be determined from the individual data alone. Some individuals reported contributions greater than $2000—primarily at $2250 and at $4000, apparently confusing individual contributions with the family total. When the individual data are used, contributions above $2000 are not explicitly recorded at that level, rather any reported contribution above $2000 is treated as a contribution at the $2000 limit. Under the model assumption, this procedure still yields unbiased parameter estimates; it simply does not use all the information.

Family data were created by matching and combining information for individuals in the same household. This allows estimation of family income and of family IRA contribution limits based on the employment status of the husband and wife. Estimated marginal tax rates were also calculated for the family. The estimates were based on average marginal tax rates by income and family status reported by the IRS. As mentioned above, IRA contributions for each family member are reported only by intervals. The intervals for a family were obtained by inferring the possible family intervals from the possible individual reporting intervals. There are twelve possible family intervals in total. Details of the procedures used to create the family data and the tax rates are reported in appendix B.

1.3.2   Parameter Estimates: Single-Equation Models

Individual Data

Estimates by three methods of estimation are reported in tables 1.6 and 1.7. Summary statistics for the variables included in each equation are presented in appendix C. Table 1.7 includes variables indicating whether a person was covered by a private pension plan and whether the worker participated in a salary reduction plan (401[K] or 403[B] plans which permit workers to defer compensation); these variables are not included in table 1.6. Column 1 in each table presents estimates based on the two-limit Tobit specification. Column 2 shows probit estimates where the standard error of ϵ is set at the two-limit Tobit estimate (e.g., 5622 in table 1.6). This allows easy comparison of the two sets of estimates. It may be seen that the parameter estimates are virtually the same. Whether there is a difference between the determinants of contribution status and the determinants of the desired level

Table 1.6   Parameter Estimates, by Method of Estimation, Individual Data[a]

Variable	2-Limit Tobit	Probit, σ_ϵ from 2-Limit Tobit	1-Limit Tobit	Probit, σ_ϵ from 1-Limit Tobit
		Method of Estimation		
σ_η	.124(.012)	.120(.016)	.051(.012)	.039(.006)
σ_ϵ	5622(212)	5622	2015(210)	2015
Constant	−29712(1039)	−29196(758)	−6608(1276)	−10527(266)
Income	.839(.006)	.839(.004)	.753(.013)	.749(.004)
MTR[b]	—	—	—	—
Age	240(9)	228(8)	110(16)	81(3)
Unmarried Women	56(244)	17(247)	211(261)	5(87)
Unmarried Men	7(277)	−208(281)	1353(357)	−74(99)
Married Women	2869(209)	2768(208)	1073(238)	986(73)
Education	650(37)	653(35)	109(35)	230(12)
Private Pension	—	—	—	—
Salary Reduc. Plan	—	—	—	—
LF[c]	−9548.4	−6745.3	−2745.2	−6745.3
N	20513	20513	2999	20513
< 0	17514	17514	—	17514
> 0, < L	1003 ⎫	2999	1003 ⎫	2999
= L	1996 ⎭		1996 ⎭	

[a]Standard errors are in parentheses.
[b]Marginal tax rate.
[c]Likelihood function.

of IRA contributions may not be revealed by this comparison, however, since the preponderance of individuals make no contribution and thus the contribution status (the probit portion) will dominate the two-limit estimates. The two-limit Tobit estimates will therefore tend to look like the probit estimates.

A better way to reveal differences in the two relationships is to separate analysis of contribution amounts from the analysis of contributor status. The 1-limit Tobit estimates in column 3 of the tables are based only on the contributions of contributors, and the probit estimates of contributor status in column 4 are obtained by setting the standard error of ϵ equal to the one-limit estimate (e.g., 2015 in table 1.6). These last two columns reveal that the two sets of coefficients are quite similar. The reported coefficient on income is the estimate of $(1 + b)$. It is virtually the same in each of the alternative methods, and the estimated parameters on age seem not to be significantly different in the two cases. The estimated sex effects are also very close in the two cases, with one exception. The estimates suggest that unmarried men contribute more than married men (the omitted category)

Table 1.7   **Parameter Estimates, by Method of Estimation, Individual Data[a]**

| | | Method of Estimation | | |
Variable	2-Limit Tobit	Probit, σ_ϵ from 2-Limit Tobit	1-Limit Tobit	Probit, σ_ϵ from 1-Limit Tobit
σ_η	.124(.012)	.121(.016)	.051(.012)	.040(.006)
σ_ϵ	5621(213)	*5621*	2028(214)	*2028*
Constant	−29608(1039)	−29119(761)	−6713(1308)	−10576(269)
Income	.838(.006)	.838(.004)	.749(.014)	.749(.004)
MTR[b]	—	—	—	—
Age	239(9)	228(8)	110(16)	81(3)
Unmarried Women	42(244)	6(247)	205(264)	1(88)
Unmarried Men	6(277)	−208(282)	1350(359)	−75(100)
Married Women	2856(210)	2759(209)	1079(241)	990(74)
Education	644(37)	648(36)	108(35)	230(13)
Private Pension	23(162)	−18(165)	221(171)	−13(59)
Salary Reduc. Plan	789(346)	751(352)	239(326)	262(125)
LF[c]	−9546.0	−6743.2	−2743.9	−6743.2
N	20513	20513	2999	20513
< 0	17514	17514	—	17514
$> 0, < L$	1003 ⎫	2999	1003 ⎫	2999
$= L$	1996 ⎭		1996 ⎭	

[a]Standard errors are in parentheses.
[b]Marginal tax rate.
[c]Likelihood function.

but are apparently no more likely than married men to contribute. The constant terms in the two equations differ, although given the estimated standard errors, the difference may not be as great as the estimated values suggest.

A more formal test is to compare the sum of the likelihood values from columns 3 and 4 with the likelihood value in column 1. Under the null hypothesis is that one behavioral relationship is sufficient to describe both contributor status and the amount of contributions, the sum of the likelihoods in columns 3 and 4 will not be statistically different from the likelihood value in column 1. (Minus 2 times the difference will be distributed chi-square with 7 degrees of freedom, with a .05 level of 14.1.) Thus the hypothesis would be rejected in this case. However, the very large sample size will reveal differences even if they have rather small practical importance.

The coefficient on income of .753 implies an elasticity of desired contribution with respect to income of .63, evaluated at the mean of the data for contributors. The desired contribution increases by about $110 with each year of age according to the estimates for contributors, while the comparable estimate from the probit equation is $81. Given other variables, married women would choose to contribute about $1000 more than married men and the more educated would contribute more than those with less education. The estimated unmarried women effect is not statistically significant.

Summary statistics presented in table 1.5 suggested that employees covered by a private pension plan were more likely to contribute to an IRA. Parameter estimates in table 1.7, however, suggest that the association between pension coverage and IRA contributions can be attributed to other differences in the individual characteristics of those covered and not covered by a pension plan. After controlling for other characteristics, pension plan coverage is not significantly associated with desired contributions. Participation in a salary reduction plan (less than 4 percent of the sample) is positively associated with IRA contributions.

Both the two-limit and one-limit models fit the data rather well. This is demonstrated in table 1.8. Based on the estimates in table 1.6, the

Table 1.8   **Model Fit; Actual versus Predicted Proportions by Income Interval, Contribution Interval, and Method of Estimation[a]**

Income Interval[b]	Contribution Interval											
	Zero		Between		At Limit		$0–$500		$500–$1000		$1000–$2000	
	A	P	A	P	A	P	A	P	A	P	A	P
	2-Limit Tobit											
0–10	.95	.94	.02	.03	.03	.03	.01	.01	.01	.01	.01	.01
10–20	.89	.89	.05	.04	.06	.06	.01	.01	.01	.01	.02	.02
20–30	.81	.80	.06	.07	.13	.13	.02	.02	.02	.02	.03	.03
30–40	.68	.69	.08	.09	.23	.22	.01	.02	.02	.02	.05	.04
40–50	.56	.57	.09	.09	.35	.33	.01	.02	.01	.02	.07	.04
50–75	.47	.45	.10	.08	.43	.47	.01	.02	.02	.02	.07	.04
75+	.38	.33	.08	.06	.54	.60	.00	.01	.02	.02	.06	.03
	1-Limit Tobit											
0–10	—	—	.43	.48	.57	.52	—	—	—	—	—	—
10–20	—	—	.43	.41	.57	.59	—	—	—	—	—	—
20–30	—	—	.33	.35	.67	.65	—	—	—	—	—	—
30–40	—	—	.27	.27	.73	.73	—	—	—	—	—	—
40–50	—	—	.19	.22	.81	.78	—	—	—	—	—	—
50–75	—	—	.18	.17	.82	.83	—	—	—	—	—	—
75+	—	—	.13	.13	.88	.87	—	—	—	—	—	—

[a]A = actual; P = predicted.
[b]In thousands.

predicted proportion of individuals with contributions at zero, at the upper limit, and within selected intervals are compared with the actual proportions, by income interval. It is important in interpreting these results to realize that gross misspecification of the functional form that relates contributions to income would be revealed in the comparisons by income level. The comparisons indicate close correspondence between predicted and actual proportions. The only apparent discrepancy is that the two-limit Tobit specification underpredicts the proportion of contributions in the $1000–$2000 range and correspondingly overpredicts the proportion of contributions at the limit. Given the differences between a few of the two-limit and one-limit parameter estimates, the similarity of the predictions may be surprising. However, the major difference in parameter estimates is a larger negative constant term in the two-limit than in the one-limit specification, which is offset by a larger disturbance term variance. The likelihood function is quite flat with respect to these two parameters. Thus the sum of the last two likelihoods is not so different in magnitude from the two-limit Tobit likelihood.

Family Data

Parameter estimates based on the family data are reported in table 1.9. The variable specification is identical to that used for the individual data with two exceptions: the marginal tax rate (MTR) has been added and the dummy variable for "married women" has been deleted, with non-single-person families the norm group. Married men and women appear together in the family data, but as two separate observations in the individual data.

Where the variables are the same, the parameter estimates are very similar to those based on the individual data. For example, the estimated income coefficient based on the two-limit Tobit model is .78 using family data and .84 using individual data. The effects of age and education are also quite close.

The results suggest that the marginal tax rate has no effect on the amount of contributions but a positive effect on contributor status. The coefficient on the estimated marginal tax rate in the two-limit specification is 200 with a standard error of 39. This would suggest that an increase of ten percentage points in the marginal tax rate would increase desired IRA contributions by about $2000. On the other hand, the one-limit and probit estimates in columns 3 and 4 suggest that the tax rate has no effect on the level of contributions (column 3) but a positive effect on contributor status (column 4). The latter estimate implies that if all marginal tax rates were increased by ten percentage points—on average from about 24 percent to 34 percent—the proportion of persons who contribute would increase from .134 to .193, or by 44 percent.

Table 1.9   Parameter Estimates, by Method of Estimation, Family Data[a]

		Method of Estimation		
Variable	2-Limit Tobit	Probit, σ_ϵ from 2-Limit Tobit	1-Limit Tobit	Probit, σ_ϵ from 1-Limit Tobit
σ_η	.096(.014)	.084(.023)	.076(.017)	.042(.011)
σ_ϵ	6367(325)	6367	3219(548)	3219
Constant	−32111(1428)	−31232(1076)	−15224(4284)	−15860(548)
Income	.776(.027)	.756(.039)	.810(.033)	.701(.038)
MTR[b]	200(39)	219(38)	−15(70)	109(20)
Age	211(11)	195(12)	219(51)	98(6)
Unmarried Women	401(384)	207(421)	781(724)	118(216)
Unmarried Men	−273(436)	−645(454)	2724(1016)	−313(233)
Married Women	—	—	—	—
Education	550(45)	546(47)	142(82)	276(24)
Private Pension	—	—	—	—
Salary Reduc. Plan	—	—	—	—
LF[c]	−6727.1	−4601.9	−2089.3	−4601.9
N	15149	15149	2030	15149
< 0	13119	13119	—	13119
> 0, < L	756 }	2030	756 }	2030
= L	1274 }		1274 }	

[a]Standard errors are in parentheses.
[b]Marginal tax rate.
[c]Likelihood function.

Canadian estimates for 1981 (see section 1.4) show a much smaller statistically significant effect of the marginal tax rate on contributor status, with a smaller and not statistically significant effect on the amount of contributions. (But the difference between the two estimates is also not significantly different from zero.) Canadian estimates for 1976 show no effect of the marginal tax rate in either equation.[8] An alternative log-linear model for contributors only shows a precisely estimated zero effect of the marginal tax rate on the amount of contributions in both 1976 and 1980. Thus the estimated effect seems quite sensitive to the statistical specification.

Table 1.10 includes indicators of pension coverage and participation in a salary reduction plan. These estimates indicate that if at least one member of a family is covered by a pension plan, the likelihood of contributing to an IRA is higher. The individual data suggested essentially no relationship. A possible explanation is that married persons without pensions, but whose spouses are covered by a pension, have a high likelihood of contributing to an IRA. In the individual data, these people would be treated as not having a private pension.

Table 1.10   **Parameter Estimates, by Method of Estimation, Family Data[a]**

	Method of Estimation			
Variable	2-Limit Tobit	Probit, σ_ϵ from 2-Limit Tobit	1-Limit Tobit	Probit, σ_ϵ from 1-Limit Tobit
σ_η	.088(.014)	.063(.025)	.078(.017)	.030(.012)
σ_ϵ	6477(327)	6477	3198(550)	3198
Constant	−32687(1444)	−31470(1032)	−15522(4394)	−15607(514)
Income	.779(.025)	.745(.042)	.813(.033)	.687(.042)
MTR[b]	180(38)	781(423)	−29(71)	104(19)
Age	211(109)	192(11)	221(52)	95(5)
Unmarried Women	520(381)	196(407)	914(740)	106(205)
Unmarried Men	−98(432)	−607(444)	2824(1032)	−293(222)
Married Women	—	—	—	—
Education	538(45)	524(45)	143(83)	258(22)
Private Pension	1626(236)	1599(227)	617(513)	787(112)
Salary Reduc. Plan	791(435)	781(423)	−114(704)	385(208)
LF[c]	−6699.1	−4574.0	−2088.5	−4574.0
N	15149	15149	2030	15149
< 0	13119	13119	—	13119
> 0, < L	756 }	2030	756 }	2030
= L	1274 }		1274 }	

[a]Standard errors are in parentheses.
[b]Marginal tax rate.
[c]Likelihood function.

1.3.3 Simulations: Single-Equation Models

Simulations are obtained under three policy assumptions: the existing IRA program, the proposal contained in the administration's recent tax reform proposal (U.S. Department of Treasury 1984), and a modification of the Treasury proposal that restricts spousal IRAs. The Treasury proposal increases the limits to $2500 for both employed persons and nonemployed spouses. The modified Treasury proposal also increases the limit for employed persons to $2500 but sets the spousal limit at $500, instead of $2500.

Simulations based on the family data are presented in table 1.11.[9] To serve as a basis for comparison, the average IRA contribution under the current plan has been simulated for several demographic groups. The model yields an average predicted contribution for all families under the current plan of $312.[10] The simulations indicate that the Treasury plan would increase 1982 contributions by 30 percent to $405 per family. The largest increases are for married, one-earner families whose limit is increased by the Treasury proposal from $2250 to $5000.

Table 1.11   **Simulated IRA Contributions, by Plan and Family Type, Based on Family Data[a]**

Family Type	Current Plan ($2000/$250)	Treasury Plan ($2500/$2500)	Mod. Treas. Plan ($2500/$500)
All Families			
Avg. Contribution	$312	$405	$370
% Change	—	30	18
Unmarried Head			
Avg. Contribution	136	162	162
% Change	—	19	19
Married, 1 Earner			
Avg. Contribution	267	475	335
% Change	—	78	25
Married, 2 Earners			
Avg. Contribution	536	620	620
% Change	—	16	16

[a]These estimates are unweighted, since it was not clear what weights should be used for the "created" families.

The predicted average contribution for this group would increase from $267 to $475, about 78 percent. The smallest increase, about 16 percent, is for married, two-earner families whose limit increased only from $4000 to $5000.

The modified Treasury plan yields an overall increase of about 18 percent. The limit changes, and thus contributor responses, for unmarried heads and married, two-earner families are the same as in the unmodified Treasury proposal. The modified Treasury plan increases the limit faced by married, one-earner families by only $750, from $2250 to $3000, instead of $5000. The simulated increase in average contributions by this group is 25 percent, about a third as large as the simulated increase under the Treasury plan.

Simulations based on the individual data are shown in table 1.12. Unlike the family data, the individual data do not provide enough information to completely specify the limit faced by each person. Employed single persons face a limit of $2000. For married couples the limits are $2000 per person if both work and $2250 if only one works. If both work, then both will appear in the sample and the appropriate limit for each is $2000. If only one is employed, however, the nonemployed spouse will not be present in the sample, since only employed persons received the CPS pension supplement questionnaire. The appropriate limit for the employed spouse is $2250. The problem is to assign the "correct" limit ($2000 or $2250) to each married person in the sample, given that we do not know if the spouse is employed. [11] If the married person is a woman, a limit of $2000 is assigned, assuming that her spouse also works. If the married person is a man, the limit

Table 1.12   **Simulated IRA Contributions, by Plan Based on Individual Data[a]**

Individual Type	Current Plan ($2000/$250)	Treasury Plan ($2500/$2500)	Mod. Treas. Plan ($2500/$500)
All Persons			
Avg. Contribution	$246	$326	$296
% Change	—	33	20
Unmarried Males			
Avg. Contribution	120	142	142
% Change	—	18	18
Unmarried Females			
Avg. Contribution	134	158	158
% Change	—	18	18
Married Males			
Avg. Contribution	323	469	395
% Change	—	45	22
Married Females			
Avg. Contribution	280	332	332
% Change	—	18	18

[a]Weighted to reflect national population.

is randomly assigned. With probability P it is set at $2000 and with probability $1-P$ at $2250, where P is the proportion of wives of working husbands that are employed.

The individual data simulations based on this procedure are quite close to those obtained using the family data. For all persons, the simulations indicate that the Treasury plan would increase 1982 contributions by about 33 percent and that the modified Treasury plan would increase contributions by about 20 percent. The largest effects are for married men, the group facing the largest change in limits.

1.3.4   Parameter Estimates: Two-Equation Model

The above results suggest that the observed outcomes can in general be described well with a single behavioral relationship. If two relationships are required, the one-limit Tobit and the probit models together, even if estimated independently, should provide a reasonably accurate description of the determination of contributions. The two-equation model described in appendix A, however, distinguishes between a "potential" contributor behavioral relationship and the level of desired contributions, were one to contribute. Under this representation, a potential contributor could be observed with zero contributions not because the person was a noncontributor, but rather, say, because income was too low for the person to devote current income to future consumption. To the extent that the parameters in the two relationships differ, the single-equation probit estimates, for example, will not provide accurate estimates of potential contributor status. As the parameters in the two relationships become close, and the correlation between them approaches 1, however, the two-equation model approaches the two-limit Tobit specification. If only the variable coefficients were the same, the results could differ if the correlation between the disturbance terms in the two relationships were not unity.

Estimation of several two-equation models indicated only minor differences between parameters based on the single-equation models and those derived from two relationships estimated jointly. The two-equation model is of the form

$$S = a_s + Y^{b_s} + \eta_s Y + \epsilon_s \qquad \text{Contributor Status}$$

$$C = a_c + Y^{b_c} + \eta_c Y + \epsilon_c \qquad \text{Contribution Amount}$$

The details of the specification and estimation procedure are described in section 2 of appendix A. The key distinction between the specification used here and the common sample-selection specification is that even potential contributors can have zero contributions, while others would not contribute under any circumstances. Only the latter are "noncontributors" in the strict sense.

Illustrative estimates for this model are presented in table 1.13. In this specification, $V(\eta_c) = V(\eta_s)$, $V(\epsilon_c) = V(\epsilon_s)$, and all covariances

Table 1.13   **Parameter Estimates, Two-Equation Model, Individual Data[a]**

Variable	Level of Contribution (C)		Contributor Status (S)
σ_η		.037(.005)	
σ_ϵ		2034(115)	
$\rho(\eta_c,\eta_s)$		.095(.094)	
Constant	−4293(463)		−9547(464)
Income	.758(.009)		.744(.007)
MTR[b]	—		—
Age	92(8)		65(4)
Unmarried Women	423(177)		−111(50)
Unmarried Men	1347(248)		−410(110)
Married Women	998(168)		825(92)
Education	—		250(19)
Private Pension	—		
Salary Reduc. Plan	—		—
LF[c]		−9497.8	
N		20513	
< 0		17514	
> 0, < L		1003	
= L		1996	

[a]Standard errors are in parentheses.
[b]Marginal tax rate.
[c]Likelihood function.

other than $\text{cov}(\eta_c, \eta_s)$ are set to zero. Education is excluded from the contributions equation. In practice, covariance or exclusion restrictions were required for identification of key parameters. Because the likelihood function was so flat, more restrictions were necessary than were in principle required.

The parameter estimates indicate that the correlation between η_c and η_s is not significantly different from zero.[12] This suggests independence of the contributor and contributions relationships, given measured individual characteristics. Thus these estimates are very close to the single-equation results presented in columns 3 and 4 of table 1.6.[13]

In principle, however, this specification allows estimation of the proportion of persons who are potential contributors but, because of a liquidity constraint, for example, are observed not to contribute. The probability that a person does not contribute is given in this specification by $1 - \Pr[S < 0] + \Pr[S > 0 \text{ but } C < 0]$. Averaged over all observations in the sample, the proportion of noncontributors is .854, the same as in the probit estimates based on individual data. A proportion of .146 contribute. The proportion of potential contributors, $\Pr[S > 0]$, is estimated to be .182. Thus, the proportion of potential contributors who do not contribute, $\Pr[S > 0 \text{ but } C < 0]$, is estimated to be .036, about 20 percent of potential contributors.

1.4   Comparison of Results for the United States and Canada

Since the Canadian and the U.S. systems are very similar in their general outlines, it is informative to compare the model estimates for the two countries. The Canadian equivalent of IRA and Keogh plans is the Registered Retirement Savings Plan (RRSP). RRSP contributions are also tax-deferred and have upper limits determined both by income and by a maximum level. The Canadian rules also provide for different limits depending on whether a person is a member of a private pension plan.

Since the Canadian tax system is on an individual basis, the most appropriate comparison is with the individual estimates for the United States. Estimates analogous to those in table 1.6 for the United States are shown in table 1.14 for Canada. While the general model specification is identical in the two countries, the specific variables do not correspond precisely. In particular, the variables for women, married, and education are not included in the Canadian version, and there is no marginal tax rate variable in the U.S. version. The comparable parameter estimates, however, are surprisingly similar, based on a comparison of the one-limit Tobit and the corresponding probit estimates in the two countries. The coefficient on income is .75 in the United States, while it is approximately .81 in Canada. The estimated effect

Table 1.14   RRSP Contribution Parameter Estimates, by Method of Estimation, Totals, 1981[a]

Group and Variable	2-Limit Tobit	Probit, σ_ϵ from 2-Limit Tobit	1-Limit Tobit	Probit, σ_ϵ from 1-Limit Tobit
σ_η	.106(.006)	.096(.014)	.125(.032)	.103(.015)
σ_ϵ	2999(183)	—	3199(632)	—
Constant	−9151(561)	−8951(466)	−11657(4690)	−9539(498)
Income	.794(.008)	.789(.009)	.807(.036)	.795(.009)
MTR[b]	37(8)	39(8)	28(40)	42(8)
Age	62(9)	61(9)	79(47)	65(10)
Govt. Employee	—	—	—	—
Employee w/RPP	—	—	—	—
Self-Employed	—	—	—	—
Professional	—	—	—	—
Farmer/Fisherman	—	—	—	—
LF[c]	−6583.8	−1763.9	−4818.9	−1763.9
N	4038	4038	1083	4038
< 0	2955	2955	—	2955
> 0, < L	516 }	1083	516 }	1083
= L	567 }		567 }	

[a]Standard errors are in parentheses.
[b]Marginal tax rate.
[c]Likelihood function.

of age is approximately $80 to $110 in the United States, while it is $65 to $80 in Canada. The estimates for Canada also show a close correspondence between the one-limit Tobit and the probit estimates, indicating that a single behavioral relationship apparently describes the observations rather well. Indeed, for Canada the estimates in the two equations are not statistically different, based on the chi-squared test described above.

As already discussed, the estimated effect of the marginal tax rate in Canada is not statistically different from zero in the contributions equation; the estimate for the United States, reported for the family data in table 1.9, is also not statistically different from zero. In both countries the effect of the tax rate on contribution status is positive, although it is much smaller in Canada. As emphasized earlier, these results are very sensitive to model specifications and it may not be possible to distinguish the effect of the marginal tax rate from a nonlinear effect of income.[14]

The parameter estimates from a more highly parameterized model for Canada are shown in table 1.15. The variable "employee w/RPP" indicates individuals in Canada with a private pension plan. Neither

Table 1.15   **RRSP Contribution Parameter Estimates, by Method of Estimation, Grouped, 1981[a]**

Group and Variable	2-Limit Tobit	Probit, σ_ϵ from 2-Limit Tobit	1-Limit Tobit	Probit, σ_ϵ from 1-Limit Tobit
σ_η	.113(.004)	.105(.009)	.080(.082)	.088
σ_ϵ	2978(125)	—	2523(227)	—
Constant	−8918(371)	−8702(300)	−6527(1209)	−7390(253)
Income	.797(.005)	.790(.006)	.812(.082)	.776(.006)
MTR[b]	33(5)	34(5)	16(13)	29(4)
Age	60(6)	59(6)	42(14)	50(5)
Sex	−45(138)	24(139)	−478(385)	19(117)
Govt. Employee	−693(220)	−796(219)	322(602)	−672(185)
Employee w/RPP	−33(171)	81(170)	−721(403)	68(144)
Self-Employed	31(163)	−101(164)	724(405)	−86(139)
Professional	3995(255)	3133(303)	5312(710)	2644(256)
Farmer/Fisherman	−347(255)	−582(268)	2067(641)	−490(226)
LF[c]	−17566.7	−4996.0	−12513.9	−4995.3
N	11019	11019	3169	11019
< 0	7850	7856	0	7856
> 0, < L	1339 }	3169	1339 }	3169
= L	1830 }		1830 }	

[a]Standard errors are in parentheses.
[b]Marginal tax rate.
[c]Likelihood function.

estimate is statistically different from zero, although the one-limit estimate is quite negative. In the United States, there appears to be no relationship between pension coverage and IRA contributions based on individual data, although there is some evidence of a positive pension relationship in the family data.

Because data in Canada are available for several consecutive years, it is possible to check the validity of the model specifications for that country. Between 1976 and 1981, the Canadian Consumer Price Index increased by about 60 percent, but RRSP limits did not change over the period. Thus in real terms the limits declined very substantially between those years. Thus a good external check of the predictive validity of the model is to use estimates for one of the years to predict contributions in the other, when the limit was either considerably higher or much lower. Such predictions, using the two-limit and the one-limit estimates reported in table 1.15, are shown in table 1.16. In general, the predicted values are very close to the actual ones. For example, one-limit estimates for 1981 underpredict 1976 contributions by only 1.7 percent, and one-limit estimates for 1976 underpredict 1981 contributions by only 1.1 percent. Estimates based on the two-

Table 1.16   **Predicted Total Contributions for 1976 Based on 1981 Estimates and Predicted Total Contributions for 1981 Based on 1976 Estimates, by Estimation Method, Using Estimation Files[a]**

For 1976 Based on 1981 Estimates
Actual: 2149
Predicted:

		Difference
Two-Limit	1920	−10.7%
One-Limit	2133	−1.7%

For 1981 Based on 1976 Estimates
Actual: 4810
Predicted:

		Difference
Two-Limit	4940	+2.7%
One-Limit	4754	−1.1%

[a]Estimates are based on parameter estimates in table 1.15.

limit model also yield predicted values very close to actual values. Since the parameter estimates in the two countries are rather close, this suggests that the model also should predict rather well in the United States.

1.5 Conclusions

Persons with low incomes are unlikely to have IRA accounts. In addition, after controlling for income, age, and other variables, persons without private pension plans are no more likely than those with them to contribute to an IRA. Indeed, if anything, those with private plans contribute more than those without them. Both contributor status and the amount of positive contributions are determined in large part by income and, to a lesser extent, by demographic characteristics. The marginal tax rate may have a positive effect on whether one contributes, but it does not appear to influence the contribution amount. Results based on different specifications suggest that it may be difficult to distinguish the effect of the marginal tax rate from a nonlinear income effect. Simulations based on the estimates suggest that the current U.S. Treasury Department proposal would lead to about a 30 percent increase in IRA contributions.[15] Model estimates based on Canadian data for RRSPs are very similar to those for the United States. External checks of the predictive validity of the model for Canada indicate that predictions of the effects of limit changes are quite accurate.

Appendix A
Estimation of IRA Contributions

To estimate IRA contributions, there are two possible methods. The first is to assume that one underlying behavioral relationship leads to all of the observed outcomes. In this case there are three ways to estimate the same parameters, and the difference between the estimates can serve as a basis for a test of the assumption that one behavioral relationship is sufficient. If it is not, the second method is to assume that observed behavior results from two behavioral relationships, one pertaining to the decision to be a contributor and the other describing the desired amount of contributions, were one a contributor. These two methods are described in turn. The first is familiar to many readers, and the goal here is simply to make clear that, under the maintained hypothesis, the three approaches all yield estimates of the same parameters. The second method is not as familiar but is a generalization of a similar procedure in Deaton and Irish (1984).

1.   A Single Behavioral Relationship

Assume the following notation:

$$s \equiv \text{Observed contribution,}$$
$$S \equiv \text{Latent contribution ``propensity,''}$$
$$X \equiv \text{Vector of individual attributes,}$$
$$L \equiv \text{Contribution limit,}$$
$$\epsilon \equiv \text{Random disturbance term,}$$
$$i \equiv \text{Individual indexes.}$$

Latent contributions are specified as

$$S_i = X_i\beta_1 + \epsilon_i,$$

where ϵ_i is assumed to be distributed normal with mean zero and variance σ^2. Precise amounts contributed by each individual to an IRA are not reported. Instead, we know if the individual did or did not contribute and, if a contribution was made, the interval in which the contribution falls. Details on the intervals are presented in appendix B. The intervals[16] may be summarized as

$$s_i \leq L_0,$$

$$L_{t-1} < s_i < L_t, \qquad t = 1, T,$$

$$L_T \leq s_i,$$

where, in the individual data $T = 3$ and $L_0 = \$0$, $L_1 = \$500$, $L_2 = \$1000$, and $L_3 = \$2000$. In the family data $T = 12$.

Two-Limit Tobit

When all of the observations are used, there are $T + 2$ possible outcomes—contributions at zero, contributions within each of the T closed intervals, and contributions at the upper limit. These outcomes and associated likelihoods [17] are

(1)   (i) $s_i = 0$, $\Phi\left[\dfrac{-X_i\beta}{\sigma}\right]$;

(ii) $L_{t-1} < s_i < L_t$, $\Phi\left(\dfrac{L_t - X_i\beta}{\sigma}\right) - \Phi\left(\dfrac{L_{t-1} - X_i\beta}{\sigma}\right), t = 1, T$;

(iii) $s_i = L_T$, $1 - \Phi\left[\dfrac{L_T - X_i\beta}{\sigma}\right]$;

where $\Phi[\cdot]$ denotes the standard normal distribution function.

One-Limit Tobit with Zeros Excluded

When the zero values are excluded, there are $T + 1$ possible outcomes: the contribution lies within one of the T intervals or at the upper limit. These outcomes and associated likelihoods are

(2)   (i) $L_{t-1} < s_i < L_t$, $\left\{\Phi\left(\dfrac{L_t - X_i\beta}{\sigma}\right)\right.$

$\left. - \Phi\left(\dfrac{L_{t-1} - X_i\beta}{\sigma}\right)\right\} / \Phi\left[\dfrac{X_i\beta}{\sigma}\right], \quad t = 1, T$;

(ii) $s_i = L_T$, $\left\{1 - \Phi\left[\dfrac{L_T - X_i\beta}{\sigma}\right]\right\} / \Phi\left[\dfrac{X_i\beta}{\sigma}\right]$.

The denominator in each expression, the probability of a positive contribution, reflects the fact that noncontributors have been excluded from the analysis. In a single-equation model, the underlying distribution of contributions is truncated at zero when the one-limit Tobit specification is used, while there is a mass point at zero when the two-limit version is used.

Simple Probit

Finally, estimates can also be obtained with a simple probit specification (up to the scale factor σ). In this case the outcomes and associated likelihoods are

(3)   (i) $s_i = 0$, $\Phi\left[\dfrac{-X_i\beta}{\sigma}\right]$;

(ii) $s_i > 0$, $\Phi\left[\dfrac{X_i\beta}{\sigma}\right]$.

Likelihood Function

If there are N_0 observations at zero, N_t observations in interval t, and N_{T+1} observations at the upper limit, the log-likelihood function in each of the three cases is:

(A) $$\ln L = \sum_{}^{N_0} \ln\Phi\left[\frac{-X_i\beta}{\sigma}\right]$$

$$+ \sum_{t=1}^{T} \left\{ \sum_{}^{N_t} \ln\left[\Phi\left(\frac{L_t - X_i\beta}{\sigma}\right) - \Phi\left(\frac{L_{t-1} - X_i\beta}{\sigma}\right) \right] \right\}$$

$$+ \sum_{}^{N_{T+1}} \ln\left[1 - \Phi\left(\frac{L_T - X_i\beta}{\sigma}\right) \right].$$

(B) $$\ln L = \sum_{t=1}^{T} \left(\sum_{}^{N_t} \ln\left\{ \left[\Phi\left(\frac{L_t - X_i\beta}{\sigma}\right) - \Phi\left(\frac{L_{t-1} - X_i\beta}{\sigma}\right) \right] / \Phi\left(\frac{X_i\beta}{\sigma}\right) \right\} \right)$$

$$+ \sum_{}^{N_{T+1}} \ln\left\{ \left[1 - \Phi\left(\frac{L_T - X_i\beta}{\sigma}\right) \right] / \Phi\left(\frac{X_i\beta}{\sigma}\right) \right\}.$$

(C) $$\ln L = \sum_{}^{N_0} \ln\Phi\left[\frac{-X_i\beta}{\sigma}\right]$$

$$+ \sum_{t=1}^{T+1} \left[\sum_{}^{N_t} \ln\Phi\left(\frac{X_i\beta}{\sigma}\right) \right].$$

It is clear that (B) + (C) = (A) under the one-equation assumption. If this assumption is inconsistent with the data, the β estimated from (B) will differ from the β estimated from (C). In addition, to the extent that they differ, the sum of the likelihood values from (B) and (C) will be greater than the value from (A) since the "separated" models allow a better fit to the data. Thus a test of the one-equation behavioral assumption can be based either on a comparison of the estimated βs or on the likelihood values. If they differ, a specification with two behavioral equations may be indicated.

2.   IRA Contributors and Contributions: A Two-Equation Model

The purpose of this section is to describe a procedure that can be used to relax the one-equation constraint. It is assumed that two behavioral relationships determine the contributions that we observe. One is a relationship between individual attributes and the likelihood that a person is a potential IRA contributor. The other is a relationship between individual attributes and the level of desired contributions, were one to contribute. Of course, both of the outcome variables should be thought of initially as latent variables. In particular, if the latent contribution variable is less than zero, we shall assume that we observe no contribution, even if the contributor latent variable is greater than zero. A desirable property of the model is that it encompasses as a limiting case the standard Tobit model described in section 1 of this appendix.

The model is described by:

$$C = X\beta + \epsilon,$$

$$S = X\alpha + \eta,$$

where C is the latent contribu*tion* variable and S the latent contribu*tor* variable, X is a vector of individual attributes, β and α are vectors of parameters to be estimated, and ϵ and η are disturbance terms.[18] We assume that, given X, C and S obey the covariance matrix:

$$\Sigma = \begin{bmatrix} \sigma^2 & \rho\sigma \\ & 1 \end{bmatrix},$$

where ρ is the correlation between C and S, given X.

The bivariate distribution between S and C is represented graphically in figure 1.3. The figure includes the limit on IRA contributions L. That is, as usual, we will not observe contributions above L but will observe a concentration at the level L. We shall assume that a person is a contributor if the latent contributor variable S is greater than zero, *and* if the desired contribution amount is greater than zero. Thus when S and C are both greater than zero we observe IRA contributions greater than zero but less than or equal to L.

As in the usual Tobit case, there are three observable outcomes: IRA contributions are zero, contributions are at some level C where C is

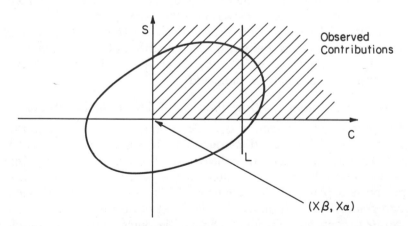

Fig. 1.3   The bivariate distribution between S, the latent contributor variable, and C, the latent contribution variable.

greater than zero but less than L, or we observe C at the limit L. The likelihoods associated with these three outcomes are now

Outcome	Likelihood
$C = 0$	$\Pr[S < 0] + \Pr[S > 0 \text{ and } C < 0]$
$L_{t-1} < C < L_t$	$\Pr[S > 0 \text{ and } L_{t-1} < C < L_t], t = 1, T$
$C = L_T$	$\Pr[S > 0 \text{ and } C > L]$

They are described in somewhat more detail by

Outcome   Likelihood

$C = 0$

$$\Phi[-X\alpha] + \Phi_2\left[X\alpha, \frac{-X\beta}{\sigma}; -\rho\right]$$

$L_{t-1} < C < L_t$

$$\Phi_2\left[X\alpha, \frac{L_t - X\beta}{\sigma}; -\rho\right]$$

$$- \Phi_2\left[X\alpha, \frac{L_{t-1} - X\beta}{\sigma}; -\rho\right], t = 1, T$$

$C = L_T$

$$\Phi_2\left[X\alpha, \frac{-(L_T - X\beta)}{\sigma}; \rho\right]$$

where $\Phi_2[\cdot]$ indicates the bivariate normal distribution function.

If indeed C and S are the same underlying stochastic variable, as in the Tobit case, β goes to α and ρ goes to 1.[19] Thus in this case, the two-equation description of IRA contributions reduces to the Tobit specification. By comparing the likelihood values in the two models, one can test explicitly whether the single behavioral equation version can be rejected. The difference between this test and those mentioned in section 1 of this appendix is that the two equations are allowed to be correlated.

Appendix B
U.S. Data Sources

All data for the United States are from the May 1983 Current Population Survey and Supplemental Survey of Pension and Retirement Plan Coverage. Two data sets were created: individual and family.

Individual Data

The CPS data are arranged by individual. The sample used includes all individuals meeting the following criteria:

1. Included in the supplement (working for pay).
2. Between the ages 16 and 65.
3. Not self-employed.
4. Containing valid responses for each of the variables used in table 1.7.

All summary tables and simulations (but not the estimated models) using individual data use the CPS weights designed to represent the nation as a whole. No adjustment to these weights was made for exclusion of observations due to invalid responses.

Several problems arose with the way the IRA variables were coded. Employed persons were asked, "Do you have an IRA?" Those answering in the affirmative were then asked, "Approximately how much of your own IRA did you credit to your 1982 Federal taxes?" Responses are coded in the intervals:

under $100
$100–$499
$500–$999
$1000–$1999
$2000–$2499
$2500

This categorization led to two problems. First, a surprisingly large number of persons reported IRA contributions in the first (under $100) category. Most of these responses probably indicate persons establishing IRAs prior to 1982 and making no contribution in 1982. We have thus interpreted the first category to indicate zero contributions in 1982.

Second, a small number of respondents (186) indicated a contribution exceeding $2500. These responses presumably reflect family rather than individual contributions. These observations have been deleted from our sample.

Family Data

For tax status the family is a more appropriate unit than the individual in the United States. Using relationship codes, ages, and marital status we have converted the CPS data to a family basis. The incidence of unclassifiable persons or otherwise inconsistent units was rather high. In such cases, the observations were deleted from the sample.[20] One consequence of this data conversion is that using the CPS weights is no longer appropriate.

There are two important advantages to forming a family-based sample. The first is that the employment status of husband and wife in two-person families can be determined. This permits unambiguous assignment of contribution limits used to simulate policy changes.

The second advantage is that marginal tax rates can be calculated based on the family information. Our calculations are based on U.S. Internal Revenue Service (1984). This source reports average adjustments and deductions by income category. The first step is to convert each family's reported total income to adjusted gross income by accounting for average adjustments (excluding IRAs and Keoghs) by income class. To obtain taxable income, personal exemptions ($1000 each for self, spouse if married, and each child) and the average itemized home mortgage interest deduction (in excess of the standard deduction if one were not to itemize) for families reporting owning a home are subtracted from gross income. Finally, 1982 tax tables by filing status provide the marginal tax rates assigned to each family. These calculated rates span the entire range from zero to 50 percent.

Appendix C
Summary Statistics

Variable	Individual Data		Family Data	
	All	Contributors Only	All	Contributors Only
Total Individual (Family) Income ($)	17403(12214)	26649(16338)	23399(15717)	38709(18985)
Marg. Tax Rate (%)	—	—	24(11)	34(10)
Age[a] (years)	37(12)	46(11)	39(13)	46(11)
Unmarried Women (%)	.17(.38)	.10(.30)	.22(.41)	.14(.35)
Unmarried Men (%)	.15(.36)	.08(.26)	.17(.37)	.10(.30)
Married Women (%)	.28(.45)	.32(.47)	—	—
Education[a] (years)	13(2.7)	14(2.6)	13(2.9)	14(2.7)
Private Pension[b] (%)	.51(.50)	.67(.47)	.53(.50)	.78(.41)
Salary Reduc. Plan[b] (%)	.03(.18)	.07(.26)	.04(.20)	.10(.29)

[a]In the family data the value for this variable pertains to the CPS reference person in the household.

[b]In the family data the value for this variable is one of either member participates; zero otherwise.

Notes

1. In general, under the Canadian plan persons can contribute 20 percent of their income up to a maximum of $3500 for those with a private pension plan and up to $5500 for those without a private plan.

2. This may be contrasted with portfolio composition analysis most recently represented in the work by King and Leape (1984) or earlier work by Feldstein (1976), for example.

3. Given current income, contributions to tax-deferred accounts could of course be taken partially or entirely from other existing asset balances. The identification problem is to determine whether this is the case. It is not possible to address this issue with the CPS data, but it will be considered in subsequent analysis based on other data sources.

4. As far as we know, a model like this one has not been estimated. In any event, data limitations and other choices in the empirical implementation would undoubtedly leave uncertainty about the effect of tax-deferred accounts, as well as the effect on tax-deferred contributions of changes in the contribution limits.

5. Answers to these questions are important in their own right and can be answered with considerable confidence.

6. By referring back to figure 1.2, one can see the difference between these procedures. If all the data are used, then there is a concentration of observations at zero and at L. If the zero observations are deleted, there is no concentration of data points at zero, but the distribution is truncated at this point and the concentration at L remains. The third procedure only considers whether contributions are zero or not.

7. The preference function that corresponds to equation (7) is

$$V(Y - S,S) = (S/\beta)e^{[a+\beta(Y-S)]/S},$$

where $a = a_0 + a_1x_1 + \ldots a_kx_k + \epsilon$, and $\beta = Y^b + \eta$.

8. The estimates are in fact negative, but not statistically different from zero.

9. Given program limits, the estimated parameters, and values of X for each member of the sample, the expected contribution of each individual or family is (following the notation of appendix A):

$$E(c) = \Pr[C \le 0] \cdot E[C \mid C \le 0]$$
$$+ \Pr[0 < C < L] \cdot E[C \mid 0 < C < L]$$
$$+ \Pr[C \ge L] \cdot E[C \mid C \ge L]$$
$$= (X\beta) \cdot \left[\Phi\left(\frac{L - X\beta}{\sigma}\right) - \Phi\left(\frac{-X\beta}{\sigma}\right) \right]$$
$$+ \sigma\left[\Phi\left(\frac{L - X\beta}{\sigma}\right) - \Phi\left(\frac{-X\beta}{\sigma}\right) \right] + \left[1 - \Phi\left(\frac{L - X\beta}{\sigma}\right) \right] \cdot L$$

10. This estimate may be compared to the average IRA deduction based on IRS wage and salary returns which was $340 for 1982.

11. This lack of information poses a problem for prediction but not for estimation. The statistical model used to obtain parameter estimates assigns all married persons an open-ended upper limit of $2000 or more.

12. The implied correlation between $(\eta_c Y + \epsilon_c)$ and $(\eta_s Y + \epsilon_s)$ is about -0.01.

13. It may be noticed that the sum of the individual likelihood functions is 9490.5, whereas the likelihood value for the joint specification is somewhat higher, 9497.8. The higher likelihood value results from the equal variance restrictions on η and the exclusion of education from the contribution equation.

14. Indeed, for some years the estimated effect in Canada is in fact negative, although not statistically different from zero.

15. Strictly speaking, the simulations indicate that had the Treasury proposal been implemented in 1982, contributions would have been 30 percent higher than they were.

16. In principle, the open intervals can be treated as closed intervals by setting limits of $-\infty$ or ∞. We treat open and closed intervals separately for expositional purposes only.

17. To simplify matters this appendix derives likelihood functions for a linear specification of S_i and a homoscedastic error structure. The estimated model is based on the parameter and error structure given by equation (5) in the text.

18. In practice, this model is also estimated with a nonlinear specification, with a heteroscedastic error structure, and with equations analogous to those in the text.

19. First consider the $C = 0$ case. Under the limiting case, the probability of S greater than zero and C less than zero goes to zero because this would be an outcome with zero likelihood. Thus, the bivariate distribution function drops out. The $L_{t-1} < C < L_t$ and $C = L_T$ cases can be rewritten as $\Pr[S > 0|L_{t-1} < C < L_t] \cdot \Pr[L_{t-1} < C < L_t]$ and $\Pr[S > 0|C > L_T] \cdot \Pr[C > L_T]$, respectively. The first term in each case goes to unity in the limiting case, since if C is greater than some positive L_t, S must also be greater than zero. Thus in both cases the bivariate distribution in the last term of likelihoods reduces to expressions containing only univariate cumulative distributions.

20. For example, we eliminated persons married but living in a single-person household. Heads living with other relatives but not married were treated as single persons.

References

Deaton, Angus, and Margaret Irish. 1984. Statistical models for zero expenditures in household budgets. *Journal of Public Economics* 23:59–80.

Feldstein, Martin S. 1976. Personal taxation and portfolio composition: An econometric analysis. *Econometrica* 44:631–50.

King, Mervyn A., and Jonathan I. Leape. 1984. Wealth and portfolio composition: Theory and evidence. NBER Working Paper no. 1468, September. Cambridge, Mass.: National Bureau of Economic Research.

U.S. Department of Treasury. 1984. *Tax reform for fairness, simplicity, and economic growth.* Vol.2. Washington, D.C.: GPO.

U.S. Internal Revenue Service. 1984. *Statistics of income, individual income tax returns, 1982.* Washington, D.C.: GPO.

Wise, David A. 1985. Contributors and contributions to Registered Retirement Savings Plans. Paper prepared for the Tax Policy and Legislation Branch of the Canadian Department of Finance.

Comment   Gary Burtless

Steven Venti and David Wise have written a very nice paper on the take-up of tax-preferred saving plans in the United States and Canada. The main objectives of the paper are stated at the outset:

- To analyze the effect of individual attributes on whether a person contributes to IRAs;
- To determine the effect of individual attributes on how much is contributed; and
- To simulate the effect of potential changes in contribution limits on the amount contributed to IRAs.

In addition, the authors very briefly consider the more interesting issue of how much IRAs and similar plans contribute to net personal saving, taking into account the fact that IRA contributions may simply substitute for other forms of saving.

The paper begins with a tabular presentation of some basic statistics on the take-up of IRAs in the United States and Registered Retirement Savings Plans (or RRSPs) in Canada. Both programs have a similar design. Wage earners are permitted to contribute designated amounts to qualified saving plans, and neither contributions nor the interest on contributions is subject to income tax until withdrawals begin during retirement. Under both the U.S. and Canadian plans, there is a maximum permissible amount that workers can contribute to tax-preferred accounts in a given year.

The authors' tabulations show, not surprisingly, that the probability of workers contributing to a plan is strongly correlated with their income. In the United States the percentage of workers contributing to an IRA is about 5 percent in the lowest income class (under $10,000 per year in 1982 earnings), but approaches 60 percent in the highest income class (earnings above $70,000). The percentages are quite similar in Canada, though there is evidence that Canadian taxpayers in the highest income class contribute somewhat less than taxpayers in the upper-middle-income classes. Nor surprisingly, the average contribution per worker—among workers making a contribution—tends to be closer to the permitted maximum in the higher income classes.

How much of the strong correlation between contributions and income is due to an income effect and how much is due to a price effect is difficult to say. The price of retirement consumption (or, equivalently, the price of preretirement saving) can be dramatically reduced by an IRA. Because wage-earners temporarily escape income taxes on both the contribution out of current earnings and the interest on the con-

Gary Burtless is a senior fellow at the Brookings Institution.

tribution, they can essentially buy a greater level of retirement consumption from a $1 increase in current saving. However, the amount of the price change is determined by workers' current and expected future income tax rates. The price reduction is thus determined by workers'marginal tax rates, which are in turn determined by their incomes.

One odd aspect of these tabulations is the finding that workers in jobs covered by private pensions are more rather than less likely to contribute to IRAs than are uncovered workers, holding earnings levels constant. Even when the authors use a formal statistical model to control for the effects of other factors, they never find evidence that uncovered workers are any more likely to contribute to IRAs than are covered workers. Using family data, in fact, they find that uncovered workers are *less* likely to contribute to IRAs (see tables 1.7 and 1.10).

Why this should be is difficult to explain; the authors do not attempt an explanation. Under a private pension plan the firm is saving on its workers' behalf. For at least a few of its workers the firm must be "oversaving" for their retirement. These workers would be expected to compensate for the oversaving by saving less outside of their pension plan. Hence, these workers should save less in the form of IRAs, which are in fact no more tax-preferred than are firms' contributions to private pension plans. By contrast, uncovered workers have no employer which saves on their behalf. One would expect them to do their own saving for retirement, and IRAs are the cheapest way for them to do so. Conceivably, workers with strong preferences for retirement saving sort themselves into pension-covered jobs. Their demand for retirement income is not satisfied by their employers' saving in pension plans, so they salt away additional savings in IRAs. This explanation, while somewhat plausible, is nonetheless surprising.

In the following section, Wise and Venti consider the estimation problem confronting them. Their discussion of the statistical issues is a model of lucidity. Essentially, there are three issues to be dealt with:

- How to model the decision to contribute to an IRA;
- How to estimate the demand function for contributions, given that some amount is going to be contributed; and
- How to deal with the limits on contributions set by current law.

Although the authors discuss three or four solutions, and in fact estimate the IRA demand function using more than one of them, the doubly-truncated Tobit model seems to perform about as well as more elaborate alternatives. That is, the more elaborate alternatives do not yield meaningfully different estimates of participation rates in IRAs, demand for IRAs, or the number of persons at the maximum contribution level.

For those not familiar with the Tobit model, the idea is very simple. For any particular individual, an index of the desire to make contributions to an IRA can extend over the entire range of real numbers— including negative numbers (for workers wishing to reduce their IRA holdings) and high positive numbers (for workers wishing to contribute an amount in excess of the legal maximum). However, there is an upper and lower bound on the *observed* distribution of demands because workers are prevented from reporting withdrawals and are not permitted to make contributions in excess of the maximum. Assuming normality in the distribution of the error terms, it is straightforward to obtain maximum likelihood estimates of the parameters that predict both the *desired* and the *observed* demand for IRA contributions. The model here is somewhat more clever than the usual Tobit model because it properly treats the issue of heteroscedasticity.

Venti and Wise obtain maximum likelihood estimates for both U.S. and Canadian workers. The U.S. data are examined in two different ways. The authors consider individual-level data on contributions and then look at family-level data. The main difference between the two statistical specifications is that the marginal tax rate is excluded as an explanatory variable when the authors estimate individuals' demand for IRAs. I have no idea why this critical variable is excluded for individuals. As mentioned earlier, the marginal tax rate is the main determinant of the marginal price of retirement saving in terms of current consumption foregone. To estimate a demand function that includes only income but excludes price seems odd, but I presume this was motivated by some defect in the data set. It seems clear to me that the marginal tax rate is as well defined for an *individual* in a joint filing unit as it is for the full filing unit. (In fact, it may be better defined if two members face differing tax rates on marginal earnings, as they sometimes will.)

The estimates for both the United States and Canada appear plausible. In the United States, the results indicate an elasticity of contributions with respect to income of 0.63—which doesn't seem unreasonable to me. But this estimate is subject to the qualification that it may be capturing some of the effect of varying the *price* of IRA contributions. As I mentioned above, income and price will be highly correlated under a progressive income tax scheme. In the individual-level specification, Venti and Wise exclude the price (or its proxy— MTR), implying that much of the effect of the price variation must be captured by the income term. In the family-level specification, the price term is included, but is so highly correlated with income (and possibly mismeasured because of the imputation procedure) that its coefficient must be at least a bit suspect. I think this has implications for the simulation results.

Essentially, we have two variables—income and the price of saving—which are highly correlated. Both variables probably have an important and independent effect on the demand for and attractiveness of IRA savings. The statistical procedure must somehow divide up the explanation of overall variance into a part explained by income and a part explained by price. Since the two variables are so highly correlated, this may be difficult to do. The highly erratic estimates of the effect of MTR are apparent in tables 1.9 and 1.10. I'm not sure we can trust those estimates, and for that reason, I'm not sure the simulations (especially those for the new Treasury tax plan) are entirely trustworthy.

The authors, however, are extremely careful to show the correspondence between their findings (1) using different models; (2) for the United States and Canada; and (3) from cross-sectional and time-series analysis of Canadian data. Those comparisons add considerably to the believability of the results.

The simulations in the paper show the effect of raising the present limits on IRA contributions. Since limit changes are frequently proposed, I think the results are interesting. Although I know little about past IRA research or simulations, these simulation predictions seem quite reasonable.

In closing, I wish to consider whether the questions dealt with in the simulations lie at the heart of the IRA issue. The critical question about IRAs and other tax-preferred saving plans is whether they contribute to or subtract from net personal saving. Because they reduce the price of saving for retirement, many Congressmen blithely assume that IRAs must eventually raise the amount of private saving that is done. The more sophisticated members of Congress would agree that in the *short run* most of the contributions to IRAs may come out of non-tax-sheltered savings. But in the long run—so the argument goes—workers will salt away something extra because retirement saving is so cheap.

As economists we cannot be so sanguine. The issue is deeper than the average Congressman imagines. If the price of obtaining $1 of consumption during retirement is reduced by enough, workers may actually engage in less not more saving for retirement; less saving is needed to attain a target level of retirement consumption. In fact, if everyone contributes at the maximum level, the marginal price of saving has not even been reduced. The net effect of IRAs on personal saving is the critical issue economists must address. This paper briefly raises the subject, but because of data limitations is prevented from formally addressing it. What would be useful here is a clear exposition of this main issue and an explanation of how the results in this paper—or extensions of those results—contribute to our understanding of the issue.

This paper, however, generally ignores the issue of the price of retirement saving (or retirement consumption, however you wish to view it). It ignores the objectives of retirement saving both from the point of view of the individual utility maximizer and the typical member of Congress.[1] And it does not treat the problem of saving in the relevant framework of lifetime utility maximization within a lifetime budget constraint that is affected by nonlinear taxes.

Can this paper tell us anything about the fundamental question just mentioned? I think it can. If we look over the tabular results, we notice that only a small minority of wage earners are at or near the maximum contribution level for IRAs or Canadian RRSPs. Even at the highest income (and marginal tax rate) levels, only a bare majority of U.S. and Canadian men make contributions equal to the legal maximum. This implies that the marginal price (not just the average price) of retirement saving has unambiguously been reduced for virtually all wage earners. The IRA does not represent a windfall drop in taxes which has no net effect on the marginal price of saving. In the case of the United States, the reduction in marginal price was sharp and discontinuous. If IRAs on balance *encourage* retirement saving, by reducing its marginal price, we should see some immediate population response, discernible in the aggregate statistics on personal saving. In fact, however, the U.S. personal saving rate has fallen precipitously since 1982, when IRAs were first extended to all wage earners, and in 1986 stood at 3.9 percent— less than half the rate of the 1970s.[2] The net impact of IRAs on personal saving, if any, has evidently been small or swamped by other factors.

In sum, I like the empirical work very much, and I admire the exposition and statistical modeling. But I would be interested in learning the authors' views on the relative importance of the issues raised and formally treated in this paper. Without treating the question of the *net* impact of IRAs on personal saving can any research on IRAs hold broad interest for economists? I realize that the U.S. and Canadian tax authorities will be very interested in these findings. But will the findings interest most public finance economists?

1. If the goal of a typical Congressman is to raise the net *national* saving rate, IRAs are an even poorer instrument than suggested in the previous paragraph. Even if an IRA succeeds in raising the private saving rate, it will reduce the public saving rate, at least initially, because it must reduce government tax revenue. Unless the net private saving response is fairly substantial, the loss in government saving can easily exceed the rise in private saving, leading to a reduction in net national saving.

2. U.S. Council of Economic Advisors, *Economic Report of the President, 1987,* (Washington, D.C.: U.S. Government Printing Office) 1987, p. 274.

2   Annuity Prices and Saving Behavior in the United States

Benjamin M. Friedman and Mark Warshawsky

One of the most puzzling contrasts between observed behavior and the implications of standard economic theory is the fact that, at least in the United States, few elderly individuals purchase life annuities. The conventional life-cycle model, based on the appealing concept that people save so as to smooth their consumption over their lifetimes, suggests that elderly retired individuals would seek to dissave out of their available resources as their remaining life expectancy shortens. Instead, observed age-wealth profiles among the elderly are more nearly flat.[1] Given the uncertainty associated with any individual's life expectancy, this reluctance to dissave would be a natural consequence of risk aversion if individuals could not avoid that risk by buying annuities. Since a well-developed individual life annuity market does exist in the United States, however, the challenge is to explain why so few people actually avail themselves of it.[2]

In an earlier paper, the authors offered an explanation for this phenomenon based on a combination of the cost of annuities and a bequest motive.[3] Annuities are costly, in the first instance, because the insurer must price them to defray ordinary costs of doing business and then earn a competitive profit. In addition, the typical individual in the population finds annuities even more costly because of adverse selec-

Benjamin M. Friedman is a professor of economics at Harvard University and a research associate of the National Bureau of Economic Research. Mark Warshawsky is an economist in the Capital Markets Section of the Division of Research and Statistics of the Board of Governors of the Federal Reserve System.

We are grateful to Andrew Abel, Glenn Hubbard, Laurence Kotlikoff, and Lawrence Summers for helpful comments on an earlier paper; to Amy Bassan, Robert Rubinstein, Francis Schott, Mark Slutzky, Michael Winterfield, as well as the Equitable Life Assurance Society, A. M. Best Publishers, and the American Council of Life Insurance, for help in gathering data; and to the National Bureau of Economic Research and the Alfred P. Sloan Foundation for research support.

tion—in other words, the tendency of longer-lived people to buy more annuities than people facing shorter life expectancies. Both kinds of costs understandably discourage the purchase of individual life annuities within the context of the familiar life-cycle model. By contrast, if individuals choose not to buy annuities because they have accumulated wealth to leave to their heirs, rather than to finance their own consumption after retirement, then the life-cycle model—and with it, a variety of well-known implications for economic behavior and economic policy—fails to withstand scrutiny. The principal finding of the authors' earlier research was that during the early years of retirement the observed cost of annuities can independently account for the absence of purchases of individual life annuities, while at older ages the combination of the observed cost of annuities and a bequest motive of plausible magnitude can account for this phenomenon.

The object of this paper is to experiment with an alternative form of the authors' earlier analysis by representing the cost of annuities as the (positive) differential between the premium on an annuity and its implicit expected value, rather than as the (negative) differential between the implicit expected yield on an annuity and the available yield on alternative forms of wealth holding. Given the inverse relationship between price and yield for any fixed-income investment vehicle, in principle these two forms of analysis are simply the duals of one another. The difference here stems from the need to compromise with reality in order to investigate the implications of life annuities within the context of a readily tractable model of the consumption-saving and portfolio-allocation decisions. In effect, the analysis both here and in the authors' earlier paper represents these annuities as if they were one-year contracts. Here, however, the analysis represents the cost of annuities as a one-time proportional charge to enter a market in which actuarially fair annuities are available, while in the earlier paper this cost consists of a continual unfairness in the pricing of the (one-year) annuity contracts. One advantage of the approach taken here is that, because large short-sales of annuities are no longer optimal, the nonnegativity constraint that was necessary in the earlier paper is no longer required. Because these formulations of the problem imply alternative opportunity sets, the results given by the two approaches differ.

Section 2.1 presents raw data on the prices of individual life annuities sold in the United States during 1968–83, together with transformations of those data that correspond to familiar concepts in economic discussions of consumption-saving behavior. Section 2.2 reviews the model of consumption-saving and portfolio-allocation behavior, for an individual with an uncertain lifetime, developed in the authors' earlier paper. Section 2.3 uses simulations of this model, based on the observed pricing of annuities, to draw inferences about the respective roles of annuity costs and a bequest motive in accounting for the typical elderly retired individual's preference for maintaining a flat age-wealth profile instead of buying annuities. Section 2.4 briefly summarizes the paper's principal findings and reemphasizes some limitations that apply to the analysis here as well as to the authors' earlier work.

2.1 Prices of Individual Life Annuities

Table 2.1 presents data for 1968–83, compiled from successive annual issues of the *A. M. Best Flitcraft Compend,* on the per-dollar prices of guaranteed single-premium immediate annuities offered in the United States for 65-year-old males. In each case the value shown is the price (premium) charged to purchase a stream of payments equaling $1 per month, to begin in the month immediately following the purchase and to continue for the life of the annuitant.

Column 1 of table 2.1 indicates the mean premium charged on this basic annuity contract by the ten largest insurance companies in the United States. These data are probably the most relevant for analyzing economy-wide individual behavior. The largest insurers usually do business in all regions of the country, so that the typical 65-year-old U.S. male has access to annuities at this mean price with little or no search costs. As would be expected, the average annuity premium has fallen over time, as the effect of rising interest rates has predominated over the effect of increasing life expectancy.

Table 2.1   **Premiums for Immediate $1 Monthly Life Annuities**

| | Ten Largest Insurers | | | Complete Sample |
Year	Mean	High	Low	Low
1968	$132.10	$136.20	$128.60	$127.20
1969	129.90	134.30	125.20	123.90
1970	127.40	133.70	119.30	116.70
1971	124.60	133.70	115.80	115.80
1972	124.70	133.70	117.70	117.70
1973	123.20	131.00	117.70	117.70
1974	121.70	127.60	115.80	115.50
1975	118.70	123.80	113.30	113.30
1976	116.60	123.30	111.40	107.90
1977	116.60	122.10	113.30	109.10
1978	116.60	122.10	113.30	109.10
1979	117.20	122.40	113.30	105.90
1980	113.40	119.90	105.70	101.80
1981	109.00	116.60	103.20	92.30
1982	104.90	116.60	87.60	75.30
1983	103.70	116.60	90.80	81.80

NOTE: Quotations are for 65-year-old males.

The remaining columns of table 2.1 indicate the potential returns to market search by showing the dispersion of premiums charged for this same basic contract by different insurers.[4] Columns 2 and 3 show data for the highest and lowest premiums charged for this contract by any of the ten largest insurers. Presumably most 65-year-old males have access to the lowest premium in this group at only modest search cost. Column 4 shows the lowest premium charged for this contract by any of the fifty-odd insurers in Best's sample. Because the smaller companies in the sample do not necessarily maintain sales forces in all parts of the country, however, there is no presumption that the typical 65-year-old male has ready access to this complete-sample lowest premium.

Table 2.2 presents calculations of the present expected value of an immediate $1 monthly annuity for the life of a 65-year-old male. The two key ingredients in such calculations, of course, are the assumed interest rate and the assumed structure of mortality probabilities.[5] The table reports annual calculations of present expected value based on two different interest rates, the 20-year U.S. government bond yield and the average yield on corporate debt directly placed with major life insurance companies. In the calculations underlying columns 1 and 2, the assumed mortality probabilities are the general population mortality probabilities for 65-year-old males reported in the 1970 and 1980 U.S. Life Tables, adjusted by a factor of .985 to reflect the 1.5 percent annual

Table 2.2   **Present Expected Values of $1 Monthly Life Annuities**

	General Population		Annuity Purchasers	
Year	Government Bonds	Direct Placements	Government Bonds	Direct Placements
1968	$104.80	$92.19	$120.81	$104.80
1969	99.49	87.64	113.81	98.92
1970	96.67	80.14	110.04	89.50
1971	101.41	85.84	116.59	96.86
1972	102.74	88.48	118.06	100.00
1973	96.16	88.25	109.46	99.53
1974	91.23	82.23	103.07	91.91
1975	90.93	79.49	102.52	88.41
1976	93.23	83.67	105.20	93.37
1977	94.83	87.88	107.01	98.39
1978	90.66	85.04	101.65	94.75
1979	86.64	80.67	96.56	89.29
1980	77.43	70.21	85.61	76.92
1981	69.31	63.24	75.75	68.57
1982	72.25	65.57	79.15	71.23
1983	78.69	74.38	86.77	81.58

NOTE: Calculations are for 65-year-old males.

improvement in U.S. male mortality probabilities that has occurred over the last two decades, and by a further factor of .9925 to reflect the assumption of a future 0.75 percent annual improvement in male mortality probabilities for all ages.[6]

Which of the two interest rates used in table 2.2 is most relevant depends upon the perspective taken in the analysis. From the standpoint of the actuarial "fair" value to an insurer who has access to (and typically owns) direct placement securities, the associated higher yield is the correct one to choose. Alternatively, from the standpoint of an individual's opportunity cost of funds, the lower yield on U.S. government bonds is relevant if the individual has no better investment vehicle. Because direct placements bear higher yields than do government bonds, the present expected values calculated using this yield are smaller than the corresponding values calculated using the government bond yield. Nevertheless, the present expected values calculated on either basis, including the government bond yield, are always smaller than even the lowest premium charged in the same year by any insurer in Best's sample.

If all individuals had identical mortality probabilities, a comparison between the calculated present expected values shown in columns 1 and 2 of table 2.2 and the actual premiums shown in table 2.1 would indicate the "load factor" by which the pricing of these annuities differs from their fair actuarial value. In fact, many individuals have information that leads them to expect either a shorter or a longer life than the population-wide average. Insurers, however, typically charge a uniform premium to all individuals of the same age and sex, presumably because information about individual mortality probabilities is either impossible or too costly to obtain and use. Individuals expecting longer (shorter) than average lifespans will therefore perceive life annuities as more (less) attractively priced, and hence will be more (less) likely to buy them.[7] This adverse selection—adverse from the viewpoint of the insurer, that is—will lead to underwriting losses if the insurer continues to charge a premium that is actuarially fair to the population as a whole.

Columns 3 and 4 of table 2.2 therefore present the results of further annual calculation of the present expected value of the same basic annuity contract for a 65-year-old male, based on the same two interest rates as before, but now based on alternative mortality probabilities compiled from the actual company experience on individual life annuity contracts issued in the United States during 1971–75, again adjusted as indicated above to reflect the improvement in mortality probabilities.[8] Figure 2.1 illustrates the extent to which the subpopulation who choose to buy annuities in fact have a greater survival probability than the general population. Because of this greater life expectancy, the

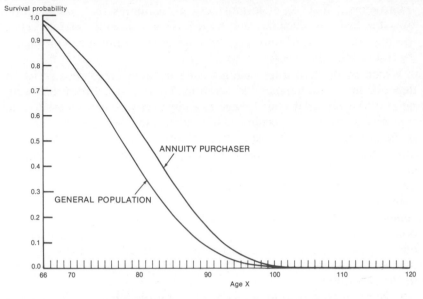

Fig. 2.1   Probability of survival to age X for males at age 65 in 1970.

present expected values shown in columns 3 and 4 of table 2.2 are greater than the corresponding values shown in columns 1 and 2, based on the same two interest rates but on general population mortality probabilities. For each year, however, even the greater values resulting from the actual company experience mortality probabilities are still uniformly smaller than even the lowest corresponding premiums shown for that year in table 2.1. Even within the subpopulation who voluntarily buy annuities, therefore, the price is not actuarially fair.

Table 2.3 summarizes the differences between the actual premiums charged on this basic annuity contract and the corresponding actuarially fair values by showing the 1968–83 average of the ratio of premium charged to present expected value for each of the four premiums re-

Table 2.3   **Average Load Factors on Life Annuity Premiums**

	General Population		Annuity Purchasers	
Premium	Government Bonds	Direct Placements	Government Bonds	Direct Placements
Ten-Largest Mean	1.32	1.48	1.18	1.33
Ten-Largest High	1.39	1.55	1.24	1.40
Ten-Largest Low	1.24	1.39	1.11	1.25
Complete-Sample Low	1.20	1.34	1.06	1.20

NOTE: Calculations are for 65-year-old males.

ported in table 2.1 and each of the four present expected value calculations reported in table 2.2. The resulting average load factors range from a low of 1.06 for the smallest premium charged by any company in Best's sample, compared to the present expected value based on government bond yields and actual company experience mortality probabilities, to a high of 1.55 for the largest premium charged by any of the ten largest insurers, compared to the present expected value based on direct placement yields and general population mortality tables.

The comparisons in table 2.3 that are probably most relevant for studying economy-wide individual behavior are those shown in row 1 for the mean premium charged by the ten largest insurers versus the present expected value based on either government bond yields or direct placement yields, and on either general population or company experience mortality probabilities. The load factor of 1.32, for the first case considered, means that a 65-year-old U.S. male, randomly selected from that population, and for whom the government bond yield represents the opportunity cost of capital, typically pays $1.32 for each $1.00 of expected present value when he purchases a life annuity. Among the (on average longer-lived) subpopulation of 65-year-old U.S. males who actually choose to buy life annuities, the load factor based on the same opportunity cost is only 1.18. In other words, of the 32¢ per dollar load factor to the general population, 14¢ represents the effect of adverse selection and the remaining 18¢ the combination of transaction costs, taxes, and profit to the insurer. If the annuity purchaser's opportunity cost of capital is instead the direct placement yield—for example, because of ability to buy shares in packages of intermediated private securities—then the load factor per dollar of expected present value is 48¢, of which 15¢ represents the effect of adverse selection and the remaining 33¢ the insurer's costs, taxes, and profit.[9] As the appendix shows, these results for 65-year-old males are similar to those for females or for males of different ages.

The question for consumption-saving behavior, then, is whether an average load factor of 1.18 (or even 1.48) is sufficient to account for the small participation in the individual life annuity market in the United States. In short, do most elderly retired people choose not to consume out of their wealth, and therefore leave unintentional bequests, merely because they are reluctant to pay $1.18 (or $1.48) for every $1.00 of present expected value of annuities?

It is difficult to answer this question on the basis of casual evidence only. At first thought, a load factor of this magnitude seems a large price to pay for pooling risk. Nevertheless, it is not out of line with loads charged elsewhere in the insurance business, in product lines that almost everyone buys. For example, data from *Best's Key Rating Guide: Property-Casualty* indicate that the recent average load factor in premiums charged for property and casualty insurance written by large companies has been 1.37—essentially the same as that on individual life annuities.

Moreover, despite the apparently large load factor, individual life annuities are not a "dominated asset" in the sense that the cost per unit of payoff, unadjusted for mortality probabilities, is greater than the analogous cost of alternative investment vehicles. Table 2.4 shows the present value of a 35-year certain $1 monthly annuity, calculated using the two interest rates used in tables 2.2 and 2.3 for each year during 1968–83.[10] As comparison to column 1 of table 2.1 shows, the value of the certain annuity based on the government bond yield exceeded the mean premium on the life annuity charged by the ten largest insurers in all years of the sample except 1980–82, while the value based on the direct placement yield exceeded the mean premium in most years until 1979.

Hence some more formal approach to this issue is necessary. Section 2.2 develops a framework for such an analysis, and section 2.3 applies that framework in the context of the premium and load factor data reported here.

2.2   A Model of Saving and Annuity Demand

The model used in Friedman and Warshawsky (1985)[11] to analyze the demand for individual life annuities in the context of life-cycle saving and a bequest motive is an annuity analog of Fischer's (1973) model of the demand for life insurance, generalized to incorporate fixed mandatory holdings of socially provided annuities.[12] The individual's

Table 2.4   Present Value of a 35-Year Certain $1 Monthly Annuity

Year	Government Bonds	Direct Placements
1968	$190.41	$153.04
1969	172.26	139.60
1970	162.68	120.14
1971	176.32	133.88
1972	178.51	139.47
1973	158.30	137.77
1974	144.21	122.38
1975	142.28	115.40
1976	146.91	123.96
1977	149.69	132.79
1978	138.42	125.35
1979	128.12	115.03
1980	108.21	93.95
1981	91.80	80.87
1982	96.86	84.62
1983	108.96	100.45

decision problem in this expanded life-cycle context is to maximize expected lifetime utility:

(1)
$$E(U) = \sum_{t=0}^{w-x-1} [p_t U_t(C_t) + p_t q_{t+1} V_{t+1}(G_{t+1})],$$

where w is the assumed maximum length of life, x is the individual's age as of time $t = 0$, p_t is the probability that an individual of age x at $t = 0$ will be alive at any time $t > 0$, q_{t+1} is the (conditional) probability that such an individual who was alive at time t will die at time $t + 1$,[13] $U_t(C_t)$ is utility received from consumption C at time t, and $V_{t+1}(G_{t+1})$ is utility received from (anticipation of) a bequest G at time $t + 1$. Following Fischer (1973), it is convenient to specify the two utility functions in the isoelastic form:

(2)
$$U_t(C_t) = \frac{C_t^{1-\beta}}{1 - \beta} \cdot \alpha^t \quad ,$$

(3)
$$V_t(G_t) = \frac{G_t^{1-\beta}}{1 - \beta} \cdot b_t \quad ,$$

where β is the Pratt-Arrow coefficient of relative risk aversion, α is the time preference parameter, and b_t (in comparison to α^t) indicates the relative utility attached to bequests left in period t.

The usual life-cycle specification of behavior with no bequest motive is therefore just the special case of this model with $b_t = 0$ for all $t > 0$. In general, however, people may value bequests, and they may value them differently at different times. The application of the model in section 2.3 below follows Yaari's (1965) suggestion that b_t follows a hump-shaped pattern with higher values during the years when family dependency is important, so that b_t is declining during retirement years when children have typically become independent.

The individual's problem is to maximize $E(U)$ subject to a given initial wealth position and to a nonnegativity constraint on wealth in each subsequent time period, given the menu of available investment opportunities (including any mandatory holding of socially provided annuities) and their respective yields.[14] In each period the individual must decide not only how much of current wealth to consume but also how to allocate the remainder among the available investment vehicles. The specific asset menu considered here includes a riskless one-period bond bearing gross rate of return R_t, a one-period social annuity bearing gross rate of return Q_t^S to survivors, and a one-period market annuity bearing gross rate of return Q_t^A to survivors.[15] Both annuities are actuarially fair—that is, there is no load factor on either—if

(4)
$$(1 - q_{t+1})Q_t^S = (1 - q_{t+1})Q_t^A = R_t.$$

With little relevant loss of generality, it is convenient to set R_t constant at R for all $t > 0$.

The dynamic programming solution to this problem proceeds from the final period $t = w - x - 1$, in which the certainty of death at the end of the period ($q_{w-x} = 1$) simplifies the problem of an individual who has survived to that date to merely choosing C_{w-x-1} to maximize the sum of utility from current consumption $U_{w-x-1}(C_{w-x-1})$ and utility from bequests $V_{w-x}(G_{w-x})$, subject to then-remaining wealth W_{w-x-1} and the constraint

$$(5) \qquad G_{w-x} = R \cdot (W_{w-x-1} - C_{w-x-1}).$$

Given the isoelastic utilities assumed in equations (2) and (3), the solution is just

$$(6) \qquad C_{w-x-1} = k_{w-x-1} \cdot W_{w-x-1} \quad,$$

where

$$(7) \qquad k_{w-x-1} = \frac{R(Rb_{w-x})^{-1/\beta}}{1 + R(Rb_{w-x})^{-1/\beta}} \quad,$$

and the corresponding indirect utility function,

$$(8) \qquad J_1[W_{w-x-1}] = \max_{C_{w-x-1}} [U_{w-x-1}(C_{x-x-1}) + V_{w-x}(G_{w-x})] \quad,$$

is

$$(9) \qquad J_1[W_{w-x-1}] = \delta_{w-x-1} \cdot \frac{W_{w-x-1}^{1-\beta}}{1-\beta} \quad,$$

where

$$(10) \qquad \delta_{w-x-1} = k_{w-x-1}^{-\beta}.$$

The consumption decision in equation (5) represents the entire solution for $t = w - x - 1$, since in that period the availability of annuities is irrelevant to the analysis.

The dynamic programming solution next proceeds to the individual's optimal consumption and portfolio decisions for the immediately prior period, given wealth remaining at that time. An individual alive at $t = w - x - 2$ will die at the end of that period with probability q_{w-x-1}. Hence the relevant maximand governing the decisions to be taken as of $t = w - x - 2$ is $U_{w-x-2}(C_{w-x-2})$ plus the bequest motive $V_{w-x-1}(G_{w-x-1})$ with probability q_{w-x-1} and the indirect utility function in equation (9) with probability $(1 - q_{w-x-1})$. The indirect utility function for $t = w - x - 2$ is therefore

$$J_2[W_{w-x-2}] = \max_{C_{w-x-2}, A_{w-x-2}} \left\{ \frac{C_{w-x-2}^{1-\beta}}{1-\beta} + (1 - q_{w-x-1})\alpha\delta_{w-x-1} \right.$$

(11)
$$\cdot \frac{(W_{w-x-2} - C_{w-x-2})^{1-\beta}}{1-\beta} \cdot [R(1 - A_{w-x-2} - S_{w-x-2})$$

$$+ Q_{w-x-2}^A A_{w-x-2} + Q_{w-x-2}^S S_{w-x-2}]^{1-\beta} + q_{w-x-1} b_{w-x-1}$$

$$\left. \cdot \frac{(W_{w-x-2} - C_{w-x-2})^{1-\beta}}{1-\beta} \cdot [R(1 - A_{w-x-2} - S_{w-x-2})]^{1-\beta} \right\} \quad ,$$

where A and S are the proportions of saving $(W - C)$ invested in market annuities and in (mandatory) social annuities, respectively. The usual life-cycle model with no market for annuities is therefore just the special case represented by $A_t = 0$ for all $t \geq 0$ (and, if there are no social annuities either, $S_t = 0$ for all $t \geq 0$ also).[16]

The first order conditions for equation (11) then give the optimal values of consumption and purchases of market annuities at $t = w - x - 2$ as

(12)
$$C_{w-x-2} = \delta_{w-x-2}^{-1/\beta} \cdot W_{w-x-2}$$

and

(13)
$$A_{w-x-2} = \frac{R\left[\left(\dfrac{Rb_{w-x-1} q_{w-x-1}}{(1 - q_{w-x-1})\alpha\delta_{w-x-1}(Q_{w-x-2}^A - R)}\right)^{-1/\beta} - 1\right]}{Q_{w-x-2}^S + R\left[\left(\dfrac{Rb_{w-x-1} q_{w-x-1}}{(1 - q_{w-x-1})\alpha\delta_{w-x-1}(Q_{w-x-2}^A - R)}\right)^{-1/\beta} - 1\right]}$$
$$- S_{w-x-2} \quad ,$$

and the corresponding value of the indirect utility function as

(14)
$$J_2[W_{w-x-2}] = \delta_{w-x-2} \cdot W_{w-x-2} \quad ,$$

where

(15)
$$\delta_{w-x-2} = \left[\frac{k_{w-x-2}}{1 + k_{w-x-2}}\right]^{-\beta} \quad ,$$

and

(16)
$$k_{w-x-2} = \{\alpha\delta_{w-x-1} [R(1 - A_{w-x-2} - S_{w-x-2})$$
$$+ Q_{w-x-2}^A A_{w-x-2} + Q_{w-x-2}^S S_{w-x-2}]^{1-\beta}$$
$$+ b_{w-x-1}q_{w-x-1}[R(1 - A_{w-x-2} - S_{w-x-2})]^{1-\beta}\}^{-1/\beta}.$$

The remainder of the dynamic programming solution proceeds backward to the initial period $t = 0$ in an analogous way. The expressions for each period's optimal consumption and purchases of market annuities, and for each period's value of the indirect utility function, are of the same form (but with subscripts adjusted accordingly) as equations (12), (13), and (14), respectively.

2.3 Simulation Results

The model developed in section 2.2 generates lifetime streams of consumption and annuity purchase values that are optimal for given values of parameters describing preferences (β, α, and b), the market environment (R, Q^A, and Q^S), and mortality probabilities (p and q). The principal focus of interest in this paper is on one aspect of preferences and one aspect of the market environment—the bequest motive and the availability of market annuities, respectively.

The strategy adopted here for representing the bequest motive (confronting a 65-year-old male) follows Fischer (1973) by assuming that b_t in equation (3) varies according to

$$(17) \qquad b_t = (1.04 - .01t) \cdot \theta, \qquad t = 0, \ldots, 35 \ ,$$

where θ is a non-age-specific parameter indicating the individual's lifelong preference for bequests relative to current consumption, given the other parameters of the model, including in particular the interest rate (R), the curvature of the utility function (β), and—because θ implicitly gives the relative weight of a stock (the bequest) versus a flow (consumption)—the assumed time unit of analysis. For any given value of θ, however, b_t declines linearly with t.[17] Given θ and b_t, the bequest amount is larger as R is higher, and smaller as β is higher. For example, from equations (5)–(7) and (17), θ takes the value $(G_{w-x}/C_{w-x-1})^\beta \cdot (.69)/R$, where (G_{w-x}/C_{w-x-1}) is just the ratio of the final-period bequest to the prior-period consumption. The normally limiting case for altruistic bequests, in which an individual provides for his heirs' consumption at the same level as his own, indicates $(1/R - 1)^\beta \cdot (.69)/R$ as the logical upper bound on θ.[18] In the simulations reported below, the strength of the bequest motive is indicated initially by θ, and subsequently by the corresponding bequest/saving ratio (G_{w-x}/C_{w-x-1}), given the other assumed parameters.

The strategy used here to represent the market for private annuities follows Kotlikoff and Spivak (1981) by assuming that private annuities are either available at the actuarially fair price $Q^A = R/(1 - q)$, or, alternatively, not available at all ($A = 0$). The object of the analysis, therefore, is to determine what load factor an individual would be willing to pay in order to have access to market annuities under the assumed values of all of the model's other parameters. By comparing this critical load factor with the typical load factors summarized in table 2.3, in light of the observation that in fact very few individuals actually purchase life annuities, it is then possible to assess the reasonableness of the assumed values of the model's other parameters—including, in particular, the strength of the bequest motive.

This treatment of the cost of annuities captures the chief implications of the fact that, although the model in principle refers to one-period annuities, in fact the annuities available for purchase are life annuities. Even when an individual makes monthly annuity purchases over time, as in many defined contribution retirement plans, what he is buying each month is an additional life annuity. It is therefore plausible to treat the load factors on annuity premiums shown in table 2.3 in a lump-sum fashion, not as a load to be repeated in every period.

The simplest place to begin is the special case of the model developed in section 2.2 corresponding to the standard life-cycle model with neither bequest motive nor Social Security (which is equivalent to the model in Kotlikoff and Spivak [1981]). Table 2.5 summarizes the results of two simulations of the model, both based on the assumptions that $b_t = 0$ and $S_t = 0$ for all t. As in Kotlikoff and Spivak (1981), the assumed time preference parameter is $\alpha = .99$, and the assumed market interest rate is constant at $R = 1.01$. The assumed coefficient of relative risk aversion is $\beta = 4.$[19] The assumed mortality probabilities are those for a 65-year-old male reported in the 1980 U.S. Life Tables, adjusted as described in section 2.1. For each simulation, table 2.5 shows the relevant solution values for the initial year (age 65) and every fifth year thereafter until the assumed maximum life span (age 110).

Table 2.5   **Simulation Results for the Standard Life-Cycle Model**

Age	No Annuities		Annuities Available		
	Consumption	Bonds	Consumption	Bonds	Annuities
65	4.08%	100.00%	7.20%	.00%	100.00%
70	3.90	84.43	7.20	.00	83.36
75	3.67	69.06	7.20	.00	68.49
80	3.37	54.26	7.19	.00	55.58
85	2.98	40.44	7.19	.00	44.55
90	2.49	28.13	7.19	.00	36.00
95	1.95	17.81	7.19	.00	29.70
100	1.41	9.78	7.19	.00	25.23
105	.96	3.96	7.19	.00	19.61
110	.00	.00	.00	.00	.00

NOTES: Assumed values are $\alpha = .99$, $R = 1.01$, and $\beta = 4$. Calculations are for 65-year-old males. Values are percentages of initial wealth. Annuity values are present expected values.

The first simulation considered within this traditional life-cycle context represents the case in which market annuities (like social annuities here) are unavailable. The individual's only choice is therefore how much to consume in each period, since the unconsumed portion of initial wealth is automatically invested in one-year bonds. Column 1 of table 2.5 shows the optimal age-consumption profile, while column 2 shows the corresponding implied profile of remaining wealth (consisting entirely of bonds), with both sets of values stated as percentages of initial wealth. These simulated values immediately indicate the important contrast between reality and this set of assumptions, in that they show the optimality of a declining age-consumption profile and a sharply declining age-wealth profile—phenomena not observed in available data.

The second simulation within this traditional life-cycle context, summarized in columns 3–5 of table 2.5, shows that simply relaxing the assumption that market annuities are unavailable avoids this strikingly counterfactual result only at the expense of leading to another. This simulation differs from the first one in assuming that individual life annuities are available in the private market at an actuarially fair price $[Q^A = R/(1 - q)]$, and the table reports values for optimal consumption as well as optimal wealth holdings in bonds and annuities, respectively.[20] In this case, the individual's optimal course of action is to hold no bonds at all but to stabilize the age-consumption profile almost completely by investing all wealth in annuities. The implied flat age-consumption profile is roughly consistent with the available evidence, but the implied large demand for market annuities is sharply counterfactual.

Following Kotlikoff and Spivak (1981), it is possible to infer the lump-sum value to the individual, under the conditions assumed in the simulations reported in table 2.5, of having access to a market for actuarially fair life annuities. From equation (14), the initial value of the indirect utility function in each simulation is

$$(18) \qquad J_{w-x}[W_0] = \delta_0 \frac{W_0^{1-\beta}}{1 - \beta} \quad,$$

for given initial wealth W_0. The proportional increment in the individual's initial wealth required to render the individual as well off, in the sense of an equal initial value of the indirect utility function, in the absence of an annuity market as with such a market is therefore just

$$(19) \qquad M = \left[\frac{\delta_0 | Q^A = R/(1 - q)}{\delta_0 | A = 0} \right]^{\frac{1}{1-\beta}} - 1 \quad,$$

where $\delta_0|Q^A = R/(1 - q)$ is the value of δ_0 in equation (18) in the simulation with a market for fair annuities, and $\delta_0|A = 0$ is the analogous value in the simulation with no annuity market.

For the pair of simulations reported in table 2.5, the calculation in equation (19) yields $M = 1.13$. Under the conditions assumed in these simulations, therefore, it would still be preferable to put all initial wealth into annuities than to buy none at all, as long as the load factor did not exceed $L^* = 2.13$.[21] Because $L^* = 2.13$ far exceeds the load factors in actual annuity prices calculated on any of the bases reported in table 2.3, and yet in fact there is little individual demand for life annuities, some other assumption common to the two simulations shown in table 2.5 must be importantly counterfactual.

One possibility, of course, is that $\beta = 4$ overstates the coefficient of relative risk aversion. Alternative simulations with a smaller risk-aversion parameter show that this is not the source of the problem, however. Table 2.6 summarizes a pair of simulations that are identical to those reported in table 2.5 except for the new assumption $\beta = 2$.[22] Although the specific age-consumption and age-wealth profiles shown in table 2.6 differ somewhat from those in table 2.5, the same counterfactual implications are again readily apparent. Indeed, because of the lower risk-aversion, the optimal age-consumption and age-wealth profiles when annuities are unavailable decline even more sharply. When actuarially fair annuities are available, it is again optimal to invest all of initial wealth in them. Most importantly, even with lower risk aversion the proportional increment in initial wealth required to render the

Table 2.6   **Simulation Results for the Standard Life-Cycle Model (Low Risk Aversion)**

	No Annuities		Annuities Available		
Age	Consumption	Bonds	Consumption	Bonds	Annuities
65	5.25%	100.00%	7.20%	.00%	100.00%
70	4.81	78.91	7.20	.00	83.36
75	4.26	59.21	7.20	.00	68.49
80	3.58	41.63	7.19	.00	55.58
85	2.79	26.89	7.19	.00	44.55
90	1.96	15.57	7.19	.00	36.00
95	1.20	7.86	7.19	.00	29.70
100	.63	3.33	7.19	.00	25.23
105	.29	1.03	7.19	.00	19.61
110	.00	.00	.00	.00	.00

NOTES: Assumed values are $\alpha = .99$, $R = 1.01$, and $\beta = 2$. Calculations are for 65-year-old males. Values are percentages of initial wealth. Annuity values are present expected values.

individual as well off in the absence of an annuity market as with such a market is still $M = .88$. Even with lower risk aversion, therefore, it would still be preferable to put all of initial wealth into annuities rather than to buy none at all, as long as the load factor did not exceed $L^* = 1.88$—a critical value again well in excess of any of the observed load factors reported in table 2.3.

A further possible explanation for the counterfactual results in both tables 2.5 and 2.6 is that Social Security not only exists but is a large part of wealth for most individuals. Table 2.7 presents a pair of simulations of the more general model developed in section 2.2—first without, and then with, a market for actuarially fair annuities—based on the assumption that actuarially fair Social Security constitutes half of total wealth ($S = .5$).[23] In all other respects, including the absence of a bequest motive, these simulations are analogous to those reported in table 2.5.

The results shown in table 2.7 again exhibit largely the same counterfactual patterns as in table 2.5 and, therefore, suggest that merely allowing for Social Security cannot account for the observed behavior. In the absence of an annuities market, the optimal age-consumption and especially age-wealth profiles decline fairly sharply, although not so much as in table 2.5. If actuarially fair annuities are available, it is optimal to invest all of total wealth other than Social Security in purchasing them. Most importantly, even with a sizeable role for Social Security, the proportional initial wealth increment required to render the individual as well off without as with a private annuity market is $M = .33$. Hence it would still be preferable to put all of total wealth other than Social Security (that is, one-half of total wealth) into private

Table 2.7   **Simulation Results for the Model Including Social Security**

	No Annuities			Annuities Available			
Age	Consumption	Soc. Sec.	Bonds	Consumption	Soc. Sec.	Bonds	Annuities
65	5.81%	50.00%	50.00%	7.20%	50.00%	.00%	50.00%
70	5.68	41.62	41.62	7.20	41.68	.00	41.68
75	5.51	33.83	33.83	7.20	34.25	.00	34.25
80	5.28	26.79	26.79	7.20	27.79	.00	27.79
85	4.97	20.57	20.57	7.19	22.27	.00	22.27
90	4.57	15.42	15.42	7.19	18.00	.00	18.06
95	4.06	11.30	11.30	7.19	14.85	.00	14.85
100	3.50	7.99	7.99	7.19	12.61	.00	12.61
105	2.92	4.73	4.73	7.19	9.80	.00	9.80
110	.00	.00	.00	.00	.00	.00	.00

NOTES: Assumed values are $\alpha = .99$, $R = 1.01$, $\beta = 4$, and $S = .5$. Calculations are for 65-year-old males. Values are percentages of initial wealth. Annuity values are present expected values.

annuities rather than buy none at all, as long as the annuity load factor did not exceed $L^* = 1.66 = 1 + (.33/.5)$—again far greater than the load factors actually observed. An analogous simulation based on the lower risk-aversion value of $\beta = 2$ (not shown in the table) produces almost identical results, with $M = .31$ and a critical load factor $L^* = 1.62$.

The potential explanation for the observed behavior that is of greatest interest in the context of this paper is that, in general, people may value not just their own consumption but also bequests. Table 2.8 presents three further pairs of simulations of the fully general model developed in section 2.2, in each case based on the same assumptions as in table 2.7 (including the prominent role for Social Security) and, in addition, a positive bequest motive. The first of these three pairs of simulations assumes the bequest motive $\theta = 2$, which is quite modest given the stock-flow dimension of θ and the model's use of an annual time unit, and $\beta = 4$. The second pair of simulations assumes $\theta = 8$, the third $\theta = 24$.

The simulation results reported in table 2.8 show that even a very modest bequest motive is sufficient to eliminate one of the importantly counterfactual aspects of the earlier simulations. In particular, because of the bequest motive it is no longer optimal to invest all of total wealth other than Social Security in private annuities. The fraction of wealth invested in bonds varies positively with the strength of the bequest motive, but even $\theta = 2$ is sufficient to make optimal bond holdings neither zero nor trivially small. Moreover, optimal bond holdings do not decrease (until the final year they actually increase slightly) with age. Hence the general model, with even a modest positive bequest motive, is consistent with observed behavior in implying an approximately flat age-wealth profile for the part of wealth held in nonannuity form.

By contrast, the results for all three pairs of simulations shown in table 2.8 continue to be counterfactual in implying that, when private annuities are available, it is optimal to use a large fraction of total wealth other than Social Security to purchase them. Further analysis, however, indicates that here the load factor in annuity pricing is potentially very important.

For the weak bequest motive $\theta = 2$, the proportional initial wealth increment required to render the individual as well off without as with a private annuity market is $M = .22$. The critical load factor necessary to make buying no annuities at all preferable to investing 41 percent of initial wealth in annuities is there $L^* = 1.53 = 1 + (.22/.41)$, again above the observed load factors reported in table 2.3 for the mean premiums charged by the ten largest insurers, regardless of the mortality probabilities and the interest rates used in the calculations.

Table 2.8   Simulation Results for the General Model

	No Annuities			Annuities Available			
Age	Consumption	Soc. Sec.	Bonds	Consumption	Soc. Sec.	Bonds	Annuities
$\theta = 2$							
65	5.80%	50.00%	50.00%	6.72%	50.00%	8.56%	41.44%
70	5.68	41.64	41.64	6.72	42.31	8.57	33.74
75	5.51	33.87	33.87	6.72	35.42	8.60	26.83
80	5.28	26.86	26.86	6.71	29.44	8.66	20.78
85	4.97	20.69	20.69	6.71	24.31	8.78	15.54
90	4.57	15.61	15.61	6.71	20.33	8.92	11.41
95	4.08	11.61	11.61	6.71	17.37	9.08	8.29
100	3.54	8.54	8.54	6.71	15.25	9.22	6.03
105	3.04	5.79	5.79	6.71	12.60	9.62	2.98
110	.00	.00	3.18	.00	.00	7.01	.00
$\theta = 8$							
65	5.78%	50.00%	50.00%	6.54%	50.00%	11.76%	38.24%
70	5.66	41.67	41.67	6.53	42.54	11.76	30.79
75	5.49	33.95	33.95	6.53	35.86	11.78	24.08
80	5.27	26.99	26.99	6.53	30.06	11.85	18.21
85	4.96	20.90	20.90	6.53	25.08	11.97	13.11
90	4.58	15.93	15.93	6.53	21.20	12.11	9.09
95	4.12	12.10	12.10	6.53	18.31	12.26	6.05
100	3.66	9.30	9.30	6.53	16.24	12.39	3.85
105	3.29	6.94	6.94	6.53	13.64	12.76	.88
110	.00	.00	5.57	.00	.00	9.65	.00
$\theta = 24$							
65	5.76%	50.00%	50.00%	6.35%	50.00%	15.01%	34.99%
70	5.64	41.75	41.75	6.35	42.78	14.99	27.79
75	5.47	34.12	34.12	6.35	36.31	15.01	21.31
80	5.25	27.27	27.27	6.35	30.69	15.06	15.62
85	4.96	21.31	21.31	6.35	25.85	15.17	10.68
90	4.60	16.55	16.55	6.35	22.09	15.30	6.79
95	4.22	13.02	13.02	6.35	19.28	15.42	3.85
100	3.89	10.65	10.65	6.34	17.24	15.51	1.73
105	3.76	8.90	8.90	6.34	14.71	15.83	-1.12
110	.00	.00	9.54	.00	.00	12.33	.00

NOTES: Assumed values (other than θ as shown) are $\alpha = .99$, $R = 1.01$, $\beta = 4$, and $S = .5$. Calculations are for 65-year-old males. Values are percentages of initial wealth. Annuity values are present expected values.

For $\theta = 8$, the initial wealth increment required to render the individual as well off without as with a private annuity market is only $M = .18$, so that the critical load factor that would make buying no annuities at all preferable to investing 38 percent of initial wealth in annuities is $L^* = 1.47$. As table 2.3 shows, this load factor is approximately equal to that charged on average by the largest ten insurers if the underlying present expected value calculation relies on general population mortality probabilities and the interest rate on corporate direct placements. Nevertheless, it still exceeds the implied load factor confronting an individual who knows that his mortality probabilities are characteristic of other annuity purchasers, or whose opportunity cost of funds is the government bond yield (or who searches for the lowest available premium).

Finally, for $\theta = 24$, the initial wealth increment required to render the individual as well off without as with a private annuity market is $M = .14$. Hence the critical load factor that would make buying no annuities at all preferable to investing 35 percent of initial wealth in annuities is $L^* = 1.40$, about in the middle between the actual load factor based on general population mortality probabilities and the direct placement yield and the actual load factor based on alternative assumptions.

Under some sets of plausible assumptions, therefore, importantly including a positive bequest motive, the actual load factor included in the premiums on individual life annuities sold in the United States is sufficient to make people prefer buying no annuities at all over buying the amount that would be optimal if annuity prices were actuarially fair. Although this finding is hardly without interest, since it indicates a joint role for the bequest motive and for annuity load factors in explaining the observed behavior, it still does not fully explain the fact that almost no one buys *any* individual life annuities. Nothing forces people to choose between buying either the amount of annuities that would be optimal at actuarially fair prices or buying none at all. Hence showing under what conditions people would prefer no annuities at all to the amount they would purchase at actuarially fair prices still does not establish the conditions under which they would not buy some amount that is significant albeit less than the actuarially fair optimum. For the assumed values of α, R, β, and S underlying the simulations reported in table 2.8, for example, and for an assumed annuity load factor of $L = 1.40$ (the critical value for $\theta = 24$), the strength of the bequest motive required to make the individual indifferent between purchasing private annuities equal to 1 percent of initial wealth (including Social Security) and purchasing none at all is $\theta = 343$—far above $\theta = 24$, yet still below the logical upper bound for θ given the assumed parameter values. Table 2.9 summarizes the results of analogous simulations based on various values of S, R, and β, reporting in each case the value of θ that renders the individual just indifferent between investing 1 percent of initial wealth (including Social Security) in private annuities and purchasing none at all when the load factor is $L = 1.40$.[24]

Both because the quantitative importance of bequests in overall saving is a question with major implications for both positive and normative

Table 2.9   **Bequest Motive Strength Needed to Eliminate Annuity Purchases**

	$S = .4$	$S = .5$	$S = .6$
$R = 1.01$			
$\beta = 2$	18	9	4
$\beta = 3$	169	58	18
$\beta = 4$	1488	343	74
$R = 1.04$			
$\beta = 2$	10	5	3
$\beta = 3$	66	24	7
$\beta = 4$	419	105	22

NOTES: Values shown are for θ, just sufficient to eliminate initial annuity purchases equal to 1 percent of initial wealth. Assumed values (other than S, R, and β as shown) are $\alpha = .99$ and $L = 1.40$. Calculations are for 65-year-old males.

issues,[25] and because there is little other way to evaluate the plausibility of values of θ within the logically admissible range, it is interesting to see just how large these results suggest that the typical bequest should be. Table 2.10 shows, for each of the combinations of parameter values considered in table 2.9, and in each case for the value of the bequest motive parameter θ (as shown in table 2.9) needed to render the individual indifferent between investing 1 percent of initial wealth in private annuities and purchasing none at all when the load factor is $L = 1.40$, the corresponding bequest/consumption ratio (G_{w-x}/C_{w-x-1}). For the most part these estimates are closely bunched, despite the wide variation in the underlying parameter values, typically indicating a bequest equal to 2–4 times the final year's consumption. Especially for the lower end of the range, these estimates appear to be empirically plausible.[26]

Table 2.10   **Ratio of Expected Bequest to Final Period Consumption**

	$S = .4$	$S = .5$	$S = .6$
$R = 1.01$			
$\beta = 2$	3.40	2.40	1.60
$\beta = 3$	4.77	3.34	2.25
$\beta = 4$	5.56	3.85	2.63
$R = 1.04$			
$\beta = 2$	2.57	1.82	1.29
$\beta = 3$	3.52	2.51	1.67
$\beta = 4$	4.08	2.89	1.95

NOTES: Values shown are ratios of expected bequest to final period consumption, given θ just large enough to eliminate initial annuity purchases equal to 1 percent of initial wealth. Assumed values (other than S, R, and β as shown) are $\alpha = .99$ and $L = 1.40$. Calculations are for 65-year-old males.

Given the respective roles of S, R, and β in affecting the demand for annuities in the model developed in section 2.2, their corresponding roles here in determining the strength of bequest motive necessary to eliminate that demand (for a given load factor) is straightforward. The demand for individual life annuities is smaller as Social Security is more important, smaller as the rate of return is higher, and greater as people are more risk averse. Hence the bequest motive implied by the fact that few people buy individual life annuities is weaker as Social Security is more important, weaker as the rate of return is higher, and stronger as people are more risk averse.

In sum, the results shown in tables 2.9 and 2.10 indicate that for plausible sets of assumed parameter values the combination of an annuity load factor in the observed range (see again table 2.3) and an empirically plausible positive bequest motive in the theoretically admissible range for altruistic bequests is sufficient to explain the absence of purchases of individual life annuities. This finding lends strength to the view that desired bequests are an important element in consumption-saving behavior. Moreover, when Social Security is less important and people are more risk averse, the bequest motive assumes an especially large role in explaining why so few people buy annuities. Under these circumstances the indicated bequest is at least 4 times final consumption.

2.4 Conclusion and Further Thoughts

The observed reluctance of most individuals in the United States to buy individual life annuities, and the concommitant approximately flat average age-wealth profile, stand in sharp contradiction to the standard life-cycle model of consumption-saving behavior. The analysis in this paper lends support to an explanation for this phenomenon based on the interaction of an intentional bequest motive and annuity prices that are not actuarially fair.

Premiums charged for individual life annuities in the United States do include a load factor of 32¢–48¢ per dollar, or 18¢–33¢ per dollar after allowing for adverse selection, in comparison to actuarially fair annuity values. Load factors of this size are not out of line with those on other familiar (and almost universally purchased) insurance products. Simulations of an extended model of life-cycle saving and portfolio behavior, allowing explicitly for uncertain lifetimes and Social Security, show that the load factor charged would have to be far larger than this to account for the observed behavior in the absence of a bequest motive. By contrast, the combination of a load factor in this range and a positive bequest motive can do so for some plausible values of the assumed underlying parameters. Moreover, if this combination of factors is leading elderly individuals to avoid purchasing life annuities, it implies a typical bequest that is fairly large in comparison to their annual consumption.

As the authors' earlier work has already emphasized, caution is appropriate in relying on these conclusions without further research. Although the model used here does generalize the standard life-cycle model in several potentially important ways, it still excludes *a priori* a variety of further possible explanations for the observed behavior.[27] First, many people at least say that they choose stable age-wealth profiles, rather than either buying annuities or simply consuming out of wealth, not because of mortality considerations but from fear of the consequences of catastrophic illness. Second, while the analysis here follows the recent literature by implicitly working in real terms, the individual life annuities available in U.S. markets guarantee specified nominal payments. Third, the analysis here does not allow for several more complex kinds of possible interactions within families, including, for example, either nonaltruistic ("manipulative") bequests or intra-family risk sharing.[28] Finally, in contrast to the reliance here (and in just about all of the available literature on the subject) on the standard theory of expected utility maximization, there is evidence that, especially when the prospect of rare events is involved, individuals systematically overweight the probability of rare events.[29]

These further possible explanations for the fact that few people purchase individual life annuities are subjects for future research.

Appendix

Average Load Factor for Life Annuity Premiums

Premium	General Population		Annuity Purchasers	
	Government Bonds	Direct Placements	Government Bonds	Direct Placements
65-Year-Old Females:				
Ten-Largest Mean	1.26	1.42	1.18	1.35
Ten-Largest High	1.34	1.52	1.26	1.44
Ten-Largest Low	1.18	1.33	1.11	1.26
Complete-Sample Low	1.15	1.30	1.08	1.23
70-Year-Old Males:				
Ten-Largest Mean	1.30	1.43	1.16	1.29
Ten-Largest High	1.37	1.51	1.22	1.36
Ten-Largest Low	1.24	1.36	1.11	1.23
Complete-Sample Low	1.18	1.30	1.06	1.17
75-Year-Old Males:				
Ten-Largest Mean	1.29	1.40	1.15	1.26
Ten-Largest High	1.35	1.47	1.21	1.33
Ten-Largest Low	1.23	1.34	1.10	1.21
Complete-Sample Low	1.15	1.25	1.03	1.13

Notes

1. See, for example, Mirer (1979) and Hubbard (1983).
2. The Retirement History Survey indicates that only 2 percent of the elderly population own individual annuities of any sort; see, for example, Friedman and Sjogren (1980).
3. See Friedman and Warshawsky (1985).
4. This dispersion probably reflects search costs; see, for example, Pratt et al. (1979). Alternatively, it could reflect different marketing choices by different insurers.
5. The exact expression used is

$$\sum_{t=1}^{w-x-1} (1 + r)^{-t} p_{xt},$$

where w is the assumed maximum length of life (here taken to be 110 years), x is the age at the date of issue (here 65 years), r is the relevant interest rate, and p_{xt} is the probability that an individual of age x at the time $t = 1$ will survive to any year $t > 1$. These annual calculations are then converted to a monthly basis.
6. The calculations rely on the 1970 tables for years 1968–70, on the 1980 tables for years 1980–83, and on both tables (weighted) for the years 1971–79. See Faber (1982) for a complete discussion of the U.S. Life Tables, and Wetterstrand (1983) for a discussion of improvements in mortality probabilities. In the calculations for females summarized in the appendix, the corresponding adjustment factors are .98 and .99.
7. See Rothschild and Stiglitz (1976) for an analysis of the principles underlying this kind of adverse selection.
8. See Society of Actuaries (1983) for the actual company experience tables.
9. This latter comparison is the relevant one from the perspective of the insurer. Informal discussions with the insurers suggest that, of this 33¢ per dollar, roughly 11¢ reflected transaction costs (narrowly defined), 8¢ taxes, and 14¢ return to capital at risk. This breakdown is at best only suggestive, however.
10. The small probability that a 65-year-old male will survive past age 100 is simply ignored for purposes of this comparison.
11. This section draws heavily on Friedman and Warshawsky (1985); see that paper for additional details and references to relevant literature.
12. In fact, Fischer's model is really an annuity model, despite his application of it to the demand for life insurance.
13. Probabilities p_t and q_{t+1} are, of course, conditional on initial age x. Writing them as $p(x)_t$ and $q(x)_{t+1}$ would be appropriate but would clutter an already cumbersome notation. Conditionally on x is to be understood, here and below.
14. In a more general context it would also be necessary to take account of labor income. The focus of this paper, however, is on the elderly retired population.
15. As in Fischer (1973), the assumption of one-period annuities makes the analysis tractable. The annuities actually available for purchase in the United States are instead life annuities.
16. The model as written here imposes no nonnegativity constraint on choice parameter A—that is, it does not explicitly preclude short sales of annuities. For most reasonable values of the given parameters, however, large short sales are not optimal anyway. If they were, imposing a nonnegativity constraint in solving the model would be straightforward.

17. The time profile in equation (17) is from Fischer's (1973) appendix table A2, extended to age 110. Reasoning analogous to that underlying Abel's (1984) model of life insurance markets suggests that the results could be very sensitive to whether the value of bequests is rising or falling with t. In particular, a sufficiently negatively sloped bequest motive can, under some circumstances, give rise to a negative demand for annuities. The after-age-65 portion of Fischer's time profile, used here, makes b_t decline approximately in step with α^t for $\alpha = .99$ as assumed below.

18. Friedman and Warshawsky (1985) indicate other circumstances under which θ would not be bounded. See also Abel and Warshawsky (1987) for a theoretical analysis in which the "joy of giving" bequest motive assumed in this chapter is interpreted as the reduced form of an altruistic bequest motive to derive a relation between the value of the altruism parameter and the value of the "joy of giving" parameter.

19. Grossman and Shiller (1981) found evidence consistent with a relative risk-aversion coefficient roughly equal to 4. Bodie et al. (1985) also used this value.

20. Wealth held in annuities is valued at the present expected value.

21. In other words, any approximately flat consumption stream exceeding 3.3 percent of initial wealth each year (7.20 percent as in column 3 of table 2.5, divided by 2.13) would be preferable to the declining stream shown in column 1.

22. Friend and Blume (1975) found evidence indicating a relative risk-aversion coefficient roughly equal to 2.

23. One-half is about the fraction of total wealth constituted by Social Security and private pensions for the average retired elderly individual in the United States; see the evidence provided by Kotlikoff and Smith (1983, table 3.7.19, p. 127).

24. The results shown in table 2.9 follow from searching over θ, given the assumed values of the other parameters. For purposes of comparison to the analysis by Kotlikoff and Spivak (1981), the θ values corresponding to $\beta = 1.25$ are (in order, from top to bottom in the table) 3, 2, 1, 2, 1.5, and 1.

25. See, for example, Kotlikoff and Summers (1981).

26. For males, Menchik and David (1982, table 1, p. 193) reported a median bequest equal to 2.1 times annual median labor income (defined as one-fortieth of total lifetime labor earnings), and a mean bequest equal to 4.2 times mean annual labor income.

27. See Friedman and Warshawsky (1985) for a brief discussion of several of these other possible explanations.

28. See, for example, Bernheim et al. (1985) on nonaltruistic bequests and Kotlikoff and Spivak (1981) on intrafamily risk sharing.

29. See, for example, Kahneman and Tversky (1979).

References

Abel, Andrew B. 1984. The effects of Social Security in the presence of perfect annuity markets. Harvard University. Mimeo.

Abel, Andrew B., and Mark Warshawsky. 1987. Specification of the joy of giving: Insights from altruism. *Review of Economics and Statistics*, forthcoming.

Bernheim, B. Douglas, Andrei Shleifer, and Lawrence H. Summers. 1985. The strategic bequest motive. *Journal of Political Economy* 93:1045–76.

Bodie, Zvi, Alex Kane, and Robert McDonald. 1985. Inflation and the role of bonds in investors' portfolios. In *Corporate capital structures in the United states*, edited by B. M. Friedman. Chicago: University of Chicago Press.

Faber, J. 1982. *Life tables for the United States: 1900–2050*. Office of the Actuary, Actuarial Study no. 87. Washington, D.C.: Social Security Administration.

Fischer, Stanley. 1973. A life-cycle model of life insurance purchases. *International Economic Review* 14 (February): 132–152.

Friedman, Benjamin M., and Mark Warshawsky. 1985. The cost of annuities: Implications for saving behavior and bequests. National Bureau of Economic Research. Mimeo.

Friedman, Joseph, and Jane Sjogren. 1980. Assets of the elderly as they retire. Social Security Administration. Mimeo.

Friend, Irwin, and Marshall E. Blume. 1975. The demand for risky assets. *American Economic Review* 65 (December): 900–922.

Grossman, Sanford J., and Robert J. Shiller. 1981. The determinants of the variability of stock prices. *American Economic Review* 71 (May): 222–27.

Hubbard, R. Glenn. 1983. Uncertain lifetimes and the impact of Social Security on individual wealth holding. Harvard University. Mimeo.

Kahneman, Daniel, and Amos Tversky, 1979. Prospect theory: An analysis of decision under risk. *Econometrica* 47 (March): 263–92.

Kotlikoff, Laurence J., and Daniel E. Smith. 1983. *Pensions in the American Economy*. Chicago: University of Chicago Press.

Kotlikoff, Laurence J., and Avia Spivak. 1981. The family as an incomplete annuity market. *Journal of Political Economy* 89 (April): 372–91.

Kotlikoff, Laurence J., and Lawrence H. Summers. 1981. The role of intergenerational transfers in aggregate capital accumulation. *Journal of Political Economy* 89 (August): 706–32.

Menchik, Paul L., and Martin David. 1982. The incidence of a lifetime consumption tax. *National Tax Journal* 35 (June): 189–203.

Mirer, Thad W. 1979. The wealth-age relation among the aged. *American Economic Review* 69 (June): 435–43.

Pratt, John W., David A. Wise, and Richard Zeckhauser. 1979. Price differences in almost competitive markets. *Quarterly Journal of Economics* 93 (May): 189–212.

Rothschild, Michael, and Joseph Stiglitz. 1976. Equilibrium in competitive insurance markets: An essay on the economics of imperfect information. *Quarterly Journal of Economics* 90 (November): 629–49.

Society of Actuaries. 1983. Report to the committee to recommend a new mortality basis for individual annuity valuation (derivation of the 1983 table a). *Transactions of the Society of Actuaries* 33:675–750.

Wetterstrand, W. H. 1983. Parametric models for life insurance mortality data: Gompertz's law over time. *Transactions of the Society of Actuaries* 33:159–79.

Yaari, Menachem E. 1965. Uncertain lifetime, life insurance, and the theory of the consumer. *Review of Economic Studies* 32:137–50.

Comment   R. Glenn Hubbard

It is difficult to think of more important items on the research agendas of public finance and macroeconomics than explaining personal saving behavior (especially the role of intergenerational transfers) and the impacts of social insurance programs on national saving and individual welfare. With respect to both areas, it is now well recognized that, for all its theoretical clarity, the life-cycle model has not tested out very well vis-à-vis predictions about the shape of the wealth-age profile or the impact of pensions on the level of nonpension wealth. While there is evidence that the model, in its most general context of forward-looking intertemporal optimization, is not at variance with the observed saving behavior of most households, many studies have concluded that there exists a nontrivial fraction of households for which the model does not appear to be an adequate description of saving behavior.

One element missing from most of these studies is the wealth allocation choice between assets which can be transferred to heirs upon death (e.g., stocks, bonds, or life insurance proceeds) and those which cannot (e.g., annuities). Analyses of the impact of the introduction of Social Security are typically conducted either under the assumption of a perfect private market in life annuities—in which annuity prices are actuarially fair—or complete market failure in the provision of annuities. Such polar extremes are hardly innocuous.[1]

A key advance of the paper by Benjamin Friedman and Mark Warshawsky is its attempt to quantify the extent to which annuity contracts are "unfairly" priced (in an actuarial sense). After all, the empirical finding that wealth-age profiles do not decline significantly in old age is consistent with the basic life-cycle model (when lifetime is uncertain and there is no bequest motive) only if there are no annuity markets. As Friedman and Warshawsky point out, there are well functioning life annuity markets in the United States, but very few individuals (in the present or the past) have chosen to purchase them.

Consistent with the organization of the Friedman-Warshawsky paper, my comments can be divided into three parts: (i) pricing life annuities and computing "load factors," (ii) modeling the impact of different

R. Glenn Hubbard is an assistant professor of economics and urban affairs at Northwestern University and a faculty research fellow of the National Bureau of Economic Research.

1. For example, if the prices of market annuity contracts were actuarially fair and there were no restrictions on the quantities purchased, then exogenous increases in mandatory Social Security annuities would displace annuity purchases with no effect on bequeathable nonpension wealth. With no market annuities, such increases would displace marketable nonpension wealth. For discussions of implications of these assumptions for models of individual saving, see Bernheim (1984), Hubbard (1987), and Sheshinski and Weiss (1981).

assumptions about annuity pricing on individual saving, and (iii) considering the implications of the modeling approach for more general discussions of individual saving behavior and public policies toward retirement saving.

First, Friedman and Warshawsky have made a real contribution in calculating the load factors associated with the purchase of life annuity contracts in the United States. Their comparison of the present expected values of identical annuities for 65-year-old males for the "general population" and "annuity purchasers" reveals a premium most likely traceable (as they note) to the classic adverse selection problem.[2] That is, annuity prices are not actuarially fair for those individuals who choose to purchase life annuity contracts.[3]

In their table 2.3, Friedman and Warshawsky present the mean load factors under various assumptions. These implied charges are substantial, ranging up to 55 percent for individuals in the "general population." In a particularly interesting calculation, they isolate "the effect of adverse selection" by subtracting the mean load factor for individuals actually purchasing annuities from that for individuals in the general population. This calculation is not conclusive, however, as theoretical treatments of adverse selection have seldom found pure price equilibria to be optimal. That is, quantity rationing may occur. Whether such rationing is in fact important in the market for life annuities is an empirical question, and one worthy of mention in the paper.

Second, the core of the Friedman-Warshawsky paper is an extension of Fischer's (1973) model of the demand for life insurance to examine the extent to which the combination of actuarially unfair market annuities, mandatory social annuities (e.g., Social Security), and bequest motives can explain observed patterns in annuity purchases and consumption in old age. The extension of the dynamic programming model is straightforward, and the authors use the solution expressions as the basis for a simulation model.

Their modeling strategy is clever, namely, to calculate the maximum load factor an individual would be willing to pay to purchase market

2. Recent theoretical contributions to the literature on adverse selection as applied to annuities include Eckstein, Eichenbaum, and Peled (1985) and Judd (1984). The Judd paper in particular points out the potential importance of general equilibrium analysis—since the annuity market equilibrium affects incentives to save, the level of savings and the supply of capital will be affected, altering the supply of goods and the real interest rate. He shows that private insurance markets afflicted by adverse selection generally cannot internalize this spillover into the goods market, the competitive equilibrium will in general not be efficient, and that some sort of compulsory contract will be Pareto-improving.

3. In a companion paper, Friedman and Warshawsky (1985) present information on yield differentials between life annuities and marketable securities; as with the load factors, these differentials are substantial.

annuities and compare that with the actual load factors calculated earlier.[4] Because we do not observe many actual annuity purchases, such a comparison can be used to justify the appropriateness of other assumed parameter values (particularly that for the strength of the "bequest motive"). The results in table 2.4 illustrate (not surprisingly) that the no-annuities-available and market-only-annuities cases yield counterfactual results for consumption-age and wealth-age profiles in old age.

More reasonable results are obtained when Social Security annuities are introduced (based on the assumption that Social Security wealth constitutes half of total wealth). I do, however, have two reservations about the choice of parameter values. First, the values used for the annual rate of time preference and market rate of interest (1 percent for each) seem very low. We are not told how sensitive the simulation results are to this choice of parameter values (in particular with respect to the more likely case wherein the interest rate exceeds the rate of time preference), though an alternative value for the market interest rate is reported later in table 2.9. Second, while the assumption that Social Security wealth and nonpension wealth are roughly equal may be true on average, it is certainly not true for high-income and wealthy

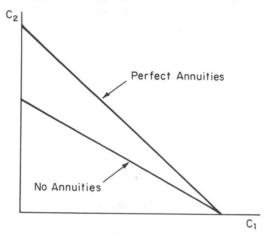

Fig. 2.2   Intertemporal budget constraints implied by no-annuity and perfect-annuity cases.

4. Friedman and Warshawsky consider the load factors on market annuities as fixed, "upfront" fees. An alternative approach would be to consider a continuous rate of return on annuities which is less than the actuarially fair return. Consider for simplicity a two-period model with consumption (C_1, C_2) in the two periods. The intertemporal budget constraints implied by the no-annuity and perfect-annuity cases are illustrated in figure 2.2. The availability of annuities expands the budget set, and compensating or equivalent variation calculations can be made. Actuarially unfair annuities could be considered by drawing an intermediate budget line between the two sketched above. Friedman and Warshawsky (1985) do focus on yield differentials.

individuals, for whom bequest motives are most frequently observed (Menchik and David 1983).[5] I will discuss this point further later.

Since across all cases prior to the introduction of bequests, the "critical load factors"calculated by the model are greater than those actually observed, there remains a puzzle as to why individuals are not more active participants in private annuity markets. The logical next step is to consider the extent to which planned bequests can rationalize the model's predictions with observed annuity purchases. Bequests are indexed by a parameter θ, which represents the ratio of a bequest to current annual consumption.

Table 2.8 is most interesting in this respect, in that the inclusion of a bequest motive, by lowering the difference between critical and observed load factors, removes the feature of earlier simulations that it is optimal to invest all non-Social-Security wealth in market annuities. While this modification does not yet explain the fact that almost no annuities are purchased by anyone in the United States, the authors' table 2.9 summarizes the model's implications very well by calculating the strength of the bequest motive (again indexed by the parameter θ) required to eliminate market annuity purchases.

For parameter values that seem sensible on average—say, an interest rate of 4 percent, a ratio of Social Security wealth to total wealth of 0.5, and a coefficient of relative risk aversion of 2—a relatively modest bequest motive (θ = 5) is required. This still seems troublesome, however, for any claim that a bequest motive per se is all that is needed to explain observed behavior in private annuity markets. Plausible increases in relative risk aversion, reductions in the market interest rate, or declines in Social Security wealth relative to total wealth[6] would require implausibly high bequest motives to eliminate annuity purchases.

These results are even more pronounced in the calculations of the impact of the yield differential between annuities and government bonds. That differential on average is sufficient to eliminate annuity purchases by 65-year-old males (given a coefficient of relative risk aversion of 4 and a ratio of "social annuities" to total wealth of 0.5) irrespective of any bequest motive. For lower values of the coefficient of relative risk aversion (e.g., 2), the combination of even lower differentials and plausible bequest motives can explain the absence of market annuity purchases.

Finally, I would like to devote the remainder of my remarks to three factors that may shed further light on the stimulating findings in the

5. More subtly, the inclusion of Social Security annuities might have been better modeled by using the entire life cycle to capture the effects of Social Security on preretirement consumption and wealth accumulation. For example, these effects would not in general be invariant to the way in which the system is financed.

6. Again, such a decline in Social Security wealth relative to total wealth is perfectly plausible, given that it is wealthy individuals—with comparatively little Social Security wealth—who are most likely to leave a bequest.

Friedman-Warshawsky paper. The first relates to the definition of annuities. While the annuities described in the paper are real annuities, annuities available in the market are subject to inflation risk.[7] Moreover, when a model of the entire life cycle is considered, the lack of fungibility of annuities (e.g., because of problems in intertemporal reallocation of resources and liquidity constraints) may be important. Other "contracts" not considered in the analysis might act as proxies for market annuities, namely, private pension annuities[8] (Hubbard 1987) or implicit intrafamily contracting arrangements (Kotlikoff, Shoven, and Spivak 1987). These added considerations could account for some remaining annuity purchases in the presence of a bequest motive in table 2.8, or for a lower bequest motive required in table 2.9 to "eliminate" market annuity purchases (by augmenting "exogenous" annuities relative to total wealth).

Second, two modeling considerations might increase the robustness of the results. Solving for steady-state values of national saving and individual welfare would permit comparison of the impacts of alternative "social annuity" policies on individual welfare given different assumptions about bequest motives. In addition, it would be useful to know the size of bequests relative to life-cycle resources implied by the values in table 2.9. Such calculations could shed additional light on the importance of intergenerational transfers in accounting for the size of the capital stock.

Finally, and most important, the ultimate relevance of the simulation exercises depends on the extent to which lifetime uncertainty is the dominant form of uncertainty present in individual consumption optimization problems. I am reminded of the cry by Maggie in Tennessee Williams's *Cat on a Hot Tin Roof:* "You can be young without money, but you can't be old without money."

Uncertainty in old age is a general phenomenon. While there is no doubt that uncertain longevity is important, one can easily imagine that uncertainty over health or disability is a significant worry for the elderly.[9] That is, "uncertainty" broadly defined may account for stable wealth-age profiles in retirement. For example, Friedman and Warshawsky point out that market annuities have never been very significant in the United States, yet the past two generations of Americans have witnessed a dramatic expansion in the coverage and generosity of the Social Security and private pension systems. Extrapolating from

7. It is not clear, for example, that individuals prefer real (market) annuities given the existing structure of Social Security benefits (Feldstein 1983).

8. In addition, private pension annuities receive favorable tax treatment relative to market annuities.

9. See the discussion in Diamond and Hausman (1984).

table 2.9, an implausibly high bequest motive would have been required to eliminate life annuity purchases.[10]

Recent papers on the influence of lifetime uncertainty on national saving and this contribution by Friedman and Warshawsky suggest the importance of recognizing and modeling the effects of uncertainty on individual saving decisions and the size of the capital stock. Measuring the size of uncertainty saving may help to reconcile the life-cycle model with observed saving behavior and to reevaluate the importance of intergenerational transfers for the size of the capital stock (as in Kotlikoff and Summers 1981). Such an approach will facilitate welfare analyses of social insurance programs and complementary private programs. Finally, data permitting, cross-country comparisons of the influence of social and private annuities on the capital stock would be useful in empirically disentangling motivations for saving behavior.

References

Bernheim, B. D. 1984. Life-cycle annuity valuation. NBER Working Paper no. 1511. Cambridge, Mass.: National Bureau of Economic Research.

Diamond, P. A., and J. A. Hausman. 1984. Individual retirement and savings behavior. *Journal of Public Economics* 23 (February-March): 81–114.

Eckstein, Z., M. Eichenbaum, and D. Peled. 1985. Uncertain lifetimes and the welfare-enhancing properties of annuity markets and Social Security. *Journal of Public Economics* 26 (April): 303–26.

Feldstein, M. S. 1983. Should private pensions be indexed? In *Financial aspects of the United States pension system*, edited by Z. Bodie and J. B. Shoven. Chicago: University of Chicago Press.

Fischer, S. 1973. A life-cycle model of life insurance purchases. *International Economic Review* 14 (February): 132–52.

Friedman, Benjamin M., and Mark Warshawsky. 1985. The cost of annuities: Implications for saving behavior and bequests. National Bureau of Economic Research. Mimeo.

Hubbard, R. G. 1987. Uncertain lifetimes, pensions, and individual saving. In *Issues in pension economics*, edited by Z. Bodie, J. B. Shoven, and D. A. Wise. Chicago: University of Chicago Press.

Judd, K. L. 1984. Adverse selection, efficiency, and production. Northwestern University. Mimeo.

Kotlikoff, L. J., J. B. Shoven, and A. Spivak. 1987. Annuity markets, savings, and the capital stock. In *Issues in pension economics,* edited by Z. Bodie, J.B. Shoven, and D.A. Wise. Chicago: University of Chicago Press.

Kotlikoff, L. J., and L. H. Summers. 1981. The role of intergenerational transfers in aggregate capital accumulation. *Journal of Political Economy* 89 (August): 706–32.

10. Problems remain, however. Empirical studies finding "oversaving" among some groups (e.g., the elderly) have also found a nontrivial fraction of the population whose saving is completely "inadequate" by usual life-cycle standards.

Menchik, P. L., and M. David. 1983. Income distribution, lifetime savings, and bequests. *American Economic Review* 73 (September): 672–90.

Sheshinski, E., and Y. Weiss. 1981. Uncertainty and optimal social security systems. *Quarterly Journal of Economics* 96 (May): 189–206.

3 Pension Funding and Saving

B. Douglas Bernheim and John B. Shoven

The private saving rate in the United States in 1984 has to be considered disappointing. After the enactment of a large number of policies to make investment/saving more rewarding (such as liberalized Individual Retirement Accounts and Keogh Plans, the special tax treatment of some reinvested dividends, capital gains taxes which have been reduced twice in the past six years, and certainly increased investment incentives at the corporate level), the preliminary Bureau of Economic Analysis (BEA) estimate for the 1984 personal saving rate is 6.1 percent of disposable personal income. This is lower than the average personal saving rate in the 1970s of 7.3 percent, and only imperceptibly better than the 6.0 percent of the first four years of this decade. With all of these incentives, plus a robust economy and record high real interest rates, why was the personal saving rate so low? We are not going to attempt to answer this general question here. Rather, we suggest that personal saving needs to be examined in a disaggregated manner. Some of the policies just mentioned do not really provide incentives to save at the margin, but only serve to channel the existing quantity of saving

B. Douglas Bernheim is an associate professor of economics at Stanford University and is a faculty research fellow of the National Bureau of Economic Research. John B. Shoven is a professor of economics at Stanford University and a research associate of the National Bureau of Economic Research.

The research for this paper was greatly assisted by the work of Tim Wilson of Stanford. We would also like to thank Dan Beller (Department of Labor), Greenwich Research Associates, Marty Murphy (Bureau of Economic Analysis), Emily Andrews, Sophie Korczyk, Bonnie Newton, and Joe Piacentini (Employee Benefit Research Institute), Sylvester Schieber (the Wyatt Company), Steve Taylor and Judy Ziabro (Federal Reserve Board), and David Walker (Pension Benefits Guarantee Corporation) for providing us with valuable empirical information. Eugene Steuerle (U.S. Treasury) was most helpful as a discussant of an earlier draft, and David Starrett's comments were also appreciated.

or wealth through particular vehicles. Undoubtedly, this accounts for at least some of the apparent sluggishness in private saving.

Our topic, however, is the behavior of personal saving which results from the funding of pension plans. In this country, most covered workers participate in defined benefit plans, where the promised pension annuity is based on years of service and level of compensation, and not directly on the funding status of the plan or the return on the investments which have been previously acquired to fund the plan. However, while the worker may be able to separate his or her accumulation of pension rights or wealth from the funding of the plan, it is the aggregate funding contributions less outlays (i.e., benefits) which constitute a component of personal saving, and which generate loanable funds to finance investment or government deficits. Thus, the structure of defined benefit plans may produce a divergence between the apparent saving of workers through the accumulation of pension rights and the actual creation of loanable funds through net contributions to pension plan reserves.

This can be an important phenomenon if only because pension funds are so large relative to financial markets and because pension contributions constitute such a large fraction of personal saving. Also, net corporate pension contributions fell sharply in 1984. They amounted to 4.02 percent of personal disposable income in 1984, down from 6.02 percent in 1982. Thus, the decline in pension funding was large enough to be responsible for the disappointing level of aggregate personal saving. Indeed, these figures raise the possibility that, had pension contributions remained at their 1982 level, the personal saving rate might have risen by as much as 2 percent, to perhaps 8 percent in 1984. Had this indeed occurred, various policies designed to stimulate saving might have been judged more successful.

To understand why corporate pension contributions dropped so significantly in 1984, one simply has to examine the defined benefit pension contract from the firm's point of view. The liability of the firm is to pay for retirement annuities for its vested workers. To calculate the present value of this obligation, the firm typically predicts the magnitude of those annuities (making some assumptions regarding wage growth until retirement, labor turnover, etc.) and then discounts the future obligation to the present using an assumed interest rate. The resulting present value of liabilities is then compared to the value of the assets in the plan to arrive at the net unfunded liability. By law, contributions are related to the unfunded liability of the plan, although the companies have substantial discretion both as to the speed with which unfunded liabilities are amortized and in the assumptions which are made in arriving at the value of unfunded liabilities. However, the key point is that from the company's point of view, the funding of pension liabilities is a target—the higher the earnings of the assets funding the plan, the lower the contributions needed to meet the obligations. If the assets earn more than the assumed discount rate used to value the liabilities (or if the assumed interest rate is raised or the assumed rate of growth of wages is lowered), the unfunded liability will be reduced (or, more relevantly for many companies, become negative) and the contributions will tend to decline. In the not-so-rare case (in 1984) of an overfunded plan, the law may force a reduction or an elimination of contributions. The very factors which have been hailed as the economic achievements of the past few years (e.g., a rising stock market and a reduction in wage inflation), combined with those high real interest rates which may encourage other kinds of saving, are the primary reasons behind the reduction in the number of underfunded plans and the sharp drop in pension contributions. As with the classic target saving examples, defined benefit pension contributions have a negative elasticity with respect to (real) interest rates. With pension contributions so large a part of total personal saving, the negative elasticity of this component may significantly offset the positive responsiveness of other components of saving. This effect has not been explicitly considered in previous studies of the interest elasticity of private saving (see, e.g., Boskin 1978, Howrey and Hymans 1978, and Summers 1981).

We have not investigated potential offsets to reductions pension contributions. Clearly, resources diverted from pension funds will be employed elsewhere. Indeed, if investors penetrate all corporate and governmental veils, aggregate saving should be unaffected. While these issues no doubt merit careful consideration, they are far too complex to treat within the context of the current study. It is therefore appropriate to emphasize that the negative elasticity of contributions to a defined benefit pension plan is not the result of intertemporal optimization on the part of either the firm or the workers; it is a purely mechanical response inherent in the funding rules for these types of plans.

In section 3.1, some empirical information is given regarding pension contributions, unfunded liabilities, assumed interest rates, and recent developments in pension funding. Then in section 3.2, we present our target saving model of pension funding and derive the elasticity of contributions to changes in interest rates. Section 3.3 presents our econometric estimates of aggregate contributions as a function of lagged interest rates, inflation rates, the pattern of wage growth, and the behavior of the stock market. We summarize our findings in section 3.4.

3.1   Institutional Considerations

As table 3.1 shows, most pension plans (72 percent of them) are defined contribution. However, the defined contribution plans are typ-

Table 3.1   Basic Characteristics of Private Pension Plans,
                 By Type of Plan, 1978

	Defined Benefit	Defined Contribution	Total
Plans (#)	139,340 (28.1%)	356,505 (71.9%)	495,845
Participants	36.1 mil (68.9%)	16.3 mil (31.1%)	52.4 mil
Assets (market value)	$272.7 bil (72.3%)	$104.5 bil (27.7%)	$377.2 bil

SOURCE: U.S. Department of Labor (1983).

ically small and often supplement a defined benefit plan (a notable exception being TIAA-CREF, which is the largest pension plan in the United States). In terms of participants or assets, defined benefit plans dominate with about 70 percent of the total. To gain some appreciation of the aggregate size of private pension plans, note that the 52.4 million covered workers represent about 53 percent of all civilian employees in 1978, and the $377.2 billion in private pension assets amounts to 51 percent of the equity holdings of households in 1978. If government pensions were included, the Federal Reserve Flow of Fund figures show 1978 pension assets at $593 billion. In comparison, households held $741 billion of corporate equity.

Table 3.2 shows the number of new plans qualified and terminated by type for the years 1974–84. Prior to this period, defined benefit plans had been growing more rapidly. In every year from 1956 to 1974, the number of new defined benefit plans exceeded the number of new defined contribution plans. However, since the 1974 Employee Retirement Income Security Act (ERISA) the pattern has been reversed. In the first three quarters of 1984, the number of defined benefit terminations was at a record level and the net growth in defined benefit plans was running at a 2 percent yearly rate. The changes in the relative popularity of defined benefit versus defined contribution plans is almost certainly due to the funding, vesting, and insurance requirements of ERISA for defined benefit plans.

There are two sources of data regarding aggregate private pension contributions and benefits, the Flow of Funds data of the Federal Reserve System and the U.S. Commerce Department's National Income and Product Account (NIPA) information. As with total saving figures, the two sources do not agree particularly well on the numbers. The time series on net acquisitions of financial assets by pension funds from the Flow of Funds information is shown in table 3.3 for 1948 through 1984. The numbers for 1984 show a fairly drastic decline. The 1984 figure for private pensions alone was more than $30 billion less than

Table 3.2   **Number and Growth of Pension Plans by Type**

Year	Defined Benefit Qualified	Defined Benefit Terminated	Defined Benefit Qualified Minus Terminated	Defined Benefit Plans	
				Total Number	Growth Rate
1974	—	—	—	128,255	—
1975	6,235	2,953	3,282	131,537	2.6%
1976	4,475	5,860	(1,385)	130,152	−1.1
1977	6,953	5,337	1,616	131,768	1.2
1978	9,728	4,625	5,103	139,340	5.7
1979	15,755	3,267	12,488	157,639	13.1
1980	18,849	4,297	14,552	179,424	13.8
1981	23,789	4,536	19,253	198,677	10.7
1982	28,189	5,043	23,146	221,823	11.7
1983	22,130	7,230	14,900	236,723	6.7
84Q1–Q3	11,053	7,566	3,487	—	—

Year	Defined Contribution Qualified	Defined Contribution Terminated	Defined Contribution Qualified Minus Terminated	Defined Contribution Plans	
				Total Number	Growth Rate
1974	—	—	—	271,655	—
1975	23,804	5,155	18,649	290,304	6.9%
1976	21,454	10,053	11,401	301,705	3.9
1977	28,463	10,478	17,985	319,690	6.0
1978	55,956	10,661	45,295	356,505	11.5
1979	41,122	7,574	33,548	381,112	6.9
1980	50,493	8,982	41,511	410,469	7.7
1981	57,748	8,906	48,842	459,311	11.9
1982	57,162	10,108	47,054	506,365	10.2
1983	42,089	11,417	30,672	537,037	6.1
84Q1–Q3	24,360	9,321	15,039		

SOURCE: Employee Benefit Research Institute, Washington, D.C.

NOTE: In 1978–80, the growth in the total number of plans does not match the number of qualified plans minus the number terminated. EBRI apparently derives these numbers from different sources and does not reconcile the totals.

for 1982. The growth rate in net acquisitions is also down, though less dramatically, for pensions managed by insurance companies and state and local government pension systems. The magnitude of the drop in net acquisitions from a trend line is comparable to the total inflow of money into IRA and Keogh accounts. Thus, the effects discussed here appear to be large relative to the saving incentives mentioned earlier. The importance of net acquisitions by pension funds relative to personal saving can be judged by comparing columns 4 and 5 of table 3.3.

Table 3.3   **Net Acquisitions of Financial Assets by Pension Funds ($ billion)**

Year	Private (1)	Insured (2)	State/Local (3)	TOTAL (4)	NIPA[a] Personal Saving (5)
1948	0.6	0.6	0.4	1.6	11.2
1949	0.6	0.6	0.5	1.7	7.5
1950	1.7	0.8	0.7	3.2	11.8
1951	1.1	1.0	0.8	2.9	16.0
1952	1.7	1.1	1.0	3.8	17.3
1953	1.9	1.1	1.3	4.3	18.6
1954	2.0	1.2	1.5	4.7	17.0
1955	2.3	1.3	1.3	4.9	16.3
1956	2.7	1.2	1.3	5.2	21.3
1957	3.0	1.6	1.7	6.3	22.4
1958	3.1	1.5	1.8	6.4	23.6
1959	3.7	2.0	1.9	7.6	21.1
1960	4.0	1.3	2.2	7.5	19.7
1961	3.9	1.4	2.4	7.7	23.0
1962	4.2	1.4	2.4	8.0	23.3
1963	4.3	1.7	2.6	8.6	21.9
1964	5.5	2.0	3.0	10.5	29.6
1965	5.4	2.1	3.3	10.8	33.7
1966	6.9	2.1	4.2	13.2	36.0
1967	6.6	1.5	4.1	12.2	44.3
1968	6.5	2.3	4.8	13.6	41.9
1969	6.3	3.1	5.5	14.9	40.6
1970	6.9	2.9	6.4	16.2	55.8
1971	7.1	4.6	6.6	18.3	60.6
1972	11.5	4.4	8.5	24.4	52.6
1973	14.1	5.7	9.5	29.3	79.0
1974	21.5	6.0	9.7	37.2	85.1
1975	23.1	8.7	11.3	43.1	94.3
1976	18.9	15.0	12.9	46.8	82.5
1977	23.1	16.8	15.9	55.8	78.0
1978	28.8	19.1	20.7	68.6	89.4
1979	40.8	19.4	16.2	76.4	96.7
1980	48.9	22.3	26.5	97.7	110.2
1981	37.6	29.5	31.0	98.1	137.4
1982	54.3	39.7	37.3	131.3	136.0
1983	47.3	40.2	44.5	132.0	118.1
1984	23.5	40.8	39.3	103.6	—

SOURCE: *Flow of Funds,* Federal Reserve System.
[a]National Income and Product Account, U.S. Commerce Department.

The NIPA data for private pensions, which we use in the empirical work of section 3.2, is shown in columns 1 and 2 of table 3.4. The NIPA provides separate information on contributions and benefits paid, and we generally consider it to be more reliable than the Flow of Funds numbers. The NIPA contribution figures are based on business tax

Table 3.4   **NIPA Data on Private Pension Contributions, Benefits, and Reversions ($ billion)**

Year	Private Pension Contributions[a]	Private Pension Benefits Paid[a]	Reversions[b]
1947	—	—	0
1948	1.196	—	0
1949	1.262	—	0
1950	1.713	0.370	0
1951	2.262	0.450	0
1952	2.543	0.520	0
1953	2.861	0.620	0
1954	2.903	0.710	0
1955	3.377	0.850	0
1956	3.757	1.000	0
1957	4.153	1.140	0
1958	4.134	1.290	0
1959	4.771	1.540	0
1960	4.866	1.720	0
1961	4.966	1.970	0
1962	5.442	2.330	0
1963	5.760	2.590	0
1964	6.591	2.990	0
1965	7.646	3.520	0
1966	8.675	4.190	0
1967	9.456	4.790	0
1968	10.717	5.530	0
1969	11.823	6.450	0
1970	13.050	7.360	0
1971	15.108	8.597	0
1972	17.903	10.015	0
1973	20.934	11.235	0
1974	24.218	12.970	0
1975	28.253	14.855	0
1976	32.972	16.651	0
1977	38.764	18.761	0
1978	44.869	21.940	0
1979	48.903	27.272	0
1980	54.242	31.258	0.014
1981	55.831	37.634	0.157
1982	60.387	45.585	0.396
1983	64.821	—	1.558
1984	—	—	1.172

[a]NIPA, "Other Labor Income by Industry and Type."
[b]Pension Benefits Guarantee Corporation, Washington, D.C.

return information, while their numbers for benefits paid are based on individual tax returns netted out for government pensions. This information is not yet available for 1984, so our estimations in section 3.3 will not use the dramatic developments of that year. Column 3 of table 3.4 contains information from the Pension Benefits Guarantee Corporation on reversions. Reversions have received a lot of attention recently, partly because a few large publicly held companies have terminated their pension plans in this manner. A pension plan reversion can occur when the plan becomes overfunded. The existing plan is terminated and a new plan (usually a defined contribution plan) is adopted (often with the old obligations covered by insurance company annuities). The excess of the value of the plan assets over the cost of the annuities may revert to the company. The whole procedure is made possible because assets have previously earned more than the assumed interest rate. The case which received the most attention was the Great Atlantic and Pacific Tea Co. which recouped $272.9 million out of its $355.1 million pension fund with a reversion completed in 1984. The figures in table 3.4 show that the aggregate quantity of reversions is still relatively small, but the growth rate in this practice has been phenomenal. The reversions already pending in January for 1985 amounted to $1.824 billion, and the figure is likely to go much higher. Clearly, reversions reinforce the downward pressure on saving created by the lower net contributions. Reversions and the lower contributions actually have the same underlying cause. In both cases, assets have been earning far in excess of assumed discount rates, resulting in many pension funds which are massively overfunded if market rates were used to discount the pension obligation. Reversions amount to the company recognizing this profit suddenly, while most ongoing plans simply reduce contributions over a long period of time.

Pension plans have been slow to adjust their assumed interest rates toward market rates. The mean assumed interest rate for plans with more than 1000 participants has climbed from 6 percent in 1980 to 7.2 percent in 1984, as shown in table 3.5. However, this growth in the assumed interest rate has been matched by increases in the assumed salary growth for the 70 percent of defined benefit plans which project wage increase in determining liabilities. In fact, the spread between the interest assumption and the wage growth assumption has narrowed

Table 3.5   **Mean Assumed Interest Rates for Plans with over 1000 Participants**

1976	5.5 percent
1978	5.8 percent
1980	6.0 percent
1981	6.3 percent
1982	6.8 percent
1983	7.0 percent
1984	7.2 percent

SOURCE: The Wyatt Company (1985).

slightly in the past eight years. Since 1976, the average spread has decreased from 2.3 percent to 1.5 percent.

The adjustment toward market interest rates may be occurring somewhat faster than the previous numbers indicate, however. A strategy termed "immunization" or "dedication" has become increasingly popular. A portfolio is said to be immunized when the cash flow (interest plus principle) generated by the assets matches the cash flow of the pension liabilities. Dedication is a less precise matching strategy where the average duration of the assets matches the duration of the liabilities. By structuring the portfolio in these ways, plan managers are protecting themselves from interest rate risk. A change to a dedicated or immunized portfolio amounts to suddenly changing the assumed interest rate to the market rate. In the suddenness of the adjustment, the adoption of these strategies is similar to a reversion. Total dedications and immunizations amounted to at least $10 billion in 1984, with Ameritech leading the pack with a $2.4 billion asset dedication. Chrysler participated in a big way with a $1.1 billion immunization. The annualized yield on Chrysler's immunized portfolio exceeds 14 percent. While aggregate numbers are difficult to come up with, this phenomenon appears to be somewhat larger than reversions, and certainly it amounts to an added factor dampening pension contributions. One final example of the effect of dedication on contributions is given by the Western Conference of the Teamsters Union. The union is in the process of adopting the strategy for its entire $5.1 billion portfolio. In 1984 it placed $1.777 billion in dedicated bond portfolios yielding over 12 percent. When it completes the dedication process, the entire $1 billion of "unfunded liability" of its pension system will have been eliminated without further contributions. Basically, by structuring the portfolios in this manner, actuaries are willing to raise the assumed interest rate to the market rate, thus dramatically lowering both unfunded liabilities and contributions.

The effects of high market interest rates and high stock market returns can be seen by examining the funding status of pension plans. Table 3.6 shows the distribution of the ratio of assets to present value of accrued vested liabilities at the end of 1983 for the Fortune 500 industrials. Even using the companies' interest rate assumptions, fully 88 percent were fully funded and 34 percent were more than 50 percent overfunded. If the calculations are redone with a common 10 percent interest rate, 94 percent are fully funded and almost 70 percent are more than 50 percent overfunded. The overfunding would be even more massive at true market interest rates which ranged between 13 and 15 percent. The figures of table 3.6 were requested by the Financial Accounting Standards Board (FASB), Statement no. 36, and did not permit the use of salary growth projections. Many companies do make these

Table 3.6   Distribution of Vested Funded Ratios for the Fortune 500
                   Industrials for 1983

| | Percent of Companies | | | |
| | With Assumed Interest Rates | | With 10% Interest Rate | |
Funded Ratio	%	Accumulated %	%	Accumulated %
200% and above	7	7	30	30
175%–199%	8	15	18	48
150%–174%	19	34	21	69
140%–149%	10	44	6	75
130%–139%	11	55	7	82
120%–129%	13	68	5	87
110%–119%	10	78	4	91
100%–109%	10	88	3	94
90%– 99%	3	91	2	96
80%– 89%	4	95	2	98
70%– 79%	2	97	1	99
60%– 69%	1	98	1	100
50%– 59%	1	99	0	100
Under 50%	1	100	0	100

Source: Hewitt Associates (1984).

projections to calculate their unfunded liabilities and to determine contributions. Regardless of method, however, the funding levels of plans have dramatically improved in the last few years. Again, on the FASB no-projection basis, the percent of the Fortune 500 industrials whose assets are at least as much as accrued-vested benefits (with their discount rates) has climbed from 58 percent in 1980 to 69 percent in 1981, 78 percent in 1982, and 88 percent in 1983. The figures are not available yet for 1984, but a further gain in funding relative to liabilities is most likely.

3.2   Theoretical Considerations

In section 3.1, we described the institutional factors which largely govern the response of pension fund accumulation to changes in interest rates. Our next objective is to quantify these effects using a simple model of defined-benefit pension plans, for which we compute theoretical long-run and short-run interest elasticities. Although these calculations provide us with a sense for magnitudes, certain critical parameters are not institutionally determined. In order to refine our estimates of these interest elasticities, as well as to confirm the predictions of our theoretical analysis, we devote section 3.3 to an empirical analysis of pension fund accumulation.

Consider a firm which, in period t, accrues new pension liabilities

$$L^t = (L^t_{t+1}, \ldots, L^t_{t+T}),$$

where $L^t_{t+\tau}$ is the liability accrued in period t to be paid in period $t + \tau$. The notion of "accrual" used here corresponds to whatever actuarial convention is employed by firms under ERISA regulations. Let λ^t denote its stream of previously accrued liabilities:

$$\lambda^t = (\lambda^t_t, \lambda^t_{t+1}, \ldots, \lambda^t_{t+T}).$$

Here, $\lambda^t_{t+\tau}$ represents liabilities to be paid in period $t + \tau$, which have been recognized by period t. These streams are related as follows:

$$\lambda^t_{t+\tau} = \sum_{n=t+\tau-T}^{t-1} L^n_{t+\tau} , \tau = 0, \ldots, T - 1 ; \lambda^t_{t+T} = 0.$$

Note that λ^t_t ($\tau = 0$) represents the value of pension benefits which the firm must pay out in period t. Throughout, we will take the stream of real liabilities as given.

In what follows, for any stream $X = (X_t, X_{t+1}, \ldots, X_{t+S})$, we will denote the present discounted value of X by

$$V_t(X) = \sum_{\tau=0}^{S} X_{t+\tau}/(1 + i)^\tau ,$$

where i is the nominal interest rate. We will also denote the "duration" of X by

$$D_t(X) = \sum_{\tau=0}^{S} \tau \left[\frac{X_{t+\tau}/(1 + i)^\tau}{V_t(X)} \right] .$$

The duration of X measures its average maturity. We will use $\epsilon_i[V_t(X)]$ to denote the interest elasticity of $V_t(X)$. The following result will prove useful:

$$\epsilon_i[V_t(X)] = \frac{1 + i}{V_t(X)} \frac{dV_t(X)}{di}$$

$$= - \left[\frac{1 + i}{V_t(X)} \right] \sum_{\tau=0}^{S} \tau X_{t+\tau}/(1 + i)^{\tau+1}$$

$$= - D_t(X)$$

Thus, the elasticity with respect to the interest rate of the value of a nominal stream of payments is equal to the negative of the stream's duration. We note that this is not the conventional interest elasticity expression, but it is approximately the percentage change in value per *percentage point* change in the interest rate (precisely, it is the percentage change in value relative to the percentage change in $1 + i$). This, of course, is quite a different figure from the traditional elasticity, which would in this case be the percentage change in value relative to the percentage change in the interest rate. As an example of the difference, consider a consol which pays $1 per period as a perpetuity. Its present value is $1/i$, and the traditional elasticity of its value with respect to the interest rate is -1. The interest elasticity that we have just defined, which we should perhaps term the *sensitivity* or *responsiveness* of value to interest rate changes, is $-1/i$. We have chosen to express our elasticities in this manner only because we find it more natural to think about a 1 percentage point move in the interest rate from, say, 4 percent to 5 percent rather than a 1 percent change from, say, 4.00 percent to 4.04 percent.

In this paper, we will be concerned with changes in the *real* interest rate. To avoid unnecessary notation, we simply denote every stream in real dollars and discount by the real rate, r. Subsections 3.2.1 and 3.2.2 consider long-run and short-run effects, respectively.

3.2.1   Long-Run Effects of Changes in the Real Interest Rate

ERISA regulations permit temporary underfunding and overfunding of pension plans, but they require firms to fund their liabilities fully in the long run. It is therefore natural to begin our investigation by considering steady states, which are characterized by constant interest rates (as well as other exogenous variables), and full funding of current liabilities. Thus, at time t, pension assets (A_t) are given by

$$(1) \qquad\qquad A_t = V_t(\lambda^t) \ \ .$$

We will assume that, in the long run, the liability profile grows at a constant rate, g, by which we mean the following:

$$L^t_{t+\tau} = (1 + g)^{t-t'} L^{t'}_{t'+\tau} \ \ .$$

Note that this assumption places no constraint on the shape of the new liability profile L^t, although it does imply that benefits paid, λ^t_t, and the value of discounted liabilities, $V_t(\lambda^t)$, will grow at the rate g. Thus, pension assets, A_t, will also grow at this rate.

In steady state, pension assets always cover accrued liabilities *exactly*. Thus, to maintain full funding, current contributions, C_t, must equal the value of new accrued liabilities:

$$(2) \qquad\qquad C_t = V_t(L^t) \ \ .$$

Between equations (1) and (2), we may analyze the steady-state effects of a change in the real interest rate on pension fund contributions and total capital accumulation, given a fixed liability profile.

The assumption of a fixed liability profile is essential to our calculations. Yet, ordinarily, we would expect changes in the rate of interest to be accompanied by changes in wage rates and perhaps in levels of employment. It is, therefore, important to clarify the nature of our exercise. Ultimately, one is interested in the general equilibrium effects of any particular policy change. However, these effects are determined by partial equilibrium responses. The interest elasticity of saving, defined as the response of saving to a change in the interest rate given fixed values of other variables (such as wage rates and employment levels), often appears as a critical parameter in policy analyses. Consequently, many authors have attempted to measure personal saving elasticities. Our analysis is in the spirit of these earlier studies.

From equation (1), we see immediately that the long-run interest elasticity of pension fund assets is

$$\epsilon_r(A_t) = -D_t(\lambda^t) \quad ,$$

where, again, this elasticity is the percentage change in the value of assets for a 1 percentage point change in interest rates. While we have no data on the duration of current pension fund liabilities, it is instructive to make some rough calculations based on hypothetical values. It seems reasonable to believe that the duration of outstanding liabilities is in the neighborhood of 15 years. If so, a 1 percentage point increase in the real interest rate would *depress* the long-run value of pension fund assets by 15 percent. Given the current size of pension funds, this translates into roughly $100 billion of capital assets.

A similar calculation for yearly contributions reveals that

$$\epsilon_r(C_t) = -D_t(L^t) \quad .$$

Here we clearly see the "target saving" aspect of defined benefit pension programs: if all saving takes place to fund an expenditure in the following period [$D_t(L^t) = 1$], then the elasticity of saving is -1. Longer maturity structures will amplify the effect of interest rate changes. Again, we have no direct evidence concerning the magnitude of $D_t(L^t)$. However, we can make suggestive calculations based on hypothetical values. It seems reasonable to believe that the duration of newly accrued liabilities is in the neighborhood of 30 years. If so, a 1 percentage point increase in the real interest rate would *depress* the long-run value of pension fund contributions by 30 percent. Given current magnitudes, this translates into roughly $25 billion.

Of course, pension funds pay out significant benefits and earn interest on existing assets. Thus, net pension saving in year t, N_t, is given by

$$N_t = C_t + rA_t - B_t$$

(where benefits paid, $B_t = \lambda_t'$). Our previous calculations reveal how C_t changes with the real interest rate. By assumption, B_t is invariant. For the remaining term (reinvested interest on assets), we observe that our elasticity measure for rA_t is

$$\epsilon_r(rA_t) = \frac{1}{r} - D_t(\lambda') \quad .$$

Taking $r = 0.025$, and $D_t(\lambda') = 15$ as before, yields an elasticity of 25. If, in addition, $A_t = \$650$ billion, then a 1 percentage point increase in the real interest rate will, through this channel, bring forth approximately \$4 billion in pension fund saving.

It is useful to summarize the changes in net pension saving relative to total personal saving, S_t. Suppose that $A_t/S_t = 4$, $A_t/C_t = 8$, $A_t/B_t = 16$, and $r = 0.02$ (these magnitudes correspond roughly to historical averages). Then

$$\frac{1 + r}{S_t} \frac{dN_t}{dr} = \frac{C_t}{S_t} \epsilon_r(C_t) + \frac{rA_t}{S_t} \epsilon_r(rA_t)$$

$$= .5 \epsilon_r(C_t) + .1 \epsilon_r(rA_t) \quad .$$

Using our previous values for stream durations,

$$-.5(30) + .1(25) = -12.5 \quad .$$

Thus, in the long run, a 1 percentage point increase in the real interest rate may depress net pension fund saving by 12.5 percent of total personal saving.

If investors perfectly pierce the corporate veil, then adjustments in private portfolios will completely offset these changes. However, if the offset does not occur or is only partial, the impact on private saving elasticities may be substantial. Of course, partial offsets are much more plausible in the short run than in the long run. In addition, unexpected changes in interest rates are likely to induce short-run capital gains or losses on existing assets, leading to short-run pension fund imbalances. It is therefore essential to consider the short-run response of pension funds to interest rate changes.

3.2.2   Short-Run Effects of Changes in the Real Interest Rate

Consider a pension fund with certain assets and liabilities. Suppose that there is an unanticipated change in the real interest rate during some period. How does the accumulation of pension fund assets respond in each successive period? It is useful to divide this question into two parts. First, how would the magnitude of unfunded liabilities respond to a change in interest rates, if the full impact of this change was recognized immediately? Second, how do recognition and response lags determine the timing of compensating adjustments? These questions will be tackled in order.

The response of net unfunded liabilities to a change in the interest rate can be divided into two parts: changes in assets and changes in liabilities. First, consider liabilities. The total value of outstanding liabilities is given by $V_t(\lambda^t)$. We have already calculated that

$$\epsilon_t[V_t(\lambda^t)] = -D_t(\lambda^t),$$

and have argued that 15 is a reasonable hypothetical value for $D_t(\lambda^t)$. Thus, an increase in interest rates, if recognized immediately, generates a large decline in the value of outstanding liabilities, thereby tending to make pension plans *overfunded*.

Next, consider the effect of interest rates on fund assets. Assets can be decomposed into three categories: bonds, physical capital, and stock (leveraged physical capital). It is straightforward to calculate the effect of interest rates on the value of bonds. Suppose that, in period t, the pension fund contains bonds which provide a claim on the real income stream

$$B^t = (B^t_{t+1}, \ldots, B^t_{t+R}) \quad .$$

($B^t_{t+\tau}$ represents the income from bonds in period $t+\tau$ which the firm owns as of period t). Then, as before, for our elasticity measure,

$$\epsilon_r(B^t) = -D_t(B^t) \quad .$$

Again, we have no direct evidence of the average maturity of bonds held in pension plans. While we have noted the recent trends to "dedication" and "immunization" (section 3.1), we suspect that most plans hold bonds with short maturities relative to their liabilities. For purposes of hypothetical calculations, we will assume that the duration of bonds held in pension plans is 5 years. Thus, an increase in interest rates generates a significant decline in the value of bonds, thereby tending to make plans *underfunded*.

The case of physical assets is somewhat more complicated. Specifically, the effect of interest rates on physical asset valuation depends critically upon whether a change in interest rates represents a change in the return on all existing units, or a change in the return on marginal units only. We consider these cases separately.

Case 1: Change in return on all existing units.

In this case, the higher discount is matched by higher returns, so

$$\epsilon_r [V(P^t)] = 0 \quad .$$

(P^t represents the stream of returns associated with physical assets held by pension plans in period t.)

Case 2: Change in return on marginal assets only.

In this case, a physical asset is indistinguishable from a bond, so

$$\epsilon_r \left[V(P^t) \right] = -D_t(P^t) \quad .$$

Since real physical assets often include items such as real estate, for which durations are quite long, we choose as our hypothetical value $D_t(P^t) = 10$. Thus, in case 2, an increase in interest rates generates a large decline in the value of real physical assets, again tending to make plans *underfunded*.

Stocks can be thought of as leveraged physical assets, that is, as a combination of bonds and physical assets. To calculate the effects of interest rates on equity values, we simply combine the preceding formulas appropriately.

Let Y^t be the stream of income associated with the physical assets of firms in which our hypothetical pension plan holds common stocks. Let Z^t be the stream of outstanding liabilities arising from debt contracts of these same firms. Let E^t denote the stream of equity income:

$$E_{t+\tau}^t = (1 - C)(Y_{t+\tau}^t - Z_{t+\tau}^t) \quad .$$

(Here, C represents the corporate income tax rate.) Let α denote the debt-equity ratio of these firms:

$$\alpha = \frac{V_t(Z^t)}{(1 - C)\,[V_t(Y^t) - V_t(Z^t)]} \quad .$$

The effect of interest rates on equity values depends upon whether it involves case 1 or case 2, as defined above.

Case 1: $\epsilon_r[V_t(E^t)] = \alpha D_t(Z^t) \quad .$

Case 2: $\epsilon_r[V_t(E^t)] = \alpha D_t(Z^t) - (1 + \alpha)D_t(Y^t) \quad .$

In case 1, an increase in interest rates tends to improve the asset positions of pension plans holding stocks. In case 2, the effect is ambiguous. For our hypothetical calculations, we will take $\alpha = 1/2$, $D_t(Z^t) = 5$, and $D_t(Y^t) = 10$.

Now we assemble the various formulas given above. In year t, unfunded liabilities, U_t, are given by

$$U_t = V_t(\lambda^t) - V_t(B^t) - V_t(P^t) - V_t(E^t) \quad .$$

Thus, the change in unfunded liabilities (as a proportion of total liabilities) resulting from a change in the real interest rate is given by

$$\frac{1 + r}{V_t(\lambda^t)} \frac{dU_t}{dr} =$$

$$\epsilon_r[V_t(\lambda')] - \frac{V_t(B')}{V_t(\lambda')} \epsilon_r [V_t(B')]$$

$$- \frac{V_t(P')}{V_t(\lambda')} \epsilon_r[V_t(P')] - \frac{V_t(E')}{V_t(\lambda')} \epsilon_r[V_t(E')] \ .$$

For purposes of calculations, we will assume that pension fund assets are evenly distributed between bonds, real assets, and stocks. Using the formulas and hypothetical parameter values listed above, we calculate two predicted responses of unfunded liablities to changes in the real interest rate, corresponding to the assumptions of case 1 and case 2:

Case 1: $$\frac{1 + r}{V_t(\lambda')} \frac{dU_t}{dr} = -14\frac{1}{6} \ .$$

Case 2: $$\frac{1 + r}{V_t(\lambda')} \frac{dU_t}{dr} = - 5\frac{5}{6} \ .$$

In both cases, the response of net unfunded liabilities to a 1 percentage point change in the interest rate is large.

Now suppose that recognition and response effects were instantaneous—capitalization of the change is immediate, firms quickly switch to new interest rates for accounting purposes, and ERISA requires firms to fully fund plans at all times. Then the instantaneous response of net contributions to pension plans would be enormous. In the more conservative case, following a rise in real interest rates of 1 percentage point, contributions would fall by 25 percent of total private saving. Even if adjustments in personal portfolios offset 80 percent of this, private saving would still fall by 5 percent.

Of course, the response will not be instantaneous. While the evidence in section 3.1 suggests that interest rates employed for pension plan accounting do respond to market rates, they do so slowly. By accounting convention, the historical costs of bonds, rather than their current market values, are used to compute pension net unfunded liabilities, so relevant bond values do not immediately reflect changes in market conditions. Finally, ERISA permits firms to cover unfunded liabilities over relatively long periods. Thus, we would expect actual unfunded liabilities to be dissipated over a relatively long time horizon. Nevertheless, the magnitude of funding imbalances builds in significant downward pressure on the rate of contributions in the short run.

Rather than attempt to flesh out an explicit model of the adjustment process, we turn directly to empirical evidence. In the following section, we estimate both the short-run and long- run effects of real interest rate changes on the accumulation of pension fund assets.

3.3 Empirical Evidence

In the preceding sections, we have argued that institutional rules governing pension funds may significantly depress the response of private saving to changes in real interest rates, but no direct evidence has been offered to confirm or refute this hypothesis. In this section, we estimate a simple model of fund asset accumulation using aggregate time-series data. Our estimates corroborate the existence and magnitude of the effects described in section 3.2. However, we must stress that we provide no evidence concerning the extent of offsetting adjustments in personal portfolios. Several other papers have investigated related issues concerning the permeability of the corporate pension veil (see, e.g., Bulow, Morck, and Summers 1987, Feldstein and Morck 1983, and Feldstein and Seligman 1981); in this matter, we use existing estimates as a guide.

3.3.1 Estimation Technique

The object here is to estimate the effect of changes in real interest rates on gross contributions to pension funds and to use these estimates to compute the net effect on fund asset accumulation. To avoid problems with scaling, we will attempt to explain variations in the ratio of current contributions to current benefits. According to our model, in steady state this ratio is given by

(3)
$$\left(\frac{C_t}{B_t}\right)^* = \left[\frac{V_t(L^t)}{\lambda_t^t}\right]^* = g(X),$$

where $g(\cdot)$ is some function, X is a vector of exogenous variables, and asterisks (*) denote steady-state values. The vector X will include the interest rate, wage growth, and employment growth rates (this information determines the value of the function g) and information concerning the shape of new liability profiles. In steady state, the values of these variables remain unchanged, so we may omit a time subscript.

Since we do not observe the economy in steady state, it is impossible to estimate equation (3) directly. One must explicitly describe the process of adjustment before implementing the model with aggregate time-series data.

As stated in section 3.2.2, the adjustment to a new steady state is not instantaneous. Numerous factors induce lagged responses, including:

(1) the adjustment of expectations to a change in the current value of some variable (real interest rates or the rate of wage growth);

(2) the adjustment of assumed parameters used in pension fund accounting to changes in actual expectations concerning the corresponding market parameters;

(3) the revaluation of existing assets (such as bonds) under pension fund accounting conventions; and

(4) the adjustment of contributions to cover unfunded liabilities under ERISA regulations.

Undoubtedly, there are other sources of lags as well. Rather than model each separately to allow estimation of a structural model, we adopt a reduced form specification intended to represent the aggregate effects of these lags. Specifically,

(4) $$\frac{C_t}{B_t} = g(X_t) + \sum_{\tau=0}^{\infty} \Delta X_{t-\tau}\mu_\tau$$

Note that if the vector X_t has remained at its current rate since the beginning of time, C_t/B_t will assume the steady-state value associated with X_t.

Estimation of this relationship requires several simplifications. First, we linearize $g(\cdot)$:

$$g(X_t) = X_t\alpha \quad .$$

Second, we restrict the lag structure as follows. We allow μ_0 and μ_1 to be estimated freely and require that the effects of all right-hand-side variables thereafter decline at the common geometric rate, μ (a scalar). That is, for $t \geq 2$,

$$\mu_t = \mu_{t-1}\mu \quad .$$

Formally, it would be easy to allow additional flexibility by estimating $(\mu_0, \ldots, \mu_k)$ without restriction and requiring geometric decline thereafter. However, this consumes valuable degrees of freedom. Given the length of our sample period, a relatively restrictive specification was essential.

When these restrictions are imposed, it is possible to simplify our basic functional specification, equation (4), as follows:

(5) $$\frac{C_t}{B_t} = X_t\alpha(1 - \mu) + \Delta X_t(\mu_0 + \alpha\mu)$$

$$+ \Delta X_{t-1}(\mu_1 - \mu\mu_0) + \mu \frac{C_{t-1}}{B_{t-1}} \quad .$$

As a practical matter, we will recover estimates of μ and the parameter vectors α, μ_0, and μ_1 by estimating the following relationship:

(6) $$\frac{C_t}{B_t} = X_t\beta_0 + \Delta X_t\beta_1 + \Delta X_{t-1}\beta_2 + \mu \frac{C_{t-1}}{B_{t-1}} + \epsilon_t \quad .$$

Note that equation (6) is linear in variables and parameters. Furthermore, equation (5) implies no restrictions on the coefficients in equation

(6). Thus, we can estimate equation (6) using standard techniques (see subsection 3.3.3). This will yield an estimate of μ directly. Other primitive parameters can be recovered as follows:

$$(7) \qquad\qquad \alpha = \beta_0/(1 - \mu) \ , $$

$$(8) \qquad\qquad \mu_0 = \beta_1 - \alpha\mu \ , $$

$$(9) \qquad\qquad \mu_1 = \mu\mu_0 + \beta_2 \ . $$

Under the assumption that ϵ_t is independently and identically distributed and independent of contemporaneous right-hand-side variables (interest rates, wage rates, etc.), equation (5) may be estimated with ordinary least squares (OLS). While the second assumption does not trouble us, the first is a serious concern. Specifically, if ϵ_t is autocorrelated, C_{t-1}/B_{t-1} will be correlated with ϵ_t, and OLS estimates will be inconsistent. Consequently, we also estimate equation (6) with two-stage least squares (2SLS), instrumenting for C_{t-1}/B_{t-1} using lagged values of the other independent variables. This produces consistent estimates. However, consistency is highly sensitive to the functional specification. If our restrictions on the functional form are invalid (if, for example, the μ_t's decline geometrically after *two* lags), our instruments will be invalid. Unfortunately, there are, of necessity, no alternative candidates.

3.3.2 Data

Now the procedure described above will be implemented with aggregate U.S. time-series data. Our variables and their sources are as follows:

G_t = Annual gross contributions by employers to private pension and profit-sharing plans, as reported in the National Income and Product Accounts (NIPA) data (see *Survey of Current Business*, July issue of each year). This figure is derived from the reports of contributions on employers' tax returns. Unfortunately, a breakdown between defined benefit and other plans is unavailable. The series begins in 1951.

R_t = The dollar value of reversions to plan sponsors. Data on reversions have been collected by the Pension Benefit Guarantee Corporation since 1980, before which they were not an important phenomenon.

C_t = Annual contributions by employers to private pension and profit-sharing plans, net of reversions ($C_t = G_t - R_t$).

B_t = Benefits paid by private pension and welfare plans, as given in the NIPA data. This series is constructed primarily from data on pension income reported on individual income tax returns and is available beginning in 1952.

i_t = The nominal rate of interest, defined as the average annual rate paid on Aaa long-term corporate bonds.

v_t = The annual rate of change of wages and salaries for the average full-time equivalent employee, as measured by the NIPA.

s_t = The annual total return (dividends plus capital gains) for the Standard and Poor's 500 stock index.

p_t = The annual rate of inflation, as measured by the year-to-year percentage change in the GNP deflator.

Each of these rates (i_t, v_t, s_t, p_t) is measured in *percentage points*, rather than fractions of unity. We also define the following real rates of interest, wage-salary growth, and equity return:

$$r_t = i_t - p_t \quad ,$$

$$w_t = v_t - p_t \quad ,$$

$$e_t = s_t - p_t \quad .$$

We do not mean these to represent *expected* real rates in any period. Rather, they are actual *ex post facto* rates. Recall that our specification is designed to capture various lagged effects, including the adjustment of expectations to changes in *ex post facto* values.

Note that most of our data predate ERISA. While firms undoubtedly had greater flexibility in funding pension plans prior to federal regulation, we suspect that most firms gravitated (however slowly) toward full funding. Presumably, the existence of ERISA will make pension fund contributions more responsive to interest rates than these data suggest.

3.3.3 Estimates and Interpretation

Estimates of equation (6) are presented in this section. We took the vector of independent variables, X_t, to include a constant term, the real interest rate, the real rate of wage-salary growth, the residual real rate of equity return, and the rate of inflation (for ΔX_t we omitted the constant term, for obvious reasons). We constructed the residual rate of equity return, er_t, as follows: we regressed the current real rate of equity return on r_t, w_t, and p_t, and set er_t equal to the fitted residuals. Our justification for this procedure is that we are interested in all direct and indirect effects of changes in r_t on rates of contributions. If an unexpected rise in r_t causes a change in stock values, thereby altering the value of pension fund assets, which in turn precipitates adjustments in contributions, this is a legitimate effect.

We estimated two versions of equation (6). In the first, we imposed no constraints on coefficients. In the second, we constrained the coefficient of $r_t(\beta_6^r)$ to equal the negative of the coefficient of $w_t(\beta_8^w)$. In the long run, it is clearly the *difference* between r_t and w_t which is relevant for determining pension fund balance. Each version of equation (6) was estimated using both OLS and 2SLS techniques (see subsection 3.3.1) on aggregate annual time-series data, from 1952 to 1982 (see subsection 3.3.2). The results are presented in table 3.7.

Several aspects of table 3.7 deserve immediate comment. Note that the signs of the coefficients on r_t, w_t, er_t, and p_t determine the direction of the long-run effects of these variables on contributions (see equation [7]). Thus, we see that the long-run interest and wage growth effects have the anticipated signs. In fact, for both instrumented and uninstrumented versions, the absolute value of the coefficient on r_t is nearly the same as the coefficient of w_t, as predicted, so that imposing this constraint changes the estimates by negligible amounts. Note that the inflation rate increases long-run contributions (although the effect is not statistically significant in three out of four equations). Strictly speaking, this is inconsistent with our model—the requirement of full funding determines C_t/B_t independent of inflation. However, in practice, firms may have the ability to somewhat overfund or underfund plans in the long run. With higher inflation rates, pension funds form a more desirable tax dodge; hence, contributions may increase with inflation. Finally, observe that long-run contributions rise with er_t, although the coefficient is only marginally significant. In steady state, changes in er_t presumably reflect changes in the risk premium associated with equity. Thus, the corresponding coefficient implies that contributions increase as the risk premium associated with equity rises. Perhaps this reflects caution on the part of firms when facing greater variability on earnings from assets.

While one might be tempted to interpret the other coefficients in table 3.7 directly, this is potentially misleading. Only the primitive coefficients can be easily interpreted, and thus they must be recovered by unscrambling our estimates using equations (7), (8), and (9). Since we are primarily concerned with assessing the effects of interest rates on contributions, we recover only those primitive parameters bearing directly on this issue (μ, α^r, μ_0^r, and μ_1^r). These estimates, along with asymptotic standard errors, are presented in table 3.8.

To interpret these coefficients, recall our basic specification (equation [3]). The coefficient α^r measures the long-run impact of the real interest rate on pension plan contributions (with wages fixed, interest rates do not affect benefits, the denominator). In particular, the OLS estimates indicate that a 1 percentage point increase in the real interest rate will depress C_t/B_t in the long run by more than 0.4 (40 percent of benefits). If the long-run value of C_t/B_t is approximately 2, this implies a long-run interest elasticity of contributions in the neighborhood of -20. (Again, in this section, the elasticity is the percentage change in contributions for a 1 percentage point change in the interest rate.) 2SLS estimates imply that the magnitude of this effect is 50 percent *larger*.

Table 3.7   **Estimated Equations**

Variable	OLS Unconstrained	OLS Constrained	2SLS Unconstrained	2SLS Constrained
constant	0.398 (0.208)	0.460 (0.168)	1.45 (0.76)	1.55 (0.66)
r_t	-0.093 (0.035)	-0.097 (0.033)	-0.416 (0.076)	-0.425 (0.066)
Δr_t	-0.013 (0.043)	-0.004 (0.038)	0.153 (0.128)	0.168 (0.113)
Δr_{t-1}	-0.024 (0.048)	-0.021 (0.047)	0.240 (0.139)	0.245 (0.134)
w_t	0.118 (0.052)	0.097 (0.033)	0.460 (0.142)	0.425 (0.066)
Δw_t	-0.056 (0.040)	-0.046 (0.034)	-0.365 (0.102)	-0.347 (0.079)
Δw_{t-1}	-0.038 (0.028)	-0.033 (0.026)	-0.230 (0.076)	-0.222 (0.069)
er_t	0.0076 (0.0040)	0.0072 (0.0039)	0.029 (0.012)	0.029 (0.012)
Δer_t	-0.0065 (0.0029)	-0.0064 (0.0029)	-0.021 (0.009)	-0.021 (0.009)
Δer_{t-1}	-0.0029 (0.0019)	-0.0027 (0.0010)	-0.011 (0.006)	-0.011 (0.006)
p_t	0.027 (0.016)	0.020 (0.010)	0.062 (0.060)	0.051 (0.046)
Δp_t	-0.075 (0.036)	-0.070 (0.033)	-0.210 (0.108)	-0.201 (0.100)
Δp_{t-1}	-0.053 (0.053)	-0.054 (0.041)	0.003 (0.135)	0.0021 (0.133)
C_{t-1}/B_{t-1}	0.775 (0.057)	0.777 (0.056)	0.343 (0.195)	0.349 (0.189)
Durbin-Watson	2.66	2.68	1.54	1.56
Standard Error of Regression	0.088	0.087	0.280	0.273

NOTE: OLS = ordinary least squares; 2SLS = two-stage least squares. Standard errors given in parentheses.

The estimates of μ_0^r and μ_1^r indicate a relatively smooth, monotonic adjustment of C_r/B_t to its steady-state value. In the first year following a 1 percentage point rise in the real rate of interest, C_t/B_t changes by $\alpha^r + \mu_0^r$. For the OLS estimates, $\alpha^r + \mu_0^r \approx -0.1$, which implies a short- run impact elasticity in the neighborhood of -5 (one-quarter of the adjustment in C_t/B_t occurs in the first year). For the 2SLS estimates, the impact elasticity is much higher (approximately -13), and a larger proportion of the adjustment (more than one-third) occurs in the first year. Both OLS and 2SLS estimates imply that just under half of the

Table 3.8   Primitive Parameters

Parameter	OLS Unconstrained	OLS Constrained	2SLS Unconstrained	2SLS Constrained
μ	0.775	0.777	0.343	0.349
	(0.057)	(0.056)	(0.195)	(0.189)
α^r	−0.413	−0.435	−0.633	−0.653
	(0.089)	(0.067)	(0.146)	(0.129)
μ_0^r	0.307	0.334	0.370	0.396
	(0.085)	(0.057)	(0.370)	(0.181)
μ_1^r	0.214	0.239	0.367	0.383
	(0.048)	(0.047)	(0.139)	(0.134)

NOTE: OLS = ordinary least squares; 2SLS = two-stage least squares. Standard errors given in parentheses.

adjustment is complete by the second year. Thereafter, 2SLS estimates imply much more rapid adjustment to the steady state (compare the values of μ). It is interesting to note that, for the OLS estimates, $\mu_1^r \approx \mu\mu_0^r$, so that the additional flexibility offered through inclusion of the lagged parameter makes very little difference.

To assess more fully the implications of our estimates, we calculate implied steady-state values of (C_t/B_t) and (A_t/B_t) under different interest rate assumptions. As mentioned earlier, the implied steady-state value of (C_t/B_t) is given by substituting values of variables and parameters into equation (4), where $\Delta X_{t-\tau}$ is set equal to zero for all τ. Obtaining the implied steady-state value of A_t/B_t is only slightly more difficult. Along any path, the value of pension assets evolves as follows:

(10) $A_{t+1} = (1 + \rho_t)A_t + C_t - B_t$.

Here, ρ represents the rate of return on the pension portfolio. This may differ from r_t because of the risk characteristics of this portfolio. Equation (10) can be rewritten as

$$\frac{A_{t+1}}{A_t} = (1 + \rho_t) + \left(\frac{C_t}{A_t}\right) - \left(\frac{B_t}{A_t}\right) .$$

In steady state, $A_{t+1}/A_t = 1 + g$, the growth rate of pension benefits. Thus,

$$(1 + g) = (1 + \rho) + \left(\frac{C_t}{B_t}\right)^* \left(\frac{B_t}{A_t}\right)^* - \left(\frac{B_t}{A_t}\right)^*.$$

Solving for $(A_t/B_t)^*$,

(11) $$\left(\frac{A_t}{B_t}\right)^* = \frac{1 - (C_t/B_t)^*}{\rho - g} .$$

Given values of r, w, er, g, and the risk premium associated with pension funds ($\rho - r$), we can calculate $(C_t/B_t)^*$ and $(A_t/B_t)^*$ through equations (4) and (11).

The calculations for these steady-state contribution and asset ratios are presented in table 3.9. We set the variables appearing in our regression analysis equal to their recent (20-year) historical averages. Columns designated "initial" refer to an assumed real interest rate of 0.025. Columns labeled "final" refer to an assumed real interest rate of 0.015. We take $\rho - r = 0.03$, and $g = 0.10$. This assumed rate of real pension benefit growth may seem quite high, but it accords with historical experience, presumably because of the immaturity of most pension programs. We chose to make our calculations using the value of g which prevailed for the sample period, rather than a more "realistic" steady-state value, because our estimates may be unreliable in a regime of substantially lower pension benefit growth.

Recall from our theoretical discussion that the (absolute) long-run interest elasticity of contributions should equal the duration of newly accrued pension liabilities while the (absolute) long-run interest elasticity of assets should equal the duration of outstanding liabilities. Of course, one must adjust for the fact that approximately one-third of pension plans are not defined benefit. Nevertheless, all estimates appear to be roughly consistent with the magnitudes proposed in section 3.2. Only one anomaly appears: for the 2SLS estimates, the implied duration of outstanding liabilities slightly exceeds the duration of newly accrued liabilities. We suspect that our estimates of $(A_t/B_t)^*$ are not entirely reliable due to the maturation of the pension system during our sample period. We hope to improve these calculations in subsequent study.

3.4 Conclusion

In this paper, we have developed a simple analytical model which suggests that the long-run percentage responsiveness of contributions

Table 3.9   **Long-Run Impacts of Real Interest Rate Changes**

	$(C/B)^*$			$(A/B)^*$		
Version	Initial	Final	% Change	Initial	Final	% Change
Uninstrumented, Unconstrained	2.070	2.475	19.6	24.18	27.04	11.8
Uninstrumented, Constrained	2.026	2.460	21.4	23.19	26.76	15.4
Instrumented, Unconstrained	2.008	2.640	31.5	22.78	30.06	32.0
Instrumented, Constrained	1.982	2.635	32.9	22.19	29.97	34.8

to a 1 percentage point increase in the interest rate should equal the duration of newly accrued pension liabilities, and the responsiveness of pension assets should equal the duration of existing liabilities. The OLS and 2SLS aggregate time-series estimates of section 3.3 are remarkably consistent with this model. This analysis suggests that the operation of pension funds may significantly affect the way our economy responds to incentives for capital formation.

The importance of this target-saving/negative elasticity of contributions theory has been borne out by recent economic experience. Real interest rates have been at record levels for the past three years, and the effect this has had on pension funding has been considerable. The earnings of pension fund assets have been much greater than actuarial assumptions with the result being that a majority of pension funds are fully funded (even at their still-below-market assumed interest rates), and net contributions are down over $30 billion since 1982. Net contributions are likely to remain below the 1982 level because of the considerable lags in the pension actuarial system. Such recent and increasingly important phenomena as pension reversions, dedications, and immunizations also reflect the gap between market interest rates and the previously assumed rates, and they reinforce the downward pressure on loanable fund saving from this source. Thus, adjustments of pension fund contributions may continue to depress personal saving for years to come.

References

Board of Governors of the Federal Reserve System. 1985. *Flow of funds accounts, fourth quarter 1984*, February. Washington, D.C.
Boskin, M. J. 1978. Taxation, saving, and the rate of interest. *Journal of Political Economy* 86:S1–S27.
Bulow, J., R. Morck, and L. Summers. 1987. How does the market value unfunded pension liabilities? In *Issues in pension economics*, edited by Z. Bodie, J. Shoven, and D. Wise. Chicago: University of Chicago Press.
Bureau of Economic Analysis. *Survey of current business*. Various issues.
Feldstein, M. S., and R. K. Morck. 1983. Pension funding decisions, interest rate assumptions, and share prices. In *Financial aspects of the United States pension system,* edited by Z. Bodie and J. Shoven. Chicago: University of Chicago Press, 177–207.
Feldstein, M. S., and S. Seligman. 1981. Pension funding, share prices and national savings. *Journal of Finance* 36:801–24.
Hewitt Associates. 1984. *Pension-related financial data in the Fortune 500 industrials.* Lincolnshire, Illinois.
Howrey, E. P., and S. H. Hymans. 1978. The measurement and determination of loanable-funds saving. *Brookings Papers on Economic Activity* 3:655–705. Also in *What should be taxed: Income or expenditure?* edited by J. A. Pechman. Washington, D.C.: The Brookings Institution, 1980.

Summers, L. H. 1981. Capital taxation and accumulation in a life- cycle growth model. *The American Economic Review* 71(4):533–44.

U.S. Department of Labor. 1983. *Estimates of participants and financial characteristics of private pension plans*. Washington, D.C.: GPO

U.S. Department of Treasury. 1985. *Statistics of income bulletin*. Winter 1984–85. Washington, D.C.: GPO.

U.S. Department of Treasury, Internal Revenue Service. 1982. *Statistics of income, annual report 1981: Individual tax returns*. Washington, D.C.: GPO.

The Wyatt Company. 1985. *1984 survey of actuarial assumptions and funding: Plans with 1,000 or more active participants*. New York City.

Comment   Eugene Steuerle

In their paper, Bernheim and Shoven make a valuable contribution to recent attempts to explain both changes in personal saving rates and changes in the net flow of funds into pension plans. To the extent that pension plans are designed to meet certain target saving goals, pension funding (contributions less payments) will have a negative elasticity (or, more exactly, responsiveness) to changes in the real interest rate.

The arguments are intuitively appealing and, from my discussions with other experts on pensions, provide a rational explanation of much current activity. The tax laws limit overfunding with respect to pension plans. While higher real interest rates might eventually lead to increased benefit levels, over the short run they are likely to lead to lower levels of funding for a promised or targeted level of benefits. Regardless of the underlying reasons, both actuaries and managers of firms do fund pension plans to reach some target level of benefits.

While Bernheim and Shoven have enhanced our understanding of one important influence on pension funding, in the ideal, one would want to test the relative impact of all other influences on pension funding. Unfortunately, Bernheim and Shoven only have 31 observations of data (from an annual time series from 1952 to 1982) and have few degrees of freedom left in a model with 13 independent variables plus a constant term. With so few observations, it is not clear how alternative theories could be tested.

I will list some additional factors that I believe had a significant impact on pension funding over the period of time examined by Bernheim and Shoven.

First, the Pension Reform Act of 1974 forced funding of many plans that were underfunded prior to that time. Underfunding is advantageous to stockholders because some *expected* costs are shifted to workers

Eugene Steuerle is the deputy assistant secretary for tax analysis, U.S. Department of the Treasury.

and government as long as there is some probability of bankruptcy in the future. The passage of the 1974 Act therefore should have increased pension funding for several years, but in a declining fashion as more and more plans became fully funded.

Second, the IRS imposes limits on funding that operate differently with different rates of inflation. The tax laws not only set a maximum level of benefits that can be provided under a qualified plan, but they also disallow contributions necessary to fund future expected increases in that maximum amount due to *future* inflation. As expected inflation increases, it becomes more likely that more workers (especially younger workers) will be entitled to benefits in excess of the maximum amount allowed to be funded by the IRS. In addition, higher rates of inflation generally lower the real benefits that will be paid to workers who leave a firm before retirement. Thus, inflation might be expected to have a negative impact on funding in pension plans, although Bernheim and Shoven find the opposite (usually statistically insignificant) result.

Third, changes in income and Social Security tax rates should have a major impact on pension funding. Higher tax rates enhance the benefits of the tax preference granted to saving through pension plans. These tax rates have changed substantially over the period of time analyzed by Bernheim and Shoven.

Fourth, the changing demographic nature of the population should affect levels of funding. In general, the current tax treatment of fringe benefits tends to discriminate against secondary workers (Kosters and Steuerle 1981). In the case of pensions, the greater turnover rate for secondary workers should decrease the amount of expected benefits that would be paid out under typical defined benefit plans designed for long-term workers.

Fifth, some changes in pension funding could reflect cyclical, as well as long-term, adjustments. I have shown elsewhere how after-corporate-tax payments to owners of corporate capital tend toward constancy over the economic cycle (Steuerle 1985). A pension fund offers managers a ready device by which to steady the reported earnings stream over time. Thus, it is possible that some adjustments in payments to pension plans merely reflect cyclical, rather than long-term, responses to changes in interest rates.

Sixth, there is a substantial debate over the extent to which the increased availability of IRAs and other defined contribution options reduces the demand of workers for defined benefit plans. Certainly some offset has taken place over the same period of time that real interest rates have risen.

Finally, as noted above, increases in the inflation rate have decreased the real liabilities of defined benefit pension plans. Any model may have difficulty separating out this effect if the lag with which actuaries respond to these changes is unknown. I have argued that some of the reductions in funding in the 1980s should be attributed to this decline in real liabilities, although I have not tested this conclusion. A survey of changes in actuarial assumptions in major pension plans could help resolve the question of how long it takes for changes in inflation and real interest rates to affect funding within pension plans.

In summary, Bernheim and Shoven have enhanced our understanding of recent changes in pension funding. Changes in real interest rates are likely to have a significant impact on pension funding under any targeted benefit approach. While their logic is clear, the number of data observations is inadequate to test the relative importance of this one factor relative to other factors known to have been operating at the same time.

References

Kosters, Marvin, and Eugene Steuerle. 1981. The effect of fringe benefit tax policies on labor and consumer markets. *National Tax Journal—Proceedings of the Seventy-fourth Annual Conference.*

Steuerle, Eugene. 1985. *Taxes, loans, and inflation.* Washington, D.C.: Brookings Institution, chap. 3.

4   Poverty among the Elderly: Where Are the Holes in the Safety Net?

Michael J. Boskin and John B. Shoven

A substantial body of research, combined with aggregate and average official government statistics, documents the absolute and relative real income gains made by the elderly population of the United States in the last 15 years. The large increase in real Social Security benefits in the early 1970s, and their subsequent indexing, were a major source of this improved economic position. This period also witnessed a substantial acceleration of early retirement, a lengthening of life expectancies, and other factors affecting the welfare of the elderly.

Among the most important documented factors concerning the economic status of the elderly from 1970 to 1985 are the following:

1. A sharp reduction in the incidence of poverty among the elderly, even during the 1981–82 recession.

2. The substantial increase in absolute and relative real income of the nonpoor elderly.

3. The (historically) approximate neutrality of inflation on the cost of living of the elderly, relative to the rest of the population; and the likely lower inflation vulnerability of the elderly, given their typical asset ownership (especially housing and Social Security).

4. The substantial increase in economic resources, given various conceptual adjustments, of the elderly during their retirement years, relative to their own career average earnings.[1]

Michael J. Boskin is a professor of economics at Stanford University and a research associate of the National Bureau of Economic Research. John B. Shoven is a professor and chairman of the Department of Economics at Stanford University and a research associate of the National Bureau of Economic Research.

We wish to thank Tim Wilson of Stanford University for valuable research assistance and the NBER Pension Program for financial support for this work. We received many useful suggestions from participants of the NBER Conference on Pensions in the U.S. Economy. Special thanks go to Tom Gustafson for his comments.

115

Various other factors could be mentioned, and we do not mean to imply that more research on the factors mentioned above is unnecessary; certainly, we are in need of improved understanding of these phenomena. However, it is our tentative conclusion that subsequent research is unlikely to alter the qualitative results of this set of findings.

Previous research[1] has referred primarily to the typical, or average, situation of elderly retirees, in particular, to the younger cohorts of elderly retirees, since those are the groups for which data are most readily available. A correlative, important question is, given this remarkable social achievement of lifting the bulk of the elderly out of poverty and substantially increasing the real incomes of many of them, what fraction were not so fortunate? How many stayed poor? Who were they? Who was so unfortunate as to suffer substantial declines in their incomes relative to career average earnings? Who had particularly low or particularly high replacement rates?

The purpose of this paper is to begin to answer such questions. Again, we focus on a particular data set and a particular cohort of the elderly. Even within this data set, described in section 4.1, we must winnow our sample down for various reasons. Our analysis is nonetheless revealing. A nontrivial fraction of the elderly were left behind, and various characteristics of this group can be ascertained. Also, a modest fraction of elderly retirees, although well-off prior to retirement, suffered substantial real income declines and could now be described as relatively poor. Again, our analysis suggests that this phenomenon is not randomly distributed across the elderly population, but heavily concentrated in particular groups, for example, widows.

Thus, our goal is both to supplement previous studies of the average or typical real incomes or replacement rates of the elderly during retirement and to highlight the heterogeneity of the changes in the economic well-being of the elderly. Toward this end, section 4.1 describes our data and methodology. We basically attempt to examine three sets of phenomena using the Longitudinal Retirement History Survey. We examine (1) who among the elderly were poor in the late 1970s; (2) who among the elderly were well-off prior to retirement but suffered substantial declines in real incomes postretirement; and (3) who among the elderly had quite low or high (unadjusted) replacement rates. In our previous research, we concluded that various important adjustments should be made to the typical way replacement rates are calculated to gain a more accurate scalar measure of the economic well-being of typical, or average, elderly individuals and families, relative to their own earlier working lives. We adjusted replacement rates for such things as taxes, career average versus high three years of earnings, risk, childrearing costs, and so forth. In this paper, as described in more detail below, we take a somewhat more conventional view and just examine income during retirement unadjusted for taxes, risk, child-rearing, and other expenses. We do this both to make this research comparable with other studies and to separate the issue of finding a preferable way to approximate the well-being of typical elderly retirees and families from the detailed study of the poor elderly.

Section 4.2 presents two types of information to help address each of the questions posed above. The first consists of cross-tabulations of postretirement income by preretirement earnings by various characteristics. We examine, in this way, the fractions of the elderly who are poor, suffer substantial income declines, and have high and low replacement rates, as well as characteristics of these groups relative to the general elderly group under study. The second presents a probit analysis of some characteristics potentially correlated with each of these outcomes. This is just a richer way of examining the data. We do not present a structural interpretation of factors associated with, for example, poverty in old age, just a probabilistic analysis of factors associated with it.

Section 4.3 concludes the paper with a summary of the results, some of the potential implications of the analysis, and some avenues for further research.

4.1 Data

All of the empirical results of section 4.2 are based on the Retirement History Survey conducted from 1969 to 1979 by the Social Security Administration. The survey initially included 11,153 households whose heads were born between 1905 and 1911. There was substantial attrition (due to placement in nursing homes or loss of contact as well as to death) for each successive biennial survey, so that only 7,352 original respondents or their widows remained to answer the last survey in 1979.

Respondents were surveyed in odd-numbered years concerning current family composition, labor force participation, health, activities, assets and wealth, and the previous (even-numbered) year's income and benefits. Replacement rates are calculated here for the years *prior* to the survey years. The Social Security Administration prepared a matched data set of its records of the survey respondents' and their spouses' covered earnings through 1974. This information was used to determine the earnings histories forming the denominator in the calculation of replacement rates.

Social Security Administration records consider only the earnings for each year in each job which totaled less than the year's maximum taxable earnings. In cases where reported covered earnings equaled or exceeded the taxable maximum, the following imputation procedures were used: the few cases of covered earnings above the taxable maximum were taken as given. In these instances the person paid taxes from two or more jobs. We assumed that earnings in neither job exceeded the taxable maximum. In cases where covered earnings equaled the taxable maximum, we assumed that the taxable maximum was attained in the middle of the last quarter in which taxes were paid. If, for example, the respondents finished paying Social Security taxes in the third quarter, we imputed their year's wage income to be 8/5 times the taxable maximum. This method should prove relatively unbiased, if inexact.

A household was excluded from our tabulations if at least one of the following conditions held (number excluded in parentheses):

1. Household reports federal or military pension income in 1971, 1973, 1975, 1977, or 1979 (N = 239).

2. Respondent never reports self retired or partly retired, or the respondent's spouse is always reported either working or looking for work (N = 825).

3. Household shows no earnings subject to Social Security taxes between 1958 and 1974 (N = 553).

4. Household dies or is lost from the survey before 1977 (N = 664).

For the regressions of section 4.2, we also eliminated those households who had 1977 income, 1969 financial or nonfinancial wealth, or expected total income after retirement of less than $100. This left us with a sample of 5,644 households for 1977.

This paper reports total income replacement rates relative to career average indexed earnings. Total income was constructed by summing the household's income from wages, interest and dividends, rent, annuities, pensions, relatives, disability benefits, state welfare benefits, workers' compensation, AFDC, unemployment insurance, SSI, and Social Security (old age, disability, survivor's, and black lung benefits). Career average indexed earnings measures the average earnings during the period from 1951 to the year of retirement or 1974, whichever was earlier. The indexing was done with the Personal Consumption Expenditure deflator.

Before turning to the empirical results, it is worth mentioning that these data are not for the elderly in general, but for a particular cohort of people who were 67–72 years old in 1977. These households are not representative of the entire elderly population for many reasons. First, none of them is extremely old. Second, almost all of them benefited from the sharp increase in the level of real Social Security benefits which occurred in the 1960s and early 1970s. Third, they enjoyed the rapidly rising real wages of the 1950s and 1960s. The main point is simply that we are looking at a fairly narrow age cohort at a particular moment in time (1977 for the most part). The experiences of this group should be generalized only with extreme caution.

4.2   Analysis of Who Has Low Incomes and/or Replacement Rates

4.2.1   Cross-tabulation of Postretirement Income with Preretirement Earnings

Table 4.1 gives a cross-tabulation of 1976 postretirement income on career average preretirement indexed earnings for all retired households in the 1977 Retirement History Survey which met our selection criteria and which did not have missing information for any of the income categories. It also shows the median replacement rate for each cell, where this replacement rate is total retirement income relative to price-indexed "career average" preretirement earnings.[2] The figures are not adjusted for family size, taxes, and risk. If those adjustments were made (and we feel that there is a good case for them), the replacement rates would be significantly higher.

Of particular concern to us are the 941 households (or 23 percent of the sample) whose postretirement income was below $3000 in 1976. Of

Table 4.1   **Numbers of Households and Median Replacement Rates: Cross-Tabulation of 1976 Postretirement Income and Career Average Preretirement Earnings, for All Households**

Post-retirement 1976 Income	Career Average Preretirement Income							
	$0–$1K	$1–$3K	$3–$5K	$5–$10K	$10–$20K	$20–$30K	> $30K	Row Totals
$0–$1K	9	12	12	25	26	11	3	98
	118%	23%	10%	8%	2%	2%	1%	7%
$1–$3K	168	202	150	197	107	13	6	843
	1333%	274%	130%	78%	47%	26%	9%	138%
$3–$5K	56	100	104	281	344	54	9	948
	2304%	374%	184%	106%	68%	46%	23%	96%
$5–$10K	37	45	64	198	747	269	60	1420
	5463%	724%	329%	180%	90%	70%	46%	92%
$10–$20K	20	16	19	59	204	230	106	654
	9696%	941%	456%	306%	154%	99%	73%	120%
$20–$30K	4	2	2	6	31	25	25	95
	7221%	1534%	1021%	389%	270%	160%	104%	204%
> $30K	2	1	2	2	15	9	29	60
	8528%	2232%	1128%	641%	632%	299%	138%	249%
Column Totals	296	378	353	768	1474	611	238	4118
	1833%	348%	169%	112%	87%	78%	64%	105%

those households, 553 had career average household earnings of less than $5000, indicating that their relative poverty was a lifetime phenomenon. It is quite rare that those with above average earnings (say, those with career average earnings in excess of $20,000) end up with less than $3000 in retirement. For the entire sample this happened in only 33 instances, although the frequency of occurrence was about 4 percent for those whose earnings did, indeed, exceed $20,000.

A small minority of households end up with more real income in retirement than their career average earnings. While this is not precisely illustrated in table 4.1, that table does show that about 8 percent of those with career average earnings under $10,000, have postretirement incomes above $10,000. The corresponding figure for crossing the $20,000 threshold is 2 percent (i.e., 2 percent of those whose career average earnings were below $20,000 have retirement incomes in excess of $20,000).

Tables 4.2 and 4.3 contain the same information as table 4.1, but separately for married couples and widows. The most obvious result is that widows are far more likely to suffer a sharp fall in retirement income relative to the household's preretirement earnings. Of those widows whose households' career average earnings were between

Table 4.2   **Numbers of Household & Median Replacement Rates: Cross-Tabulation of 1976 Postretirement Income & Career Average Preretirement Earnings, for Married Couples**

1976 Income	Career Average Preretirement Income							Row Totals
	$0–$1K	$1–$3K	$3–$5K	$5–$10K	$10–$20K	$20–$30K	> $30K	
$0–$1K	2	2	3	4	5	3	1	20
	111%	10%	8%	7%	4%	7%	3%	7%
$1–$3K	12	24	26	38	18	3	2	123
	776%	207%	108%	64%	33%	19%	7%	85%
$3–$5K	13	40	52	108	112	10	3	338
	1173%	266%	151%	90%	58%	34%	20%	87%
$5–$10K	14	24	33	102	514	214	42	943
	3482%	663%	313%	158%	85%	68%	44%	83%
$10–$20K	9	10	15	45	157	195	94	525
	5778%	845%	427%	279%	143%	97%	73%	111%
$20–$30K	2	1	1	5	27	20	23	79
	7221%	2149%	1021%	389%	263%	160%	97%	193%
> $30K	1	1	2	2	11	7	27	51
	8528%	2232%	1128%	641%	628%	257%	136%	214%
Column Totals	53	102	132	304	844	452	192	2079
	1901%	334%	177%	117%	87%	79%	68%	92%

Table 4.3   **Numbers of Households & Median Replacement Rates: Cross-Tabulation of 1976 Postretirement Income & Career Average Preretirement Earnings, for Widows**

1976 Income	Career Average Preretirement Income							Row Totals
	$0– $1K	$1– $3K	$3– $5K	$5– $10K	$10– $20K	$20– $30K	> $30K	
$0– $1K	5	6	7	12	13	5	1	49
	107%	32%	13%	8%	6%	0%	0%	10%
$1– $3K	117	128	86	110	75	10	3	529
	1411%	306%	139%	82%	52%	31%	9%	160%
$3– $5K	36	47	40	112	165	40	6	446
	2716%	491%	238%	125%	75%	48%	25%	104%
$5– $10K	16	17	27	64	146	42	15	327
	5964%	765%	382%	209%	126%	78%	50%	148%
$10– $20K	7	4	3	11	27	20	8	80
	9696%	1174%	710%	417%	256%	130%	97%	247%
$20– $30K	2	0	0	0	3	2	2	9
	7023%	0%	0%	0%	391%	219%	122%	314%
> $30K	0	0	0	0	2	1	2	5
	0%	0%	0%	0%	783%	299%	169%	299%
Column Totals	183	202	163	309	431	120	37	1445
	1812%	366%	177%	118%	84%	67%	53%	133%

$10,000 and $20,000, fully 59 percent of them have retirement incomes under $5000. Thirty-nine percent of those with career average earnings between $5000 and $10,000, 39 percent wind up with retirement income under $3000. This collapse into relative poverty for widows partly reflects inadequate insurance and lack of joint survivor pension annuities.

Table 4.4 contains some detailed characteristics of households with low and high unadjusted career average earnings replacement rates. Columns 1 and 2 of the first part of the table contrasts the average figures for those with replacement rates greater than 200 percent with those whose replacement rates are under 67 percent. For those with total income replacement rates of greater than 200 percent, 1976 Social Security income amounted to 27 percent of 1976 income and 55 percent of career average earnings. For those with low replacement rates, Social Security in 1976 amounted to 67 percent of 1976 income and 15 percent of career average earnings. In absolute dollars, those with low replacement rates on average received more from Social Security than those with high replacement rates.

One aspect of table 4.4 which we find interesting is that the low and high replacement rate households expected to have roughly the same postretirement income in 1973. However, the high replacement rate

Table 4.4   **Financial & Other Characteristics of Households with High and Low Replacement Rates**

Variable	1976 Total Income Rep. Rate > 200%	1976 Total Income Rep. Rate < 67%	1976 Total Income Rep. Rate < 67%, for Married	1976 Total Income Rep. Rate < 67%, for Widowed
Income (1976)	$ 8345	$ 4712	$ 6320	$ 2845
Income Expected (73)[a]	5884	6361	7325	5236
Soc. Sec. Inc. (76)	2266	3159	4005	2185
Soc. Sec. Inc. Exp. (73)	1668	2616	2589	2365
Pension Inc. (76)	1970	854	1364	210
Pension Inc. Exp. (73)	1430	1175	1538	799
Earnings Inc. (76)	983	122	203	50
Earnings Inc. Exp. (73)	478	719	652	745
Financial Wealth (69)	10430	9288	10134	8435
Financial Wealth (76)	18559	12335	16445	8341
Non-Fin. Wealth (69)	9658	13636	15605	13608
Non-Fin. Wealth (76)	24983	23660	29358	20281
Career Average Earnings	4086	21134	24093	18611
High-3 Earnings	7808	28437	31846	26040
Race: (69)				
White	82%	92%	94%	92%
Black/Other	18	8	6	8
Sex (69)				
Male	50%	93%	98%	94%
Female	50	7	2	6
Median Age (69)	60	60	60	60
Employment Status (77)				
Retired	55%	68%	91%	33%
Keeping House	31	21	1	56
Disabled	10	6	6	7
Unemployed	1	1	0	1
Job/Not at work	0	0	0	0
Working	0	0	0	1
Other	4	4	1	3
Health vs. Others' Health (survey before retirement)				
Better	29%	28%	32%	22%
Same	44	48	47	50
Worse	22	19	15	23
Marital Status (69/77)				
Married	43% 32%	85% 54%	97% 100%	90% 0%
Widowed	40% 51%	4% 33%	1% 0%	8% 100%
Div./Sep.	11% 10%	3% 4%	2% 0%	1% 0%
Never married	5% 5%	7% 7%	0% 0%	0% 0%

Table 4.4 (continued)

Variable	1976 Total Income Rep. Rate > 200%	1976 Total Income Rep. Rate < 67%	1976 Total Income Rep. Rate < 67%, for Married	1976 Total Income Rep. Rate < 67%, for Widowed
Pension				
Yes	66%	34%	47%	17%
No	34	66	53	83
Survey Retires				
1969	34%	16%	11%	17%
1971	15	18	16	23
1973	18	29	32	24
1975	16	22	25	19
1977	16	15	15	17
1979	0	0	0	0
Preretirement Income (77 survey)				
< $7500	84%	7%	4%	10%
$7500–$12,500	9	17	10	20
$12,500–$20,000	5	37	37	38
$20,000–$30,000	2	24	28	23
> $30,000	1	16	21	9
Number of Households	994	812	435	267

NOTE: Percentages may not sum to 100% due to both rounding errors and nonresponses.
aRespondent's expected postretirement income, as reported in 1973.

group actually received 77 percent greater income in 1976 than the low replacement group. Social Security, pensions, and earnings were all well above expectations for the high replacement rate group, whereas pensions and earnings were below expectations for the low replacement rate households. Fully 29 percent of the low replacement rate group are widows who husbands died since 1969.

Table 4.5 contains the same detailed figures for those whose retirement income is low in absolute terms. Social Security and a small amount of earnings amounts to 78 percent of their income. Pension income is very low and below expectations. Earnings are also below expectations. Note that these groups with low and very low incomes are 55 percent and 61 percent widows, respectively. As was apparent in table 4.1, most of these people had low career average earnings.

Table 4.6 contains some summary information regarding those excluded from our selection criteria. Several observations can be made. First, those with military or federal pensions are very well-off, with very high pensions relative to other people. They also have more than $30,000 in financial wealth in 1977, more than any other group. Those who had not retired by 1977 also have above average incomes and substantial amounts of financial wealth.

Table 4.5   Financial and Other Characteristics of Low-Income Households

Variable (year reported)	1976 Income < Poverty Line	Very Low 1976 Income[a]
Income (77)	$ 2574	$2072
Income Expected (73)[b]	2909	2784
Social Security Inc. (77)	1966	1627
Social Security Inc. Exp. (73)	1740	1706
Pension Income (77)	158	57
Pension Income Expected (73)	279	198
Earnings Income (77)	48	29
Earnings Income Expected (73)	461	427
Financial Wealth (69)	2876	2794
Financial Wealth (77)	3575	2886
Non-Financial Wealth (69)	5637	5080
Non-Financial Wealth (77)	11082	9754
Career Average Earnings	6746	5914
High-3 Earnings	10353	9227

Race (69)		
White	79%	77%
Black/Other	21	23
Sex (69)		
Male	60%	53%
Female	40	47
Median Age (69)	60	60
Employment Status (77)		
Retired	47%	42%
Keeping House	36	41
Disabled	12	11
Unemployed	1	0
Job/Not at work	0	0
Working	1	0
Other	3	5
Health vs. Others' Health (in survey before retirement)		
Better	22%	21%
Same	45	46
Worse	27	27
Marital Status (69/77)				
Married	51%	25%	43%	15%
Widowed	30	55	34	61
Divorced/Separated	12	11	14	14
Never Married	7	7	8	8
Pension		
Yes	13%	7%
No	87	93

Table 4.5   (continued)

Variable (year reported)	1976 Income < Poverty Line	Very Low 1976 Income[a]
Survey Retires		
1969	30%	33%
1971	20	21
1973	21	19
1975	18	16
1977	12	11
1979	0	0
Preretirement		
Income (77)		
< $7500	66%	71%
$7500–$12,500	20	18
$12,500–$20,000	10	8
$20,000–$30,000	4	3
> $30,000	1	1
Total Income		
Replacement Rate (77)		
< 67%	38%	39%
67%–100%	18	15
100%–200%	18	17
> 200%	26	29
Number of Households	1320	926

[a]< $3000.
[b]Respondent's expected postretirement income, as reported in 1973.

Table 4.7 illustrates the distribution of replacement rates for six different preretirement earnings classes. Only 20 percent of the $7,500–$12,500 category had a replacement rate below 60 percent (when only Social Security and pension income are included);[3] we conclude from the second column of table 4.7 that less than 30 percent of these households are forced to make significant downward adjustments in their consumption potential. The percentages of households with low replacement rates are slightly higher for the higher earnings categories, but it should be mentioned that other sources of income certainly reduce the number of households who face these downward resource adjustments.

We can summarize some of the tabular results thus far. First, despite the high average or median replacement rates, a significant fraction of elderly households end up with very low incomes and/or with sharply lower resources than they had during their working careers. There is a wide distribution of replacement rates. A nontrivial percentage of households actually have higher real income in retirement than their career average earnings history. The group most likely to have a low

Table 4.6   Financial Characteristics of Households Excluded
                   from Main Analysis

Variable	Had Federal or Military Pension	Had No Covered Soc. Sec. Earnings	Did Not Retire	Dies or Is Lost from Survey
Income (in 1969 survey)	$11862	$ 2948	$10445	$ 6380
Income (76)	15103	5058	14470	6617
Income Expected (73)[a]	9530	3804	6277	4819
Social Security Inc. (76)	2354	1469	2080	2781
Social Security Exp. (73)	1347	741	2282	1891
Pension Inc. (76)	6337	1719	1001	1131
Pension Inc. Exp. (73)	4602	1313	1252	1212
Earnings Inc. (76)	5270	481	10569	602
Earnings Inc. Exp. (73)	1692	176	4019	1222
Financial Wealth (69)	9232	7671	12451	6921
Financial Wealth (77)	30081	10353	24487	12465
Non-Financial Wealth (69)	16019	9013	15939	9901
Non-Financial Wealth (77)	39047	14299	41697	20661
Career Average Earnings	9117	0	16359	13022
High-3 Earnings	14500	0	25067	18953
Number of Households	239	553	825	664

[a]Respondent's expected postretirement income, as reported in 1973.

Table 4.7   Distribution of 1976 Social Security + Pension Replacement Rates
                   for Married Couples

Percentile	Preretirement Career Earnings					
	$0–$7.5K	$7.5–$12.5K	$12.5–$20K	$20–$30K	$30–$50K	> $50K
95%	1574%	204%	118%	106%	93%	80%
90%	772	156	104	92	84	67
80%	338	111	90	81	71	55
70%	209	95	81	74	65	43
60%	165	86	76	68	60	40
50%	130	78	71	63	57	33
40%	115	74	66	57	47	26
30%	98	68	61	53	40	20
20%	84	60	54	47	33	12
10%	65	49	44	36	28	8
5%	7	35	32	27	18	5

*EXAMPLE: Married couples who received between $20,000 and $30,000 in career average earnings had a median replacement rate of 63 percent. Ten percent of these couples had replacement rates of 92 percent or higher.

income or to have suffered a large income decline is widows. The sharply higher incidence of poverty and income loss by widows suggests that public policy may have failed in this particular area.

Our tabular results also show that based on expectations reported in 1973, both those with high and low actual 1976 replacement rates received more Social Security income than they had anticipated. This clearly indicates that the increase in Social Security which occurred between those years conveyed a windfall gain to this population. Likewise, those with high replacement rates, most of whom have a history of low earnings levels, received more in pensions than expected and more in labor market earnings in 1976. On the other hand, those with low replacement rates received less in pensions and earnings than they had expected.

4.2.2 Probit Analysis of Low Incomes and Low Replacement Rates

Beyond the simple cross-tabulation of postretirement incomes and preretirement career average earnings and an examination of the average characteristics of poor and low replacement rate families within the general elderly population, it is worthwhile to attempt to examine the factors most closely associated with low incomes and low replacement rates. Our analysis of these phenomena are presented in tables 4.8 and 4.9. These report, respectively, probit analyses of the probability of moving from relatively high preretirement career average earnings to low postretirement income, and the probabilities of being very poor and of having low replacement rates. The analyses are performed on a relevant subset of the data described in section 4.1. For example, the analyses of movement from well-off to poor is done on the subset of individuals who had preretirement career average earnings above $20,000 (indexed).

For each of the three dichotomous dependent variables we report two probits. The first includes a large group of explanatory variables, while the second uses a smaller set of theoretically or empirically most important variables. Each of the analyses in tables 4.8 and 4.9 provides some preliminary insights into the characteristics associated with higher probabilities of the economic circumstances described.

The definitions of the variables used in the probit analyses tables are:

RICHPOOR = 1 if career average preretirement income > $20,000 and postretirement income < $5,000.
= 0 otherwise.

VPOOR = 1 if 1976 postretirement income < $3000.
= 0 otherwise.

LOWRR = 1 if 1976 total income replacement rate < 50%.
= 0 otherwise.

FEMALE   = 1 if female in 1969.
           = 0 otherwise.
NEWWSD   = 1 if marital status in 1969 was *not* widowed, sepa-
             rated, or divorced *and* marital status in 1977 *was*
             widowed, separated, or divorced.
RETSUR   = Survey in which household retires (1 = 1969, . . . ,
                                                    5 = 1977).
LCAEARN   = log career average preretirement earnings.
LEXPINC   = log total expected retirement income in 1973.
OWNHOME   = 1 if house market value > $10,000.
           = 0 otherwise.
AGE   = Age in 1969.
BLACK   = 1 if black/other in 1969.
           = 0 if white.
HSHSIZE   = Household size in 1969.
BADHLTH   = 1 if health reported as "worse than others" in the
             last survey before retirement.
           = 0 if health reported as "same as others" or "better
             than others."
SMSA   = Code for city size (goes from 1 to 7 as population
             class goes from < 25,000 to > 1,000,000).
EDUC   = Years of eduction.
WSD69   = 1 if marital status was widowed, separated, or di-
             vorced in 1969.
           = 0 otherwise.
LFW69   = log 1969 financial wealth.
SINGLE   = 1 if marital status was single,
           = 0 otherwise.

Table 4.8 presents two probit analyses of the probability of moving from high preretirement income (over $20,000) to low postretirement income (less than $5,000). Our probit coefficients tell us the change in the probability of this event that is associated with the respondent having various characteristics.

The first probit reported includes a large number of potential variables which have been discussed in the literature, such as race, health, location, and education. The most important in terms of the size of the coefficient and statistical significance appear to be newly widowed, separated, or divorced and low expected income. The coefficient for widows as of 1969 is large, but so is its standard error. Older people in this cohort are slightly less likely to move from rich to poor; those retiring later are also somewhat less likely to see their incomes collapse; and increases in the log of financial wealth appear to decrease the probability of income collapse for those with incomes above $20,000. The other variables tend to have small coefficients and are not statistically significant.

Table 4.8   **Probit Analysis of Characteristics of Households Suffering Severe Income Declines in Retirement**

	Probit 1: RICHPOOR[a]	Probit 2: RICHPOOR[a]
Constant	2.810	6.66
	(4.383)	(3.46)
AGE	−0.085	−0.084
	(0.056)	(.051)
NEWWSD	0.975	0.937
	(0.187)	(0.176)
RETSUR	−0.252	−0.257
	(0.080)	(0.075)
LEXPINC	−0.279	−0.245
	(0.081)	(0.078)
LFW69	−0.067	−0.033
	(0.054)	(0.051)
FEMALE	−0.444	
	(0.602)	
BLACK	−0.117	
	(0.616)	
OWNHOME	−0.048	
	(0.198)	
LCAEARN	0.401	
	(0.259)	
WSD69	0.645	
	(0.444)	
SINGLE	0.510	
	(0.492)	
SMSA	−0.019	
	(0.034)	
EDUC	0.018	
	(0.014)	
HSHSIZE	0.019	
	(0.081)	
BADHLTH	0.172	
	(0.242)	
No. Obs.	628	628

NOTE: The second regression includes only variables found significant in the first regression. Standard errors are given in parentheses.
[a]The mean value was 0.0780.

The second probit in table 4.8 omits the variables that had insignificant coefficients in the first probit. Again, we note that the factor associated with the greatest increase in the likelihood of moving from high preretirement career average earnings to low postretirement income is that the respondent was newly widowed, separated, or divorced in the sample period. Respondents who had high expected retirement income or who retired later, on the other hand, were less likely to suffer

Table 4.9   Probit Analysis of Characteristics of Very Poor and Low Replacement Rate Households

	Probit 1: VPOOR[a]	Probit 2: VPOOR[a]	Probit 1: LOWRR[b]	Probit 2: LOWRR[b]
Constant	6.99 (1.612)	5.377 (0.482)	−4.856 (1.714)	−4.706 (1.600)
FEMALE	0.240 (0.166)	−0.177 (0.109)	−0.104 (0.184)	— —
NEWWSD	0.481 (0.110)	0.562 (0.096)	0.541 (0.094)	0.064 (0.090)
RETSUR	−0.120 (0.033)	−0.114 (0.030)	−0.119 (0.034)	−0.110 (0.032)
LCAEARN	−0.361 (0.042)	−0.375 (0.041)	0.993 (0.089)	0.913 (0.075)
LEXPINC	−0.283 (0.039)	−0.317 (0.037)	−0.203 (0.040)	−0.232 (0.038)
OWNHOME	−0.125 (0.083)	−0.193 (0.080)	−0.017 (0.085)	
AGE	−0.022 (0.024)		−0.043 (0.024)	
BLACK	0.293 (0.177)		0.064 (0.214)	
HSHSIZE	0.017 (0.036)		−0.035 (0.040)	
BADHLTH	0.016 (0.010)		0.105 (0.104)	
SMSA	0.017 (0.016)		−0.009 (0.007)	
EDUC	0.025 (0.007)		−0.018 (0.007)	
WSD69	−0.411 (0.169)		— —	
LFW69	−0.040 (0.027)		−0.077 (0.026)	
No. Obs.	2003	2003	2003	2003

NOTE: For each dependent variable, the second regression includes only variables found significant in the first regression. Standard errors are given in parentheses.
[a]Mean value was 0.135.
[b]Mean value was 0.146.

a sharp drop in economic resources. Factors such as age (within the six years of age cohorts we examine) and the log of financial wealth in 1969 have coefficients suggesting modest negative impacts on this probability.

We should not be surprised that we are unable to identify precisely which of these many factors strongly correlate with substantial reductions in income. Among other things, there are undoubtedly a variety of case-specific considerations which cause events that cannot be captured by most of our variables. The newly widowed, separated, or divorced variable, however, is one we can observe, and it obviously has an immense impact on the probability of income collapse.

Table 4.9 presents analogous probit analyses for the probability of postretirement income roughly below the poverty line. The probit in column 1 reveals that those who are newly widowed, separated, or divorced are much more likely to be very poor than the general population. Those who retire later, have greater preretirement earnings (hardly a surprise), have greater expected retirement income, or own a home have substantially lower probabilities of being very poor. Being black and/or female also seems to greatly boost the likelihood of severe poverty, though these coefficients cannot be estimated very precisely. The coefficients of other variables measuring household size, location, poor health, widowed in 1969, and the log of financial wealth, have very small coefficients and are not statistically significant. Column 2, again, reports results for a subset of variables. Again, females and newly widowed have substantially higher probabilities of very low incomes in their retirement years than do the general population. Once again, those retiring later, with substantially greater career average earnings, or with greater expected retirement income are much less likely to be poor in old age. The probability of low income decreases substantially for the group that owns their homes.

Taken as a whole, this way of arranging the data suggests that despite the enormous reduction of the incidence of poverty among the elderly by 1977, a trend which has continued since that time, some glaring problems remain: particularly those associated with elderly females, especially those newly widowed, separated, or divorced. Perhaps this reflects the characteristics of pensions discussed above. One curiosity is that the widow's benefit was raised to 100 percent and should be replacing a very high fraction of the first few thousand dollars of earnings. Apparently for many elderly widows, there is virtually no other income source besides Social Security, and for some elderly widows, Social Security has not bridged the poverty gap.

Columns 3 and 4 of Table 4.9 provide an analysis of the population group which has a 1976 postretirement replacement rate of less than 50 percent. This is the unadjusted replacement rate, the ratio of 1976 postretirement income to preretirement career average indexed earnings. The price indexing and the career averaging are the only adjustments made to the traditional replacement rate figures (although we do look at total income, not just Social Security). We do not make any of the adjustments we made in our previous paper for factors such as risk, taxes, cost of children, and so forth. Some of a large list of characteristics come in as significant mainly because of the progressive nature of the benefit formula. The benefit formula replaces a much higher fraction of the first few thousand dollars of earnings than of subsequent earnings, and therefore, one can be poor and have a replacement rate substantially in excess of 50 percent. Thus, in examining those with low replacement rates, we are much more likely to be discussing those further up the income scale.

Turning to the results, we see that once again the newly widowed are much more likely to have low replacement rates. Also apparent, though hardly surprising in view of the progressive nature of the benefit formula, is the substantial positive impact of higher career average earnings on the probability of low replacement rates. Quite simply, those with substantial career average earnings are much more likely to have lower replacement rates due to the progressive nature of the benefit formula. The factors which appear to have a negative effect on the probability of low replacement rates are, most importantly, the retirement age, financial wealth, and expected retirement income. That those who retired later are less likely to have low replacement rates reflects both the double indexing of Social Security for several years prior to the retirement date involved and the "Gordon" effect, replacing low wage years with high wage years in the benefit computation. Most of the other variables have coefficients which are quite small and not statistically significant. Education, however, does have a small but statistically significant negative effect on the probability of having a low replacement rate.

Taken as a whole, the results reported in tables 4.7, 4.8. and 4.9 suggest, historically, some substantial gaps in the safety net for the elderly. An enormous social achievement occurred in the reduction of the incidence of poverty among the elderly, although the cost in terms of society's transferring resources to the elderly was substantial, and the target effectiveness of these transfers is open to question. Various types of conclusions can be drawn. Perhaps the most important is that females, especially widows, were much more likely to be left behind than males or intact couples.

Finally, we are not at this point able to provide a structural interpretation of these events. Is it due to problems in the annuities and survivorship rights in pensions? Or to case-specific events which we cannot identify? If the primary purpose of a social insurance program is to prevent destitution among the elderly and to provide a floor to replacement rates, we will need to generate better data and methods to answer these questions in order to design more cost-conscious and target-effective public income support systems for the elderly.

4.3 Conclusion

We have attempted to complement previous research on the general economic status of the elderly with an examination of who fell through the safety net in the 1970s. The analysis must be regarded as preliminary in some respects and as suggestive in others. Clearly, the most important finding is that a nontrivial fraction of the elderly in the age group we studied either remained poor, became poor, or had very low replacement rates in terms of their total income. This occurred despite the enormous general improvement of the economic status of the elderly, part of which was made possible by very large increases in real Social Security benefits.

Examination of the characteristics of those who fell through the safety net reveals that females, especially widows, were the most likely candidates for economic difficulty in this cohort in this stage of their lives.

A variety of other variables seems to impact the probability of low incomes and/or low replacement rates. For example, those who retired relatively early tended to be more likely to be poor and/or to have low replacement rates. This partly reflects particular institutional features surrounding Social Security and its double indexing for a brief period, but it also partly reflects factors influencing retirement in the first place.

A variety of other intriguing findings were mentioned, including the sharp differences in realizations of retirement income expectations among those who were poor and/or had low replacement rates relative to those who did well. Perhaps much of this seems self-evident in retrospect, but it is important to attempt to get behind these numbers to reasons why these events occurred. Undoubtedly, many of them had case-specific causes. The results here are suggestive of a need for further research on the structure and nature of the survivorship and annuity features of pensions; the coverage and marital status provisions of Social Security; and the relationships between actual retirement income outcomes and expectations.

We hope that this work will stimulate research on those left behind in the general improvement of the economic status of the elderly and on the private and governmental income support systems designed to assist them.

Notes

1. These facts are documented in numerous recent studies. While numerous authors have commented on various factors related to the improved economic status of the elderly, we refer the reader to the following as examples: Boskin (1986); Boskin and Shoven (1984); Hurd and Shoven (1982); Hurd and Shoven

(1985); and Boskin and Hurd (1982). These papers provide references to the research of others on the topic. The other research comes to quite similar qualitative conclusions.

2. We use average indexed earnings from 1951 to 1974 or 1951 to retirement; thus, "career average" is roughly the average over the two decades prior to retirement.

3. In Boskin and Shoven (1984), we demonstrated that an unadjusted replacement rate of around 70 percent translated into full replacement when tax, family size, and risk adjustments are included. Thus, an unadjusted replacement rate of 60 percent would be marginally below full replacement.

References

Boskin, Michael. 1986. *Too many promises: The uncertain future of Social Security*. Homewood, IL: Dow Jones-Irwin.
Boskin, Michael, and Michael Hurd. 1982. Are inflation rates different for the elderly? NBER Working Paper no. 943. Cambridge, Mass.: National Bureau of Economic Research.
Boskin, Michael, and John Shoven. 1984. Concepts and measures of earnings replacement during retirement. NBER Working Paper no. 1360. Cambridge, Mass.: National Bureau of Economic Research.
Hurd, Michael, and John Shoven. 1983. The economic status of the elderly. In *Financial aspects of the United States pension system*, edited by Zvi Bodie and John Shoven. Chicago: University of Chicago Press, 359–97.
———. 1985. The distributional impact of Social Security. In *Pensions, Labor, and Individual Choice*, edited by David Wise. Chicago: University of Chicago Press, 193–221.

Comment   Thomas A. Gustafson

Boskin and Shoven present an examination of poverty among the elderly that seeks to peer behind what has become accepted over the past several years as the new conventional wisdom, that is, (crudely put) that the elderly are no longer poor. This view, which has been developing for some time among those, the authors among them, who have been active in this area, has been gradually diffusing in the public consciousness and now appears to have achieved widespread acceptance. It received a boost in prominence as a result of an extensive discussion in the 1985 report of the President's Council of Economic Advisors (1985).

Thomas A. Gustafson is a staff economist and chief of the Medicaid Branch, Division of Policy Analysis, Office of Legislation and Policy, Health Care Financing Administration, U.S. Department of Health and Human Services.

This view holds that the elderly are, on average, about as well-off as the rest of the population. Poverty is no longer an automatic correlate of old age to the extent it was in the past. Some observers appear to have rushed from this point to the conclusion that the problem of poverty in old age needs no further attention. Boskin and Shoven provide a useful tonic to such casual thinking. There is, after all, still poverty among the elderly. The problem may no longer be systemic, but we need to examine the specific causes of the poverty that remains. Is it like poverty at other ages, or is it different in character because of the nature of the population?

Basically, what Boskin and Shoven have done is to use the 1977 wave of the Retirement History Survey to examine income poverty and replacement rates in a cohort of the elderly aged 65–71. This analysis excludes from the original sample those households in which both husband and spouse had not retired, as well as those with federal or military pensions, those with no Social Security covered earnings, and those lost to the survey through death or attrition. The authors then examine the 1976 income and a simple measure of career average earnings (that is, without making extensive adjustments) for the two-thirds of the original sample that are left. They discover a great deal of heterogeneity. Some households are poor for their whole careers, some suffer a drastic fall in income at retirement, while others maintain or improve their situations. They identify widows as a particular concern.

The study suffers from several methodological limitations, among them the way earnings are treated in the preretirement and postretirement comparisons. First, using 1976 income in the calculations creates problems because it may contain preretirement earnings and thus give a distorted view of postretirement income. (By the same token, of course, recent retirees may not report a full year of retirement benefits.) Second, Boskin and Shoven use self-description as their definition of retirement. As all who have labored in this vineyard know, selecting a definition of retirement is not straightforward, and theory usually provides little guidance (Gustafson 1982, especially chap. 4). Self-description is one way of operationalizing this definition; other obvious candidates are being out of the labor force or receiving retirement benefits from Social Security or employer pensions. A problem with the one chosen is that individuals can be working and still describe themselves as retired.

The central point is not necessarily that superior methods are available, but that both of these characteristics of the study affect the results. This problem is evident in the comparisons presented by the authors in table 4.4. For those with replacement rates over 200 percent, earnings are prominent in postretirement income. The number with earnings is not presented, but it is probably much greater than in the less than 67 percent group. On the other hand, career average earnings is much higher for the less than 67 percent group. Probably part of what is going on is that the high replacement rate group is using the "poor man's pension"—many have relatively poor earnings histories, and many are still at work. This group will probably look much different in a few years, once they have withdrawn from the labor force entirely. The high replacement rates observed for these households may thus be unstable indicators of their welfare: they may be partly an artifact of measurement lags and partly a result of use of earnings to supplement inadequate retirement benefits.

Another problem, given the prominence attached to widows in the paper, is the failure to adjust for family size in making the preretirement/ postretirement comparisons. It's hard to make much out of well-offness comparisons that do not account for the shrinkage of the household resulting from the loss of a spouse that characterizes all the cases under consideration. The extent of poverty among widows may still be clear; what we should conclude about a fall in income after retirement is clouded.

The effects of retirement on the income of widows varies greatly, as it does for the rest of the aged population. Table 4.4 reveals that half of those with replacement rates over 200 percent are widows. A simple calculation based on the results presented in tables 4.1, 4.2, and 4.3 reveals that 65 percent of all households fall in the triangle above the diagonal and thus have 1976 income at least one category lower than their career average preretirement earnings. For married couples, the figure is 68 percent, while for widows the figure is 61 percent. While one should not deny that falling income is a problem among widows, this group may do better than the population as a whole.

The authors call attention to the results about expectations of retirement benefits in comparison to what is actually received several years later. Note that these results suffer from measurement problems. The survey questions on expectations refer to benefits expected after the respondent stops working, but not all those considered retired in this analysis had stopped working in 1976, and benefits received are probably understated, both because benefits may not have started and because of the operation of the Social Security earnings test. On the other hand, expectations may have been understated by failure to account for spouse or dependent benefits in answering the original question.

The authors conclude that those who had low or high replacement rates received a "windfall" in Social Security—receipts were greater than expectations—because of changes in the system in that period. This conclusion is overstated. Divergence of expectations from realizations is widespread in these results, and we need a fuller examination and explanation of expectation formation before we conclude that the cause was a windfall. If expectations are based on fuller information, then the changes should already have been factored into expectations, since the major legal changes in Social Security predate the 1973 survey. Hence, divergence of expectations and experience must have some other cause. If we do not assume fully informed expectations, legal changes would affect expectations only slowly as they were implemented, but the divergence might be due to other aspects of imperfect information, including misunderstanding of such features of the benefit structure as the earnings test or spouse benefits.

In conclusion, I think this study is a provocative start. It suffers from some inevitable limitations imposed by the data and from some methodological shortcomings. It serves to document the substantial heterogeneity of well-offness in the face of retirement among the elderly, even among fairly recent retirees, the "young elderly." This diversity is not all that surprising, but we need to be reminded of it in the face of the new wisdom that the elderly are just fine and need little further attention.

What remains to be done, I think, is a much more systematic sorting out of the causes of residual poverty and of income collapse in this age range. To what extent are these problems associated with too early retirement, bad health, loss of spouse, and so forth? To what extent can policy solutions be crafted to deal with them? Depending on what we think the problem is, the set of solutions may differ greatly.

If the problem is poverty, is this a failure of the welfare system? Clearly some people are poor much of their lives, and we would expect this in old age as well. But the thorny question that remains is whether Supplemental Security Income, the major antipoverty program for the elderly, and other antipoverty measures are getting to those that need them.

On the other hand, retirees may also suffer from a problem of income collapse upon retirement. Although this problem may be less poignant than that of poverty—not all with sharply lower incomes become poor— our society clearly regards it as significant and has erected an extensive system of social insurance and other institutions to guard against it. If we observe a substantial problem in this area, we must look at these institutions, the various "legs" of the retirement income "stool."

The authors have rightly focused our attention on widows as a group with special problems, not that this is any great surprise (see, for instance, Warlick 1983). In time, this group's problems should be less pressing as more and more women have significant earnings records of their own on which retirement benefits will be based. Many individuals may continue to suffer a substantial fall in income, however, and we need to scrutinize further how our institutions are responding to loss of a spouse. Social Security's benefit structure suggests a not unreasonable treatment of widows, but the role of joint-and-survivor benefits under employer pensions seems to deserve further scrutiny.

The economic welfare of widows may also be substantially affected by the medical needs of their husbands in their last years, which may spell financial catastrophe depending on the nature of the needs and the operation of Medicare, Medicaid, and private health insurance. For instance, a nursing home stay of any length may have devastating effects on accumulated assets, another leg of the retirement income stool. Little empirical work has been done on this problem.

References

Gustafson, Thomas A. 1982. The retirement decision of older men: An empirical analysis. PhD. thesis, Yale University.

President's Council of Economic Advisors. 1985. *Economic report of the President*. Washington, D.C.: GPO.

Warlick, Jennifer. 1983. Aged women in poverty: A problem without a solution? In *Aging and public policy: The politics of growing old in America*, edited by William P. Brown and Laura Katz Olsen. Westport, Conn.: Greenwood Press.

5   Defined Benefit versus Defined Contribution Pension Plans: What are the Real Trade-offs?

Zvi Bodie, Alan J. Marcus, and Robert C. Merton

Although employer pension programs vary in design, they are usually classified into two broad types: defined contribution and defined benefit. These two categories are distinguished in the law under ERISA. Under a defined contribution (DC) plan each employee has an account into which the employer and, if it is a contributory plan, the employee make regular contributions. Benefit levels depend on the total contributions and investment earnings of the accumulation in the account. Often the employee has some choice regarding the type of assets in which the accumulation is invested and can easily find out what its value is at any time. Defined contribution plans are, in effect, tax-deferred savings accounts in trust for the employees, and they are by definition fully funded. They are therefore not of much concern to government regulators and are not covered by Pension Benefit Guarantee Corporation (PBGC) insurance.

In a defined benefit (DB) plan the employee's pension benefit entitlement is determined by a formula which takes into account years of service for the employer and, in most cases, wages or salary. Many defined benefit formulas also take into account the Social Security benefits to which an employee is entitled. These are the so-called integrated plans. See Merton, Bodie, and Marcus (1987) for a discussion of integration.

Zvi Bodie is professor of finance and economics at the School of Management, Boston University, and a research associate of the National Bureau of Economic Research. Alan J. Marcus is associate professor of finance and economics at the School of Management, Boston University, and a faculty research fellow of the National Bureau of Economic Research. Robert C. Merton is J. C. Penney Professor of Management at the Sloan School of Management, Massachusetts Institute of Technology, and a research associate of the National Bureau of Economic Research.

DB and DC plans have significantly different characteristics with respect to the risks faced by employers and employees, the sensitivity of benefits to inflation, the flexibility of funding, and the importance of governmental supervision. Our objective in this paper is to examine the trade-offs involved in the choice between DB and DC plans.

In section 5.1, we briefly review the mechanics governing the determination and valuation of the benefit streams under DB and DC pension plans. Section 5.2 contains an informal discussion of the relative advantages of each type of plan. In section 5.3 we develop a formal model to examine the trade-offs between the two types of plans in the face of both wage and interest rate uncertainty. Our conclusion is that neither plan can be said to wholly dominate the other from the perspective of employee welfare. Section 5.4 summarizes our results and concludes the paper.

5.1   Plan Characteristics and Valuation

5.1.1   Defined Contribution Plans

The DC arrangement is the conceptually simpler retirement plan. The employer, and sometimes also the employee, make regular contributions into the employee's retirement account. The contributions are usually specified as a predetermined fraction of salary, although that fraction need not be constant over the course of a career.[1]

Contributions from both parties are tax-deductible,[2] and investment income accrues tax-free. Often the employee is given a choice as to how his account is to be invested. In principle, contributions may be invested in any security, although in practice most plans limit investment options to various bond, stock, and money-market funds. At retirement, the employee either receives a lump sum or an annuity, the size of which depends upon the accumulated value of the funds in the retirement account. The employee thus bears all of the investment risk; the retirement account is by definition fully funded, and the firm has no obligation beyond making its periodic contribution.

Valuation of the DC plan is straightforward: simply measure the market value of the assets held in the retirement account. However, as a guide for personal financial planning, the DC plan sponsor often provides workers with the indicated size of a life annuity starting at retirement age that could be purchased now with the accumulation in their account under different scenarios. The actual size of the retirement annuity will, of course, depend upon the realized investment performance of the retirement fund, the interest rate at retirement, and the ultimate wage path of the employee.

5.1.2 Defined Benefit Plans

Whereas the DC framework focuses on the *value* of the assets currently endowing a retirement account, the DB plan focuses on the *flow* of benefits which the individual will receive upon retirement.

A typical DB plan determines the employee's benefit as a function of both years of service and wage history. As a representative plan, consider one in which the employee receives 1 percent of average salary (during the last 5 years of service) times the number of years of service. Normal retirement age is 65, there are no early retirement options, death or disability benefits, and no Social Security offset provisions. The actuarially expected life span at retirement is 80 years.

Assuming the worker is fully vested, at any point in time his claim is a deferred nominal life annuity, insured up to certain limits by the Pension Benefit Guarantee Corporation. It is a deferred annuity because the employee cannot start receiving benefits until he reaches age 65. It is nominal because the retirement benefit, which the employer is contractually bound to pay the employee, is fixed in dollar amount at any point in time up to and including retirement age.

Many people think that under final average pay plans of the sort described here, retirement benefits are implicitly indexed to inflation, at least during the employee's active years with the firm, and therefore should not be viewed as a purely nominal asset by the employee and a purely nominal liability by the firm. We examine this issue in detail in section 5.2. For now we focus on the value of the explicit claim only.

Given an interest rate and a wage profile, it is straightforward to compute the present value of accrued benefits under our prototype DB plan. Table 5.1 presents such values for workers at different ages assuming a constant real annual wage of $15,000. The present value of accrued liabilities can increase from continued service because of 3 factors: (1) as years of service increase, so does the defined benefit, (2) if the wage increases, so will the retirement benefit, and (3) as time passes, less time remains until the retirement benefits begin, so that their present value increases at the rate of interest.

To illustrate the separate contributions of each of these factors to the cumulative results reported in table 5.1, consider the case in which the benefit formula calls for 1 percent of final year's salary times years of service and that the worker lives for 15 years after retiring at age 65. The worker is 35 years old, has worked for the firm 10 years, and his current salary is $15,000. The nominal interest rate equals a real rate of 3 percent per year plus the expected rate of inflation.

Under the 7 percent inflation scenario, the sources of the change in the value of the pension benefit from the passage of an additional year are as follows. Prior to this year, the worker had accrued a life annuity

Table 5.1 Present Value of Accrued Benefits and Marginal Change in Benefits for Hypothetical Worker, No Early Retirement

| | Present Value of Accrued Benefits in Constant Dollars | | Marginal Change in Present Value of Accrued Benefits from an Additional Year's Work | | | |
| | 0% Inflation 3% Discount Rate | 7% Inflation 10% Discount Rate | 0% Inflation 3% Discount Rate | | 7% Inflation 10% Discount Rate | |
Starting Age 25 Current Age			Constant Dollars	% of Salary	Constant Dollars	% of Salary
30	$2,274	$144	$455	3.03	$41	.27
35	$5,271	$463	$527	3.51	$82	.55
40	$9,167	$1,120	$611	4.07	$158	1.05
45	$14,169	$2,404	$708	4.72	$297	1.98
50	$20,532	$4,840	$821	5.47	$546	3.64
55	$28,563	$9,354	$952	6.35	$938	6.25
60	$38,631	$17,575	$1,104	7.36	$1,768	11.79
65	$51,181	$32,329	$1,242*	8.28	$2,794*	18.63

NOTES: Worker currently paid $15,000 per year with no real wage growth.
Worker will retire at age 65.
Pension plan pays 1 percent of average salary in last 5 years times years of service.
Pension plan contains no early retirement provisions or makes correct actuarial adjustment for early retirees.
Benefits are vested after 5 years.
Real interest rate is 3 percent; nominal rate increases one for one with inflation.
*Value calculated for age 64 rather than age 65.
SOURCE: Adapted from Ellwood (1985).

of $1,500 per year (1 percent × 10 years × $15,000) beginning at age 65. With a nominal interest rate of 10% per year, the present value (PV) of this deferred annuity at age 35 is $654. The increase in pension benefits as a result of working an additional year can be broken into three parts:

Factor 1: One additional year of service at a salary of $16,050 ($15,000 × 1.07) entitles him to an additional deferred annuity of $160.50 per year, and

Factor 2: The salary increase of $1050 entitles him to an additional deferred annuity of $105 per year (1 percent × 10 years × $1,050).

The PV of these additional accrued benefits from factors 1 and 2 at the end of the year is $127. This represents the nominal value of the newly earned pension benefits, which is an annuity of $265.50 per year starting at retirement.

Factor 3: The PV of his previously accrued benefits increases by 10 percent from $654 to $719.40 because the date of their eventual receipt has drawn one year closer.

As a result of all three factors, the nominal value of his pension wealth increases from $654 to $846 and its real value to $791.

Now let us refer to table 5.1 to see how these factors manifest themselves in the time pattern of benefit accrual in the no-inflation and in the 7 percent inflation scenarios. The right-hand panel shows the constant dollar present value of benefits attributable to continued work with the same employer; these benefits are represented by factors 1 and 2 only. In the no-inflation case, there is no salary growth and hence only factor 1 is at work. For each additional year of service an additional deferred annuity of $150 per year is earned. Note, however, that the value of the incremental benefits earned at each age increases with age, from $455 (3.03 percent of salary) at age 30 to $1,242 (8.28 percent of salary) at age 64. This is a reflection of the fact that the additional $150 per year deferred life annuity has a higher PV the closer the employee is to age 65. The accrual of benefits under a DB plan is thus inherently "backloaded."

For a fixed real interest rate, this backloading effect is much more pronounced in the 7 percent inflation scenario because of the impact of inflation on the nominal interest rate. In this case the constant-dollar value of additional pension benefits earned increases from $41 (.27 percent of salary) at age 30 to $2,794 (18.63 percent of salary) at age 64. In contrast, backloading or frontloading in DC plans is independent of inflation as well as interest rates.[3] This is because employers can achieve any backloading pattern by simply choosing an appropriate pattern of contribution rates over the course of the employee's career. The left-hand panel of table 5.1 illustrates the effect of inflation on the

PV of total accumulated pension benefits under the DB plan assuming no real salary growth.

5.1.3   Funding

As mentioned before, DC plans are by their nature fully funded, that is, the market value of the plan's assets equals the liability of the sponsor to the plan's beneficiaries. In sharp contrast, the calculation of the funding status of DB plans is complex and controversial. If the plan's assets are invested in traded securities, their market value is relatively easy to ascertain. The source of difficulty is in measuring the sponsor's liability.

From a strictly legal point of view the sponsor's liability is the present value of the accrued vested benefits which would be payable if the plan were immediately terminated. But many pension experts contend that sponsors have an implicit semicontractual obligation which makes it more appropriate to take account of projected future salary growth in the computation of the firm's pension liability. The contention of a further obligation beyond the legal one makes it unclear whether a real or nominal interest rate should be used in discounting future benefits (either with or without salary growth projections) to compute their present value. To evaluate the strict obligation of the sponsor, the DB liabilities could be determined by deriving the cost of an immunized or dedicated bond portfolio using current market prices. While clearly superior to a simple interest rate assumption, this valuation procedure is itself only an approximation because the payment dates of pension liabilities typically extend far beyond the maturity range that is rich enough to extract our discount bond prices from traded coupon bonds. Hence, an exact bond-dedication scheme is not feasible. Immunization techniques that rely on duration measures are not wholly reliable because duration measures are sensitive to the specification of term structure dynamics. (See Bierwag 1977, Bierwag and Kaufman 1977, and Cox, Ingersoll, and Ross 1979). Beyond the term structure, the default risk associated with partially funded pension obligations adds the further problem of choosing equivalent-risk bonds from the securities market.

For the past several years the Financial Accounting Standard Board (FASB) has been grappling with these issues, trying to establish a uniform set of valuation standards for firms to use in their financial statements.

The government guarantees, up to a limit, employer pension benefits through the PBGC. The valuation of guaranteed benefits therefore should utilize the riskless-in-terms-of-default interest rate. However, in practice, only 80 percent of accrued benefits is vested while only 90–95 percent of vested benefits is guaranteed so that roughly one-quarter of accrued benefits is not guaranteed (Amoroso 1982). Thus, the funding status of a plan is important to employees as well as to the PBGC. In effect, adequate funding protects accrued-but-not-yet-vested benefits. See Marcus (1987) for an analysis of PBGC insurance and corporate funding policy.

5.2 Trade-Offs

Our original belief was that defined contribution plans would necessarily dominate defined benefit plans because of the flexibility of DC plan design. We would have guessed that anything that could be accomplished with a DB plan could be replicated in a cleverly constructed DC plan. However, this belief is not borne out. DB plans create implicit securities that can be welfare improving and that are neither currently available in capital markets, nor likely to be created in capital markets in the future. Some examples of these "securities" are factor-share claims, price-indexed claims, and perhaps deferred life annuities at fair interest rates.

Moreover, some of the "real-world" complications in plan design, such as incentive effects, tend to favor DB over DC plans. Thus, the optimal plan design is likely to be firm specific. At this point, all we can do is enumerate the relative advantages of each plan type and describe the circumstances in which one plan might dominate.

5.2.1 Investment Performance and Choice

The most obvious source of risk to an employee in the DC plan is the investment performance of the fund. However, this source of uncertainty can be controlled. For example, the periodic contributions of the DC plan could, in principle, be used to purchase deferred annuities which would generate retirement income streams similar to those provided by DB plans. Alternatively, it is feasible for the plan to select an investment strategy with low variance rates of *real* returns. Bodie (1980) has shown that commodity futures can be added to portfolios to successfully provide an effective hedge against inflation. Therefore, in either nominal or real terms, DC plans do not necessarily impose substantial risk on participants, given the availability of low-variance investment strategies.

There are, however, no strong *a priori* reasons to believe that most individuals would choose to invest accumulated DC funds in the lowest risk asset. DC plans typically offer sufficient flexibility to select a risk-return strategy suited to the employee's individual preferences and circumstances. In contrast, DB plans force individuals to accumulate the pension portion of retirement saving in the form of deferred life annuities and thus limit the risk-return choice.

5.2.2   Accrual Patterns

As noted and illustrated in table 5.1, DB plans are inherently back-loaded. DC plans can be backloaded too by choosing a contribution rate that rises with a worker's age and tenure.[4] Therefore, the salient inherent difference in accrual patterns between the two plan designs is that DB backloading is stochastic in the sense that real benefit accruals depend upon the rate of wage inflation. This seems to us an avoidable source of uncertainty which both parties (employer and employee) might benefit by shedding. On this score, DC plans would appear to be superior, although implicit contracting to provide employees with a protective "wage floor" (cf. Diamond and Mirrlees 1985) can be implemented more effectively with DB-type plans.

5.2.3   Termination and Portability

It is commonly asserted that considerations of portability favor DC plans. The typical justification is that the worker in a DB plan who leaves his job for reasons beyond his control forfeits future indexation of benefits already accrued. It is further asserted that there are implicit contracts between employees and firms which require larger total compensation (wage plus pension accrual) for more highly tenured workers. Hence, termination of employment causes a forfeiture of the ability to work for advantageous total compensation rates (and, in particular, indexation of total pension accruals). Under this line of reasoning, DC plans are more portable.

It should be realized, however, that the portability issue is intimately tied to the accrual pattern. For DC plans with contribution rates tied to tenure as well as age, the penalty to early termination can be as great as for any DB plan. In practice, however, contribution rates for DC plans are rarely tied to tenure and are usually not as heavily backloaded as DB plans. Therefore, in practice it would appear that portability considerations do favor DC plans over DB plans.

5.2.4   Incentives

Pension benefits in DC plans depend upon the wage trajectory over the worker's entire career. In contrast, benefits in most DB plans depend on final average salary. For this reason, workers in DB plans should have a greater incentive to sustain a high level of effort over the entire career in order to achieve a high career-end salary. Final salary has greater leverage in DB plans because of its greater effect on pension benefits.

In conclusion, it seems that there is a trade-off between the goals of portability and incentives. Portability dictates low backloading, while incentives require high backloading. While DC plans opt in practice for lower backloading than DB plans, this pattern is not an inherent property of the two plans.

5.2.5 Informational Economies in Plan Design and Implementation

Retirement income planning is one of the most complex areas of personal finance. Many employees would consider it a service to have their employer define and provide an adequate level of savings for them. Since retirement-income goals are typically defined as percentage replacement rates of salary, the benefits of DB plans which are defined in exactly those terms are easier to interpret.

One could in principle achieve the goal of a specific replacement rate with a DC plan of the so-called target benefit type. Under these plans, the contribution rate is adjusted periodically to achieve the target replacement rate, taking into account the discrepancy between actual and assumed investment return. However, such plans are rare.

5.2.6 Wage-Path Risk

The pegging of benefits in DB plans to final average wage would appear to provide employees with a type of income-maintenance insurance not available in DC plans. This observation has been used to support the selection of these plans over DC plans. This conclusion is, however, not robust. If wage paths are unpredictable at the start of a career, then individuals may view it as very risky to have their retirement benefits depend so heavily on final salary. Indeed, employees might prefer a retirement benefit tied to (inflation-adjusted) career-average earnings so as to eliminate excessive dependence on the realized wage in the final years of employment. This time-averaging feature is achieved by a DC plan because benefits will depend on the contribution in each year of service, rather than on a final wage formula. Although inflation-adjusted career-average DB plans would achieve the same goal, in practice these plans are quite rare. In fact, the only major DB plan that pays a benefit computed in such a fashion is the Social Security system. We pursue this issue further in the analysis in section 5.3.

5.2.7 Interest-Rate Risk

As noted earlier, one major source of uncertainty in DC plans concerns the terms under which the stock of retirement wealth can be transformed into a flow of retirement income. DB plans, by offering life annuities, effectively guarantee the interest rate at retirement. It should be noted, however, that without indexation of benefits, this is a guarantee of the nominal rather than the real interest rate. The value to the employee of a nominal-rate guarantee is questionable when inflation over a 10- or 20-year period can be highly unpredictable.

In principle, DC plans can offer at retirement the same nominal interest rate guarantee through the purchase of deferred life annuities as a DB plan. However, in practice, with the notable exception of the Teacher's Insurance and Annuity Association (TIAA), the capitalization rates used to compute benefits in the private annuity market are far below the interest rates available in competitive financial markets. This discrepancy is often attributed to an adverse selection problem and discourages participation in the annuity market by unhealthy individuals.[5] The adverse selection issue is largely avoided in DB plans because workers are precommitted to participation regardless of health status.

5.3 A Model of Wage and Interest Rate Uncertainty

In this section we develop a model to focus on the twin issues of wage and interest rate uncertainty using stylized versions of DB and DC plans. We find that the putative replacement rate advantages of DB plans are not supported by our model, and that the interest rate guarantee is only partially supported: specifically, DB plans do offer welfare-improving opportunities with respect to postretirement interest rate uncertainty, but *not* with respect to preretirement uncertainty.

For the most part, we will concentrate on individual welfare in a model in which all wage uncertainty is employee-specific and, from the firm's perspective, is perfectly diversifiable. This framework is at a polar extreme from Merton's (1983) model of Social Security, in which all uncertainty regarding marginal product derives from uncertainty in the aggregate production function, with no individual-specific effects. In Merton's framework, labor-income uncertainty is perfectly correlated across individuals, and in such an environment, DB plans may offer superior risk-sharing properties that are not captured in our model. Although our model focuses exclusively on uncertainty at the individual worker's level and interest rate risk, we will discuss further the implications of Merton's model for our results. As indicated earlier, interest rate uncertainty emerges as a central determinant of the relative advantages of DB versus DC plans.

5.3.1 Pension Plan Design

We consider a 3-period model in which the individual works in periods 0 and 1 and is retired in period 2. Current wage, W_0 is known, while period-1 wage, W_1, is uncertain until $t = 1$. For simplicity, we will assume that the time 0 expectation of W_1 is W_0. Trends in wage paths could easily be incorporated into the analysis, but would simply clutter the algebra; hence we ignore such trends. Wages are measured in real dollars as of time 0.

Consumption occurs at three points: $t = 0, 1, 2$. A pension benefit, P, is paid at $t = 2$. The real interest rate prevailing between $t = (0, 1)$ is denoted r_0, and is known at time 0. The real rate between $t = (1, 2)$ is r_1 and is not known until time 1. Finally, we assume that individuals have initial nonhuman wealth of A_0. The timing assumptions of the model are presented in figure 5.1.

If financial markets were complete, then, of course, the choice of pension plan would be irrelevant because the employee could use securities to trade to an optimal position. There are two important deviations from complete markets that make pension design crucial from the employee's perspective. First, there are neither markets in which wage uncertainty can be insured, nor ones in which claims to future wages can be sold. This feature of our model precludes employee-initiated risk pooling. Second, because of adverse selection problems, the market for deferred life annuities is assumed to be closed. Although such markets do in fact exist, as discussed, the rates of return typically offered are so low as to discourage widespread participation. In our model, the absence of such annuities will be captured by not allowing individuals to invest at $t = 0$ in two-period bonds which pay specified returns during the retirement period, $t = 2$.

The goal of the firm is to offer a pension plan that maximizes the utility of a "typical" worker, subject to the constraint that all pension plans considered have equal present value of costs to the firm. Subject to the firm's indifference condition, we compare the utility value of DB versus DC plans.

In DB plans, firms typically promise workers a prespecified fraction of career-end wages, possibly averaged over the last several years of working life, and this is the type of plan we model. We will assume that the pension benefit at $t = 2$ equals W_1, so that expected income in each period of life is equal. We assume further that pension benefits are explicitly linked to the price level. While this practice is uncommon in the private sector in the United States, it is true of Social Security and it serves as a useful base case from which to analyze the potential efficacy of competing pension designs.

0	1	2	Time
X ----------------------X ----------------------X			
W_0	W_1	P	Income
C_0	C_1	C_2	Consumption
A_0	A_1	A_2	Financial Wealth
----------r_0----------	----------r_1----------		Interest Rate

Fig. 5.1   Timing Assumptions

The present value at $t = 0$ of the firm's time-2 pension obligations is

(1) $$\text{PVDB} = E(W_1)B(0, 2),$$

where $B(0, 2)$ is the present value at $t = 0$ of a claim to an expected payoff of \$1 at $t = 2$, with an uncertainty equivalent to that of the wage distribution. If wage uncertainty were completely diversifiable, then $B(0, 2)$ would equal the present value of a certain dollar to be received in two periods; $B(t, T)$ would be the discount function at t for payments at T. However, for the moment, we will not restrict the nature of wage uncertainty.

In contrast to DB plans, DC plans require firms to contribute a prespecified fraction of wages into the worker's retirement saving account each period. For simplicity we will assume that explicit wages paid in each period are the same for each type of pension plan provided. Hence, the indifference condition for the firm is that the present value of periodic contributions into the DC plan equals the present value of the DB commitment. The prespecified (at $t = 0$) DC contribution schedule is set at time 0 and therefore can depend only on observed variables at $t = 0$. While the contribution rates may depend on expectations of future interest rates, they cannot be updated *ex post facto* to reflect realizations of interest rates or any other factor.

There is an infinite number of DC contribution schedules which have the same PV. Among these, we will select the one which has the same timing pattern as the PV of accruing benefits under the DB plan.

The contribution schedule, k_t, as a fraction of wages is given by:

(2) $$k_0 = \frac{1}{2}B(0, 2); \qquad t = 0,$$

$$k_1 = \frac{1}{2}B(0, 2)/B(0, 1); \qquad t = 1.$$

The present value at $t = 0$ of the DC plan contribution equals

$$\text{PVDC} = k_0 W_0 + k_1 E_0(W_1)B(0, 1)$$

$$= \frac{1}{2}W_0 B(0, 2) + \frac{1}{2}E_0(W_1)B(0, 2).$$

Since $E_0(W_1) = W_0$, the present values of the firm's contributions in the DB and DC plans are equal.

Notice that since $B(0, 1)$ is less than 1, the DC plan as specified above embodies some backloading. In fact, any degree of prespecified backloading may be built into the DC plan simply by changing the coefficients in equation (2) from their values of 1/2. Any coefficient pair for

k_1 and k_2 that sums to 1 will ensure that the present value of the DC plan equals the present value of the DB plan.

The pension benefit in the DC plan will accumulate at $t = 2$ to a value that depends on the investment experience of the plan. Call the rate of return on the pension portfolio in each period z_t and let $Z_t = 1 + z_t$. Then the pension benefit paid at $t = 2$ in the DC plan will be

$$(3) \qquad P_{DC} = \frac{1}{2}B(0, 2)W_0Z_0Z_1 + \frac{1}{2}[B(0, 2)/B(0, 1)]W_1Z_1,$$

whereas in the DB plan,

$$(4) \qquad\qquad\qquad P_{DB} = W_1.$$

Notice that there is no assurance, or even likelihood, that the expected pension benefits will be equal across the two plans, despite the fact that the ex ante present values are equal.

5.3.2   Welfare Analysis

Pension benefits are subject to uncertainty from both stochastic wage paths and stochastic investment returns. Rather than consider these effects jointly, we will examine polar cases in which one or the other source of uncertainty dominates.

Wage Uncertainty

Consider first the case in which all investment returns can be made certain by investing pension assets in default-free bonds. Therefore both r_0 *and* r_1 are known at $t = 0$. Moreover, suppose for the moment, that all wage uncertainty is perfectly diversifiable to the firm, so that $B(t, T)$ is simply the discount function for riskless future cash flows. Under these hypotheses,

$$Z_0 = 1 + r_0 = R_0 \text{ and } z_1 = 1 + r_1 = R_1.$$

Further, with no uncertainty regarding the evolution of future interest rates, $B(0, 1) = 1/R_0$ and $B(0, 2) = 1/R_0R_1$. Thus, equation (3) reduces to

$$(3') \qquad\qquad\qquad P_{DC} = \frac{1}{2}(W_0 + W_1).$$

In this simple case, it is clear that the DC plan must dominate the DB plan for any risk-averse utility function. With $E_0(W_1) = W_0$, both plans have equal expected benefits, while the DC plan imposes less uncertainty on participants because of the "wage averaging" embodied in equation (3′). Essentially the only uncertainty in this case derives from W_1. The DC plan allows for limited risk pooling of wage uncertainty through the firm (and ultimately the stock market), while the DB plan allows for none. This advantage of DC plans may be thought of as a pure efficiency gain.

The advantage of DC plans in the wage-uncertainty-only scenario does not hinge solely on the diversifiability of wage risk. Suppose that final wage is highly correlated with some marketable security, such as the value of the stock of the firm or the value of a broad market index. In this case, the DB plan implicitly forces the participant to invest a large fraction of wealth in this asset, since the pension benefit essentially duplicates the payoff to the asset. In contrast, the DC plan allows the participant to take the pension contribution each period and invest it in any security. In essence, the DC plan allows participants to get their money out of the (over)investment in W_1 and achieve superior portfolio diversification. This advantage of DC plans is incremental to the pure efficiency gain from the risk pooling opportunity that was noted above.

Interest Rate Uncertainty

In this section, we will assume that wage paths are either given or uncorrelated with the interest rate, and that the only investment vehicles are bonds. However, the future path of interest rates is not known at the time the pension contract is established. Because wages pose no systematic risk, $B(t, T)$ is simply the riskless discount function, and $B(0, 1) = 1/R_0$.

As in Merton (1983), we will assume that the lifetime utility function for the individual at time 0 is

(5) $$U_0 = \log (C_0) + E_0[\log(C_1) + \log(C_2)].$$

At time 1, all uncertainty is resolved since both W_1 and R_1 (and hence P) are known. Lifetime utility at $t = 1$ is thus

$$U_1 = \log(C_1) + \log(C_2),$$

and at $t = 2$ is

$$U_2 = \log(C_2).$$

Upon arriving at $t = 2$, the individual will consume all of his financial wealth, plus all pension benefits:

(6) $$C_2 = (A_1 + W_1 - C_1)R_1 + P.$$

Thus, at $t = 1$, the optimization problem is

$$\max[\log(C_1) + \log(C_2)],$$

which results in the first-order condition

(7) $$C_1 - C_2/R_1 = 0.$$

Using equation (6), equation (7) can be solved to yield

$$(8) \qquad C_1^* = (A_1 + W_1 + P/R_1)/2,$$
$$C_2^* = R_1 C_1^*.$$

Using the expressions for P from equations (3) and (4), we find that

$$(8\text{-DB}) \qquad C_1^{DB} = (A_1 + W_1 + W_1/R_1)/2,$$

while

$$(8\text{-DC}) \qquad C_1^{DC} = [A_1 + W_1 + (1/2)(W_0 + W_1)B(0, 2)R_0]/2.$$

As expected, the difference between equations (8-DC) and (8-DB) reflects the "wage diversification" attribute of DC plans, in that consumption depends upon a weighted sum of earnings over the entire career. A perhaps surprising feature of equations (8) is that consumption for individuals in DC plans is not a function of the realized interest rate, R_1, although it is for individuals in DB plans. This is true despite the fact that retirement *wealth* is subject to interest rate risk for DC plans, but not for DB plans.

This feature of the model turns out to be an artifact of the log utility function, but nevertheless highlights an important feature of DB versus DC plan design. Recall the first-order condition (7) for optimal consumption allocation across times 1 and 2, which requires that time-2 consumption be R_1 times time-1 consumption. For an individual in a DC plan, all wealth already is held and can be invested at rate R_1 at $t = 1$. Thus, the simple rule is to consume one-half of wealth at $t = 1$, invest the remainder, and thus consume R_1 times one-half of wealth at $t = 2$. Consumption at $t = 1$ is thus *independent* of R_1. In contrast, in a DB plan, the pension benefit to be received at $t = 2$ already is fixed at $t = 1$. Thus, a large value of R_1 requires a decrease in $t = 1$ consumption in order to satisfy the first-order condition for an optimum. Another way of seeing this is to note that, for the log utility function, consumption at $t = 1$ depends *only* on wealth, not on the interest rate. For DC plans, wealth at $t = 1$ is independent of R_1, since all assets are already in hand. For DB plans, pension benefits are still deferred at $t = 1$, and wealth depends on R_1.

For more general utility functions, consumption at $t = 1$ depends on both wealth *and* R_1. However, DC plans still offer a type of consumption smoothing that is not offered by DB plans. Specifically, the generalized first-order condition at $t = 1$ requires that the ratio of the marginal utility of consumption at $t = 1$ to that at $t = 2$ equals R_1. A larger R_1 thus induces more time-2 consumption. This can be attained with less (or no) sacrifice of current consumption when assets are already in hand since assets currently invested can earn the higher rate of interest. In DB plans, in contrast, there is no offset between income and substitution effects. A larger R_1 *decreases* pension wealth and, simultaneously, requires a reallocation of consumption to the retirement period, $t = 2$. Thus, the consumption stream in DC plans is less sensitive to the interest rate during the accumulation phase, and indeed, in the log utility case, is actually independent of the realization of the interest rate.

Using equations (8), we may now compute the derived or indirect utility function at $t = 1$:

$$\text{(9-DB)} \quad J_{DB}(A_1, W_1, t = 1) = \log(C_1{}^*) + \log(C_2{}^*)$$

$$= 2 \log[1/2(A_1 + W_1 + W_1/R_1)]$$

$$+ \log(R_1);$$

$$\text{(9-DC)} \quad J_{DC}(A_1, W_1, t = 1) = 2 \log\{1/2[A_1 + W_1 + W'B(0, 2)R_0]\}$$

$$+ \log(R_1);$$

where $W' = (W_0 + W_1)/2$, that is, career-average earnings.

As a base case to compare equations (9), consider the situation in which the expectations hypothesis for the term structure of interest rates holds. Then $B(0, 2) = (1/R_0)E_0(1/R_1)$. In this instance, with $E_0(W') = W_0$ and W_1 uncorrelated with R_1, the expectations of the arguments of the log terms in equations (9) are equal. However, the argument of the log term in (9-DC) is subject to less uncertainty (as of $t = 0$) than in (9-DB). This is due to both the wage diversification embodied in the DC plan and the interest rate risk that appears only in the DB plan.

Using equations (9), we may obtain the derived utility function at $t = 0$:

$$\text{(10)} \quad J(A_0, W_0, t = 0) = \max\{\log(C_0) + E_0 [J(A_1, W_1, t = 1)]\}.$$

From equation (10), it is easy to show that time-0 utility is higher in the DC plan (still assuming that the expectations hypothesis holds). Consider the optimizing value of time-0 consumption under the DB plan. This consumption choice is also feasible in the DC plan and will result in an identical value for A_1. However, for any given A_1, $E_0[J(A_1, W_1, t = 1)]$ is greater in the DC plan. This last point follows from the equal expected values of the arguments of the log function in equations (9), the greater dispersion of the argument in the DB plan, and the concavity of the log function. Because DC plans offer greater welfare than DB plans at consumption levels that are optimal for DB plans, they must do so *a fortiori* when C_0 is chosen to be optimal for the DC environment.

For the DB plan to dominate the DC plan, it would be necessary for it to offer a *greater* expected pension benefit at $t = 2$. This would require that $B(0, 2)$ be less than $E_0(1/R_0R_1)$, that is, that there be a positive liquidity or risk premium for investing in long-term bonds rather than rolling over shorts.

At this point, it is worth reconsidering the assumptions of our model. It should be apparent that the zero expected growth rate of real wages is not essential to the argument. Our analysis would have been similar even with a positive trend in real wages. The only major modification would involve an adjustment for the fact that a DB plan with a 100 percent replacement rate of final salary would promise retirement-period income greater than career-average wages. The per period contributions to the retirement fund in the equal-present-value DC plan would thus need to be correspondingly increased. In the nomenclature of equation (2), the sum of k_1 and k_2 would need to exceed 1.0. However, aside from this adjustment, the analysis would be similar.

The issue of interest rate uncertainty during the retirement period is more difficult and poses issues not easily treated in the above model. In our 3-period model, the individual simply consumes total retirement wealth in the last period. If, however, retirement itself is viewed as a many-period interval, then real retirement *income* and not *wealth* may be the significant determinant of welfare. Given a stock of wealth at retirement, the real consumption stream that is feasible for the retiree depends on the real long-term interest rate at the time of retirement, when the purchase of a (real) life annuity is contemplated. Even if retirement wealth can be predicted fairly precisely with a low-investment-risk DC retirement fund, the real income stream that can be generated by that wealth is subject to considerable uncertainty.[6] In contrast, by guaranteeing a specified income (and hence, consumption) stream upon retirement, the (price-level-indexed) DB plan eliminates the risk associated with the conversion, at retirement, of a stock of retirement wealth into a flow of equivalent-present-value consumption. DC plans cannot offer a guaranteed capitalization rate at retirement because of our assumption that life annuities and bonds of long- enough maturity do not exist.

In order to examine some potential effects of uncertainty in the interest rate at retirement, we will consider a simple adjustment to our model. Suppose that at $t = 2$, the financial assets of individuals are multiplied by some increasing function of R_2, $f(R_2)$, where R_2 equals one plus the postretirement rate of interest. The multiplication by $f(R_2)$ reflects the increased retirement-income stream that is available to DC participants when interest rates at retirement turn out to be high. In contrast, for DB plans, the retirement-income stream is guaranteed by the firm so that interest-rate risk is not borne by plan participants.

Reconsider now the optimal consumption program for DC plan participants. At $t = 2$,

(11) $C_2 = [(A_1 + W_1 - C_1) R_1 + P_{DC}] f(R_2),$

which now is stochastic at $t = 1$ because of the dependence on R_2. Thus, at $t = 1$, the maximization problem becomes

$$\max \log(C_1) + E_1[\log(C_2)],$$

which has first-order condition

(12) $\frac{1}{C_1} - E [\frac{1}{C_2} R_1 f(R_2)] = 0.$

But examination of equations (11) and (12) shows that $f(R_2)$ drops out of the first-order conditions so that (12) results in exactly the same consumption level at $t = 1$ as in the nonstochastic R_2 model. Lifetime utility, however, may change. For example, for an actuarially fair $f(R_2)$ adjustment, such as $f(R_2 = R_2/E_1(R_2),$[7] consumption at $t = 1$ is unchanged, while consumption at $t = 2$ has the same expected value as in the previous model, but greater uncertainty. In this case, expected time-2 utility falls. If time-2 interest rate uncertainty is sufficiently great relative to wage and time-1 interest rate uncertainty, DC plans could become inferior to DB plans from the viewpoint of plan participants. Thus, retirement-period interest rate uncertainty emerges as a potential advantage of DB relative to DC plans.

5.3.3   Factor-Share Uncertainty

Merton (1983) has examined a model in which labor-income uncertainty derives entirely from an aggregate production function in which income shares accruing to capital and labor are stochastically determined. In contrast to the model above, in which labor-income uncertainty is diversifiable, in Merton's model labor income is perfectly correlated across individuals. Given the nontradeability of human capital, economic inefficiencies arise in this economy, since early in life, individuals hold too much of their wealth in human capital relative to physical capital, while at retirement all wealth is invested in physical capital. These portfolio imbalances preclude optimal sharing of factor-share risk. Merton suggests that a Social Security system which pays retirees a share of current wage income implicitly provides diversification across factor shares and can increase welfare by improving the efficiency of risk bearing in the economy.

A similar argument can be made with regard to DB versus DC plans. In a DC plan, the income of a retired individual depends solely on investment performance and is independent of retirement-period uncertainty in factor shares. Retirees thus have no stake in labor income during their retirement period. In a DB plan, retirement income is also determined upon retirement. However, if factor-share uncertainty is primarily attributable to unforeseeable long-term secular trends (rather than to transitory business-cycle effects) then a final-salary DB plan may provide risk-sharing benefits similar to Merton's Social Security scheme. Such secular uncertainty could arise, for example, from unanticipated changes in labor-augmenting technical progress.

Since the pension benefit under the DB plan is tied to final salary, individuals participating in such a scheme are invested in an implicit security that is tied to the wage share in the neighborhood of the retirement period. To the extent that firms offer ad hoc increases in pension benefits when wages of current employees increase, the retiree's stake in aggregate labor income is further enhanced. Of course DC plan benefits also depend to some extent on end-of-career earnings. However, the career averaging properties of DC plans greatly reduce the magnitude of this dependence. Thus, if labor-income uncertainty is predominantly dependent on economy-wide factors, then this source of risk would favor DB over DC plans.

5.3.4   Inflation

In the preceding model, we assumed that wages and pension benefits were all contracted in real terms. It is clear that the vast majority of DB plans as currently implemented are not contractually indexed during the retirement period. This weakens the case for viewing DB plans as offering income-maintenance or interest-rate insurance.

Moreover, there is controversy surrounding the degree of indexation during the worker's active life. Bulow (1982) has argued that wages in firms administering DB plans should *not* be expected to keep pace with the price level. His argument is based on the notion that labor markets clear as spot markets (with respect to pension issues) and that any implicit contracts between firms and workers are independent of pension issues. In this case, the market-clearing employee compensation will determine the *sum* of wages plus accruing pension benefits. The level of either wages or pension accruals alone, however, is indeterminate.

To illustrate Bulow's point, consider the effects of an unanticipated increase in the price level. The increase imposes a real loss on workers, since their pension benefits are defined in nominal terms. Of course, the worker's loss is the firm's gain. If, however, the employees were to receive a pay raise in the subsequent period which would keep their real wage constant, then the earnings base upon which pension benefits are calculated also would rise at the inflation rate, and the worker's pension loss would be eliminated. Real compensation in the second period would in effect be higher than in the first: real wages are constant, but pension transfers have increased in order to compensate for the effects of the unanticipated inflation. The firm has, in effect, issued insurance against the effect of inflation on the value of pension benefits.

Bulow argues that firms neither behave in this way nor should they be expected to. His competing model holds total real compensation exogenous. Because pension benefits in DB plans increase with the wage level, the wage component of compensation will *not* rise at the inflation rate in the subsequent period. Instead, the sum of the partially indexed wage increase and partially indexed recovery of real pension benefits *together* will provide an increase in nominal compensation which matches the inflation rate. However, the initial loss of pension value due to inflation is borne entirely by the worker.

Under the Bulow model, DB plans pose significant risk to participants. The nominal nature of the pension contract is to be taken quite seriously; workers bear the entire brunt of inflation risk. Thus, while DB plans provide a less variable final-salary replacement rate to workers than do DC plans, the final real salary itself becomes more sensitive to inflation. Whether DB or DC plans are riskier in a utility sense is therefore an open question. Bulow's model is far from universally accepted. Several observers (e.g., Cohn and Modigliani 1983) believe that firms do in fact offer implicit indexation to workers. In this view, the wage decision is made separately from the pension decision, and the effects of wage increases on pension benefits are ignored in the determination of worker compensation.

5.4 Concluding Comments: Is There a Better Way?

The major advantage of DB plans is the potential they offer to provide a stable replacement rate of final income to workers. If the replacement rate is the relevant variable for worker retirement utility, then DB plans offer some degree of insurance against real wage risk. Of course, protection offered to workers is risk borne by the firm. As real wages change, funding rates must correspondingly adjust. However, to the extent that real wage risk is largely diversifiable to employers, and nondiversifiable to employees, the replacement rate stability should be viewed as an advantage of DB plans.

The advantages of DC plans are most apparent during periods of inflation uncertainty. These are: the predictability of the value of pension wealth, the ability to invest in inflation-hedged portfolios rather than nominal DB annuities, and the fully-funded nature of the DC plan. Finally, the DC plan has the advantage that workers can more easily determine the true present value of the pension benefit they earn in any year, although they may have more uncertainty about future pension benefit flows at retirement. Measuring the present value of accruing defined benefits is difficult at best and imposes severe informational requirements on workers. Such difficulties could lead workers to misvalue their total compensation and result in misinformed behavior.[8]

Of interest for future research is the possibility of pension plan designs that combine the best attributes of DB and DC plans. Many firms already offer DB plans supplemented by DC plans. An interesting alternative is the so-called floor plan, which is in essence a DC plan together with a guarantee of a minimum retirement income based on a DB-type formula. Employers and employees can trade off the level of guaranteed floor against the size of the expected DC benefit. These plans offer the downside protection of DB plans, yet still allow employees to take positions in high-expected-return assets. Floor plans already are offered by some firms [9] and allow for a great deal of flexibility and creativity.

Notes

1. It is important to distinguish here between several subcategories of DC plans: money purchase, profit sharing, and thrift plans. For money purchase plans, like TIAA-CREF, contributions are usually based on the employee's compensation, as stated in the text. But in profit-sharing plans employer contributions are based on the sponsor's profitability, and in thrift plans contribution levels are usually determined voluntarily by employees, with employer matching contributions at some prespecified rate. Thrift plans are usually offered as a supplement to a DB or other DC plan.

2. Until the late 1970s, employee contributions to many DC plans were not tax-deductible, the main exception being employees of certain nonprofit organizations (403[b] plans). But recently the government has expanded tax-deductibility of employee contributions to the private for-profit sector through 401(k) plans.

3. There is a separate question of whether the difference in backloading patterns is of importance to workers. Consider a scenario in which the inflation rate is fixed and only the interest rate varies. In this case, the impact of interest rates on accrual patterns would be irrelevant to workers from a welfare standpoint. The real stream of benefits to be paid starting at retirement is independent of the trajectory of the present value of accrued benefits. When inflation rates are stochastic, however, backloading patterns can have important effects on welfare. The real benefit stream during retirement moves inversely with the stochastic price level.

4. The contribution pattern for a DC plan required to match the accrual pattern of a DB plan could run into IRS limits on annual contributions at older ages, particularly for higher paid employees.

5. An alternative explanation is that insurance companies view their annuitants as members of a captive market and try to recoup past losses by offering them below-market rates.

6. As always, it is impossible to tell from first principles of welfare analysis whether an individual would necessarily choose to convert wealth into a riskless stream of retirement benefits.

7. This is an *actuarially* fair adjustment in the sense that the expected value of period-2 income would be unaffected.

8. While workers are more likely to be informationally disadvantaged than employers, the level of complication is such that employers also may make significant mistakes. All of this is perhaps an issue in evaluating the Bulow argument, since that argument turns on accurate perceptions of the "true" pension benefits and costs.

9. Among the companies offering floor plans are Xerox, Hewlett-Packard, and Georgia-Pacific.

References

Amoroso, Vincent. 1983. Termination insurance for single-employer pension plans: Costs and benefits. *Transactions, Society of Actuaries* 35:71–83.

Bierwag, G. O. 1977. Immunization, duration and the term structure of interest rates. *Journal of Financial and Quantitative Analysis* (December): 725–42.

Bierwag, G. O., and George G. Kaufman. 1977. Coping with the risk of interest rate fluctuations. *Journal of Business* (July): 364–70.

Bodie, Zvi. 1980. An innovation for stable real retirement income. *Journal of Portfolio Management* 7 (Fall): 5–13.

Bulow, Jeremy I. 1982. What are corporate pension liabilities? *Quarterly Journal of Economics* 97:435–52.

Cohn, Richard A., and Franco Modigliani. 1983. Inflation and corporate financial management. Mimeo.

Cox, John C., Jonathan E. Ingersoll, and Stephan A. Ross. Duration and the measurement of basis risk. *Journal of Business* 52 (January): 51–61.

Diamond, Peter, and James Mirrlees. 1985. Insurance aspects of pensions. In *Pensions, labor, and individual choice*, edited by David Wise. Chicago: University of Chicago Press.

Ellwood, David T. 1985. Pensions and the labor market: A starting point. In *Pensions, labor, and individual choice*, edited by David Wise. Chicago: University of Chicago Press.

Marcus, Alan J. 1987. Corporate pension policy and the value of PBGC insurance. In *Issues in Pension Economics*, edited by Zvi Bodie, John Shoven, and David Wise. Chicago: University of Chicago Press.

Merton, Robert C. 1983. On the role of Social Security as a means for efficient risk sharing in an economy where human capital is not tradeable. *Financial aspects of the United States pension system*, edited by Zvi Bodie and John Shoven. Chicago: University of Chicago Press.

Merton, Robert C., Zvi Bodie, and Alan J. Marcus. 1987. Pension plan integration as insurance against Social Security risk. In *Issues in Pension Economics*, edited by Z. Bodie, J. B. Shoven, and D. A. Wise. Chicago: University of Chicago Press.

Comment   Laurence J. Kotlikoff

This paper provides a very insightful comparison of defined contribution and defined benefit pension plans. While the authors are cautious, one is left with the impression that the defined contribution form of pension plans is superior in many, if not all, respects to the defined benefit form. I certainly concur with that conclusion. Many defined benefit plans appear to subject workers and employers to unnecessary earnings risk by tying the pension payment to the average of earnings at the end of workers' careers; while hedging inflation, such provisions mean that workers' pensions are very sensitive to earnings late in their careers. Such earnings may be unusually low for reasons including poor health, changes in market conditions, and so forth.

Other defined benefit plans relate the pension to longer averages of earnings, which make the initial real pension benefit potentially quite sensitive to inflation. Still other defined benefit pensions are independent of earnings, positing a nominal benefit that depends only on service. The real values of these latter pensions are also very sensitive to inflation.

In contrast to the defined benefit plans, defined contribution plans appear to be riskier with respect to the real rate of return. However, as the authors point out, one can devise close to riskless portfolios that get around this objection. In addition, they make the important point that defined benefit plans also are sensitive to the real rate of return because changes in real rates alter the present value of future defined benefits.

Once workers retire the defined benefit pensions are subject to considerable inflation risk. While many firms do provide cost-of-living increases on an ad hoc basis, these increases do not keep pace with inflation, as Robert Clark has shown in his study of cost-of-living increases in the 1970s. In contrast, defined contribution plans give workers the option of withdrawing their funds and investing them themselves. As mentioned, one can safely hedge inflation and secure a real, if minuscule, rate of return; the problem is, however, that many retirees may not know how to devise such riskless portfolios that involve using future commodity markets. While financial markets could provide such safe assets, they do not appear readily available at the current time.

A problem with defined contribution plans not discussed in detail by the authors is that defined contribution plans that pay off at retirement do not provide retirees with an annuity, and therefore do not provide

Laurence J. Kotlikoff is a professor of economics at Boston University and a research associate of the National Bureau of Economic Research.

retirees with insurance against life-span uncertainty. Those that do pay off in the form of an annuity provide a stream of nominal retirement benefits that are subject to inflation risk just like the benefits of defined benefit plans.

Another important issue that the authors do not consider is whether defined benefit plans are too complicated for workers—and, indeed, even employers—to understand and properly evaluate. It is not atypical to find a defined benefit plan that has (1) an age- and service-related benefit formula, (2) an average earnings base, (3) age- and service-dependent early retirement reduction formulas, (4) special early retirement supplemental benefits, and (5) actuarial reductions for workers terminating prior to early retirement. To calculate correctly one's accrual of pension benefits in such plans requires actuarial skills which typical workers do not possess. In addition, in many cases even if the workers possessed such skills, the booklets describing the pension plans are so poorly written, if not intentionally misleading, that it is very difficult to figure out what one is actually receiving. Hence, an important advantage of defined contribution plans is that they provide workers with better information about their retirement finances.

My guess is that defined benefit plans emerged because they were attractive to older union members and to employers who thought they could generate strong retirement incentives without being explicit about those incentives. In the process the country has been straddled with a very risky private pension system that provides insufficient information to both workers and employers about the benefits and costs of financing retirement.

6   Pensions and Turnover

Edward P. Lazear and Robert L. Moore

Over the past few years, a number of authors have attempted to examine the effects of pensions on retirement and worker turnover in general. Lazear (1982, 1983a, 1983b), Wolf and Levy (1984), Kotlikoff and Wise (1987), Mitchell and Fields (1984), and Frant and Leonard (1987), among others, have investigated the pattern of pension accruals and the effects of various pension provisions on worker behavior. While that literature has made definite progress toward understanding the relation of pensions to turnover, it has suffered from two basic problems.

First, for the most part (Mitchell and Fields [1984] is an exception), the empirical analyses have been unable to match workers with the exact plans in which they are enrolled. For example, in Lazear (1982, 1983b), all that was available was information on the plans, with no information on worker behavior. Even aggregate statistics on average age of retirement and the age distribution of the work force were absent. As such, it was impossible to assess the impact of the various plans on worker turnover.

Second, the specifications used in the literature are not quite correct and lead to inappropriate inferences. What most researchers do when attempting to look at the effect of pensions on turnover is to examine the value of the pension conditional on retirement at some chosen date. Thus, the pension value (or accrual amount) associated with the eighteenth year of work is based on some assumed date of retirement. Often that date is the year itself. Lazear (1982, 1983b) presented the

Edward P. Lazear is the Isidore Brown and Gladys J. Brown Professor of Urban and Labor Economics at the Graduate School of Business, University of Chicago, senior fellow, Hoover Institution, and a research associate of the National Bureau of Economic Research. Robert L. Moore is an associate professor of economics, Occidental College.

We are grateful to Michael Hurd for a helpful discussion and to Herman Leonard and David Wise for valuable suggestions.

expected present value of the pension for every age of retirement between 55 and 75. Although that information is useful and forms the starting point for this analysis, it is not the correct independent variable to use when trying to estimate the effect of pensions on worker turnover. As it turns out, the pension value, calculated in that fashion, is generally more discontinuous than the value that affects behavior. It is no surprise that trying to relate the raw pension values to worker turnover is not especially fruitful. The following example illustrates the point.

Consider a stylized military plan that vests after 20 years and provides a zero credit for any years worked after year 20. This results in a very discontinuous pension pattern. The pension value associated with retirement before 20 years of service is zero and is positive at 20 years. Beyond that, the pension value falls because fewer years are paid out and no credit adjustment is made. If $P(t)$ is the pension value associated with retirement after t years of tenure, then $P(t) = 0$ for t less than 20. Since $P(t)$ does not vary until year 20, it cannot affect turnover differentially during that period. But in reality, one would expect that the effect of this pension formula on turnover would be greater in year 19 than in year 2. Workers who have only been with the firm for 2 years still have 18 years to wait for the pension to vest. The option value of staying an additional year varies with tenure even though $P(t)$ does not.

The most obvious way to see this is to imagine that data were available only on workers whose tenure was less than 19 years. If $P(t)$ were the dependent variable, then it would be zero for all of these workers. Yet, as workers get closer to year 20, it must be true that the force of the pension on turnover rates increases. The approach that we develop picks this effect up in a smooth and more theoretically appropriate fashion. The effect of pensions on turnover could be estimated even if no workers had ever gone past the date of vesting (say, because the plan is new and workers are young). More important, the approach is dynamic; it takes into account that workers look toward the future. The current year's pension accrual is relevant, but not sufficient. The pension available 3 years hence may exert a stronger influence on this year's work decision than the current pension accrual.

This paper does two things: First, it derives the appropriate pension variable to use in a regression that relates turnover to pensions. Second, it constructs a new data set and applies the approach to those data. The data include explicit information on the pension formula and also on the workers who are currently employed. Their starting dates, birthdates, sex, marital status (in some cases), and salary history for 11 years are provided. Although no information on workers who have left the firm is available, under certain assumptions it is sufficient to examine the tenure distribution of current employees. Additionally, we have information on six different plans and their workers so that there is enough variation to obtain estimates of the effects of pensions on turnover.

The primary empirical conclusion is that pensions have a strong effect on turnover. In these data, eliminating the average worker's pension would double the turnover rate. We hasten to add that this conclusion is tentative. The current state of our data allows us to obtain estimates only under quite strong assumptions. Still, as a first guess, the results show the potential importance of the effect of pensions on turnover.

6.1 Theory: The Option Value of Working

To focus on the relevant variable, we ignore any wage payments and suppose (obviously unrealistically) that total compensation consists of pensions. Define $P(t)$ as the expected value in year t dollars of the pension flow that is available to the worker if he severs his ties to the firm at the conclusion of year t. Further, define $V(t)$ as the value associated with working during year t in year t dollars. This option value can be defined recursively:

In year T, the final year, the option value of work is

$$V(T) = P(T) - [P(T - 1)](1 + r),$$

where r is the rate of interest. This is the difference between what the worker receives in pension value if he works until time T as compared with time $T - 1$. The value of working year $T - 1$ is, correspondingly,

$$V(T - 1) = \max[P(T - 1), P(T)/(1 + r)] - [P(T - 2)](1 + r).$$

The first term says work in year $T - 1$ gives the worker the option of taking the pension available after year $T - 1$ or of going on to work year T and getting $P(T)$, discounted back to year $T - 1$ dollars. If the worker does not work year $T - 1$, he can have the pension $P(T - 2)$, which must be multiplied by $1 + r$ to put it in year $T - 1$ dollars. Note that this information assumes (relaxed below) that the worker can, with certainty, opt to work year T and receive that pension. In year $T - 2$, a similar formula gives

$$V(T - 2) = \max[P(T - 2), P(T - 1)/(1 + r),$$
$$P(T)/(1 + r)^2] - P(T - 3)(1 + r),$$

or using the first term of $V(T - 1)$, this can be rewritten as

$$V(T - 2) = \max \{P(T - 2), \max [P(T - 1),$$
$$P(T)]/1 + r\} - P(T - 3)(1 + r).$$

Define $M(t) = \max[P(t), M(t + 1)/(1 + r)]$, and $M(T) = P(T)$, so that we can write generally

(1) $$V(t) = M(t) - [P(t - 1)](1 + r).$$

Equation (1) and the definition of $M(t)$ make more obvious the intuition of the earlier example and previous paragraph. Consider a very similar example where $P(10) > 0$, but $P(t) = 0$ for $t < 10$. If $P(11) < P(10)$, $\max [P(10), M(11)/(1 + r)] = P(10)$. But $\max[P(9), M(10)/(1 + r)] = M(10)/(1 + r) = P(10)/(1 + r)$, not $P(9)$, which equals zero. Similarly, $M(8) = P(10)/(1 + r)^2$, and so forth. Thus, the $V(t)$ series is much smoother between $t = 9$, 10 than the $P(t)$ series.

The importance of this formulation can be seen even more clearly if the pension formula is such that pensions continue to accrue after year 10. In the previous example, there is a spike in $V(t)$, but it comes between 10 and 11, not between 9 and 10. This is because the value of staying to year 11 is negative. If accruals occur after year 10 so that the maximum value is achieved by retiring, say, at year 30, the spike at 11 goes away for the most part as well. There is a discontinuity only to the extent that $P(9)$, which is subtracted to get $V(10)$, is zero, where $P(10)$, subtracted to get $V(11)$, is not. But the difference between 0 and $P(10)$ is small compared with $M(10)$ or $M(11)$ in most practical situations. As will be seen below, the only time that these magnitudes are not small is when the worker is old at the year 10 vesting point. Then the option value spikes are important.

So far, we have assumed that the worker chooses and receives the branch of the maximand that is the largest. This is unrealistic for two reasons: First, the firm may sever the worker before he reaches the optimal date, t^*. Second, the worker receives wages and has alternative job possibilities as well.

To be more explicit, suppose that at time t, $R(t)$, the reservation wage, has the distribution function $G_t[R(t)]$. Suppose further that the worker does not know $R(t)$ before period t. Also, let there be an exogenous probability of separation, either due to unanticipated termination by the firm or for health reasons. Let that probability be denoted $F(t, A)$, where t reflects the worker's tenure and A his age. (This becomes important in the empirical section.) If the worker receives reservation value R_t in each year t that he does not work for the firm, and also W_t during each year that he does, then $M(t)$ must be redefined as

$$M(t) = \max\left[P(t) + \sum_{i=t+1}^{T} \frac{(R_i - W_i)}{(1 + r)^{i-t}},\right.$$

$$\left. F(t + 1, A + 1)M(t + 1)/(1 + r)\right],$$

and

(1') $V(t) = M(t) - \left[P(t - 1) + \sum_{i=t}^{T} \frac{(R_i - W_i)}{(1 + r)^{i-t}} \right](1 + r).$

The worker quits when $V(t)$ is negative. This can be rewritten. Define

$Z(t) \equiv \dfrac{M(t)}{(1 + r)} - \left[P(t - 1) + \sum_{i=t+1}^{T} \frac{(R_i - W_i)}{(1 + r)^{i-t}} \right] + W_t.$

Then equation (1') implies that the worker quits when

$R_t > Z(t),$

or he works with probability $G_t[Z(t)]$. Since everything in Z is known deterministically, or is unknown and in the future, expected values are relevant so that at time t, $Z(t)$ is merely a number that can be calculated once the distributions of the R's are known. Parameterization of the G function and observing the number of individuals who quit provide that information.

In the empirical section, it will be assumed that $R_t = W_t$ for all t, so that only $F(t, A)$ must be addressed.

The importance of treating the reservation value, R_t, correctly can be seen in the context of the standard work-leisure diagram. A number of researchers (e.g., Burtless and Hausman 1980; Hausman and Wise 1985) have used the work-leisure framework to analyze retirement decisions. Although that approach is instructive, it suffers from its static nature. This prevents analysis of many of the issues that are central to this paper. This can be seen in the context of figure 6.1.

A pension plan (ignoring wages) might result in a nonlinear budget constraint with shape ABCDE. This diagram allows us to talk about

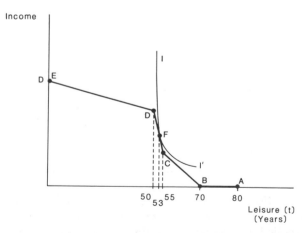

Fig. 6.1   Work/Leisure Diagram and Option Value Approach

the total number of years that an individual would choose to work if that were a one-time decision. It does not easily permit any uncertainty to be incorporated into the analysis. It cannot deal with when work occurs over the lifetime. For example, 30 years can be worked as one spell of 30 from age 20 to 50 or as two spells of 10 and 20 years separated by a 10-year hiatus. The timing is especially important for pension plans, many of which depend on dates worked either directly or indirectly by tying benefits to salary. This is particularly important for women. Finally, and most important in this context, is that the decision to leave the job is not always a decision to take leisure. More often, it is a choice of a new job over the old one. There is no way (without severely straining the interpretation of the utility function) to deal with that through a nonlinear budget constraint analysis.

The option value approach allows us to capture these effects and also nests the work-leisure analysis. But it is essential to build in the reservation wage, R_t, in an appropriate fashion. To see this, consider a worker who is deciding how long to work. If leisure has zero value, then indifference curves are functions with slope $= (1/(1 + r)^{70-t}$ at each point. (The analysis is the standard one of when to cut a tree.) Under these circumstances, it is impossible that F could dominate D. But it is clear that in the work-leisure context, F could be an optimum. This is because pure wealth maximization ignores the value of time between years 53 and 50. But if R_{51}, R_{52}, R_{53} were sufficiently high, and R_{54}, R_{55}, . . . sufficiently low (as reflected by the highly nonlinear indifference curve near F), then F could be an optimum according to equation (1'). Our view is that the option approach yields much more flexibility to analyze dynamic questions of timing of work and job switching, without sacrificing the implications of the work-leisure analysis.

6.2 Empirical Analysis

6.2.1 Data

The data consist of detailed plan descriptions and a personnel roll for six plans. The personnel data include the date of hire, birthdate, a salary history at the current firm for up to ten years, sometimes marital status, and in one case, whether the worker receives an hourly wage or salary. Additionally, accrued benefits and projected benefits have been calculated by the accounting firm that supplied the data, but those values were not used in our analysis.

Because of the proprietary nature of the data, the firms cannot be identified. However, some rough descriptions of the industry and workers are provided here along with a description of the individual plans.

Plan 1: National women's clothing retail stores, located in major urban areas; 2,083 active employees in pension plan on February 1, 1984.

Normal retirement annual flow is calculated as .0015 × (sum of annual earnings − $4,200) for each year employed. This is indexed at a CPI factor of no greater than 3 percent for past years. Early retirement can be taken at age 60 with 10 years of service. Postponed retirement is permitted, and retirement at dates other than the normal date is the actuarial equivalent of that received at age 65, conditioned on actual years of service and salaries. The plan vests after 10 years.

Plan 2: Large southwestern mining company. These workers are salaried, generally managers, who work either in the southwestern United States or in New York City; 357 active employees in the plan as of February 1, 1984.

The normal retirement annual flow is calculated as average of final 5 years' salaries = AVE. Then the flow per year is (.0175 AVE − .0125[$9,240]) × (years of service). There is a maximum flow of 2/3 of AVE. The hire date must occur before the worker turns 65. Early retirement is permitted at age 55, and late retirement to age 70 is permitted. There is an early retirement reduction of .0033 per month for each month that retirement occurs before age 60. The formula is slightly more complex for individuals who have 30 years of service by age 55 or who will reach 30 years before age 60. The plan vests after 10 years.

Plan 3: One of the companies under the corporate umbrella of the firm described in plan 2. All are salaried employees from the southwest; 821 active employees as of February 1, 1984.

The normal retirement annual flow is calculated as average of final 5 years' salaries = AVE. Then the flow per year is (.0175 AVE − .0125[$9,240]) × (years of service). Early retirement at age 55 is permitted, with the participant receiving a reduced pension actuarially equivalent to pension beginning at age 65, but for individuals who have 25 years of service (or more) and are age 60 or older at retirement, only 1/2 regular actuarial reduction is to be applied. Late retirement is permitted. The plan vests after 10 years.

Plan 4: These are the hourly rated employees of the company in plan 3 with job titles ranging from janitorial to electrician to miners. 999 active employees in plan as of February 1, 1984.

Normal retirement monthly flow (at age 62) is equal to $17 × (years of service up to 15) + $18.50 × (next 15 years of service) + $20 × (service years exceeding 30). There are three possible early retirement options: (1) at age 60 with the above amount reduced .0033 per month for each month prior to age 62; (2) with 30 years of service and no reduction, plus a monthly benefit of $300 until employee attains age

62, and a monthly benefit of $130 payable from 62 until eligible for unreduced Social Security benefits; (3) with the same benefit flow as in option (2) only the $130 supplement does not apply, under the "70/80" rule (the latter only by mutual agreement between employee and company. It requires either age 55 with sum of age + service = 70, or age less than 55 with sum of age + service = 80). Late retirement permitted. The plan vests after 10 years.

Plan 5: Salaried employees of the parent company of the major office/ home furniture manufacturing firm described in plan 6. Titles run from manager to president/owner and include employees from locations in California, New Jersey, Tennessee, and various other states; 310 active employees as of February 1, 1984.

The normal retirement annual flow (at age 65) is the sum of two parts: (1) a prior service benefit = 1.25 percent of final 5-year average pay at 1/1/84 to $20,000 plus 1.75 percent of such average in excess of $20,000, all times the number of years of service as of 1/1/84, and (2) a future service benefit = 1.25 percent of pay up to Social Security earnings limit, plus 1.75 percent of pay in excess of limit, for each year of service beyond 1/1/84. Early retirement at 60 with monthly flow reduced .005 for each month that commencement of payments precedes 65. The plan vests after 10 years.

Plan 6: Major office/home furniture manufacturer. Includes both salaried employees (managers, executives, etc.) and hourly employees (machinists, loading dock workers, etc.) under the same benefit formula. Employees are located in Mid-Atlantic states; 1,390 active participants as of February 1, 1984.

Normal retirement annual flow (at 65) is sum of two parts: (1) 1.25 percent of final 5-year average pay at 1/1/78 up to $12,000, plus 1.75 percent of this average that exceeds $12,000 for each year of service to 1/1/78, and (2) 1.25 percent of pay up to Social Security earnings limit, plus 1.75 percent of pay exceeding such limit for each year of service after 1/1/78. Early retirement at age 55, with monthly pension flow reduced .005 for each month that precedes normal reitrement. The plan vests after 10 years.

6.2.2   Simulation of Plan Values

Given the plan descriptions, it is straightforward to compute the expected present value of pension benefits for any hypothetical employee who retires at a given age. To do this, life tables must be used and the 1980 Vital Statistics tables for males or females (depending on the sex of the hypothetical individual) were selected for this purpose.

We calculated the expected present value for 72 hypothetical employees for each plan, and for each of those employees, we computed $P(t)$, the pension value after t years of service in year t dollars, for t

ranging from 0 to the t that corresponds to age 85. Note that in all plans $P(t) = 0$ for t less than 10. The 72 employees were obtained by letting sex vary, letting wage growth vary from 0 to 3 percent, letting 1984 salary take on values of $10,000, $40,000, $70,000, and $100,000, and letting the age at which the employee started with the firm take on values of 25, 40, and 55.

Although it was instructive to look at these different kinds of workers, it turns out that the following patterns were observed. Male and female workers differ only slightly in pension values. Wage growth steepened the pension accrual path and shifted it upward. Higher salaries shifted $P(t)$ upward except in the case of plan 4, which does not depend on final salary. The most interesting variation relates to the age of the worker at initial employment date. In what follows, we present results that emphasize this distinction.

6.2.3 Options

Equation (1) defines the appropriate value to examine to understand the effects of pensions on turnover (ignoring wages and other compensation). Once $P(t)$ is defined, it is straightforward to derive $V(t)$. The only additional ingredient is the assumed turnover propensity, 1 − F, for which we made the following assumptions:

F varies with tenure such that $F(1) = .7$, $F(2) = .8$, $F(3) = .9$, $F(4) = .95$, $F(t) = .98$ for $t > 4$. However, since the probability of turnover is also a function of age, especially after 55, we multiplied what would otherwise be the probability of continuation by $[1 - 1/(72 - \text{age at time } t)]$ so that the probability of continuation is F at 54, but falls to 0 at 71, irrespective of tenure. This assumption is admittedly arbitrary, but it captures the spirit of declining turnover rates with tenure and increasing turnover rates with age above 55.

Figure 6.2 best summarizes what can be learned from looking at $V(t)$ profiles so derived. It displays the $V(t)$ and $P(t)$ profiles for one hypothetical employee—a male, with wage growth equal to 3 percent, with a salary of $40,000 and starting age of 25 ("a" panels), and 55 ("b" panels) in each of the six plans. The most striking point is that even though the pension does not vest until year 10, so that $P(t)$ is the same and equal to zero for all years less than 10, the $V(t)$ profile is upward-sloping in that range. Thus, the value of working year 8 exceeds the value of working year 1 not only because it brings the worker closer to the vesting year, but also because the optimal pension taking year is closer.

The empirical importance of this is perhaps obvious. Suppose, for example, that one had data only on workers who had less than 10 years of tenure. If $P(t)$ were used as the dependent variable, there would be no effect of pensions on turnover in any regression. On the other hand,

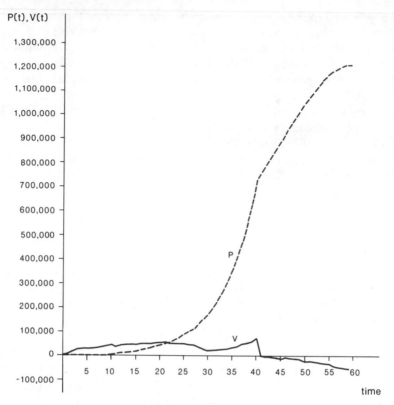

Fig. 6.2   Panel Ia. Pension Values (*P*) and Option Values (*V*) for Hypothetical Worker Hired When "Young" (Plan 1)

if $V(t)$ were used, it is expected that a negative coefficient would be
obtained since $G(R)$ increases in R. As $V(t)$ rises with t, the probability
of turnover decreases. (This should be true even holding the normal
effect of tenure on retirement constant.)

A second point that is clear from looking at the $V(t)$ profiles is that
the downward spike in $V(t)$ at the vesting year is much more important
for the old workers than for the young workers. The reason is that
young workers are likely to wait to take their pension until some year
far after 10 years. For example, for plan 1, the likely retirement date
is 40 years of tenure. For old workers, the likely retirement date is
much closer since the probability of exogenous reasons for quitting is
higher.

At the empirical level, this implies that there should be a much greater
proportion of old workers who quit immediately following the vesting
year than young workers. It would not be surprising to find no effect
of vesting on young workers since this discontinuity is so small.

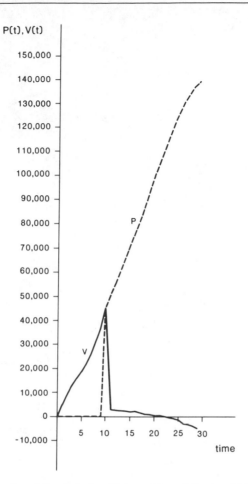

Panel Ib.   Pension Values (*P*) and Option Values (*V*) for Hypothetical Worker Hired When "Old" (Plan 1). *Figure 6.2 continues on next page.*

The third point comes from comparing the $P(t)$ profiles to the $V(t)$ profiles. For workers who begin employment with the firm when young, there is sometimes a discontinuity in the $V(t)$ profile that is not mimicked by the $P(t)$ profile. For example, in plan 1 (panel Ia), there is a very large discrete jump downward at the 40th year of tenure. The $P(t)$ profile is much smoother at that point. This implies that there should be significant retirement at $t = 40$. This would be the prediction if $V(t)$ were the independent variable, but it would appear as noise if $P(t)$ were the independent variable.

The last point is that the distinction between workers who start when old and those who start when young is lost if the $P(t)$ profile is used.

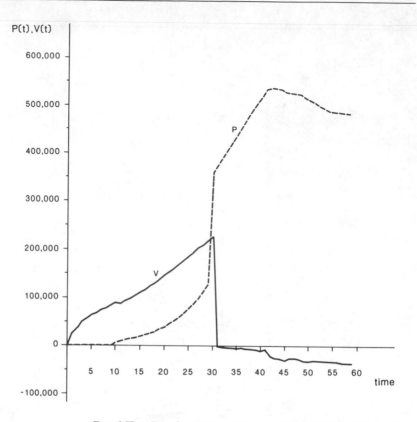

Panel IIa. Pension Values (*P*) and Option Values (*V*) for Hypothetical Worker Hired When "Young" (Plan 2)

The shape of the $P(t)$ profile is basically quite similar in the "a" panels of figure 6.2 as it is in the "b" panels. This comes back to the earlier point that the incentives to remain on the job are different for old and young hires. That is obscured by looking at the $P(t)$ profile.

6.2.4   Regressions: Turnover and Pensions

The formulation in equation (1) says that the value of working another year can be calculated from the pension stream, conditional on retirement at a given date. Given a density of reservation prices at each age/ tenure level, the higher the option value the less likely a worker is to leave in that given year. This can be modeled more rigorously as follows:

Recall that if the reservation price R at tenure t and age A is distributed as $G(R; t, A)$, then the probability that the worker chooses to continue is

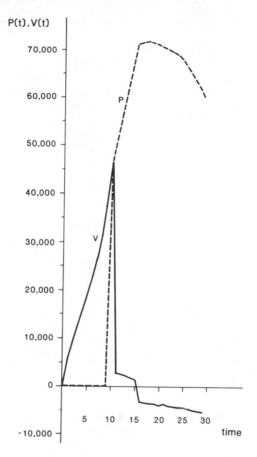

Panel IIb. Pension Values (P) and Option Values (V) for Hypothetical Worker Hired When "Old" (Plan 2). *Figure 6.2 continues on next page.*

$$G(V_t; t, A).$$

Let us parameterize G such that $G(V_t; t, A)$ can be approximated by

(2) $$G(V_t; t, A) = \exp(a_0 + a_1 V_t + a_2 t + a_3 A).$$

Having written equation (2) in this way implies that $F(t, A)$ is subsumed in G and suppressed. If N_0 workers are hired in each period, then today (1984), the tenure of those workers $t = 1984 -$ start year. The number with t years of tenure is then

(3) $$N(t) = N_0\{\exp[a_0 + a_1 V_1 + a_2 + a_3(A_{0+1})]\} \{\exp[a_0 + a_1 V_2 + a_2(2) + a_3(A_{0+2})]\} \ldots \{\exp[a_0 + a_1 V_t + a_2(t) + a_3(A_{0+t})]\},$$

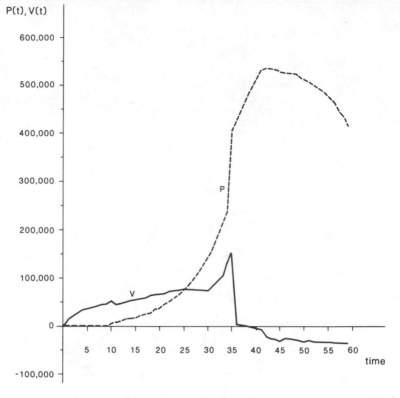

Panel IIIa. Pension Values (*P*) and Option Values (*V*) for Hypothetical Worker Hired When "Young" (Plan 3)

where A_0 is the age at which the workers are hired. (This ignores the fact that workers are hired at different ages. This is dealt with below.)

Taking logs, equation (3) can be written as

$$\ln N(t) = \ln N_0 + a_0 t + a_1 \sum_{i=1}^{t} V_i + a_2 \sum_{i=1}^{t} i + a_3 \sum_{i=1}^{t} (A_{0+t}),$$

or

$$\ln N(t) = B_0 + B_1 t + B_2 \left(\sum_{i=1}^{t} V_i \right) + B_3 \left(\sum_{i=1}^{t} i \right) + B_4 \sum_{i=1}^{t} (A_{0+t}),$$

or

(4) $$\ln N(t) = B_0 + B_1 t + B_2 X + B_3 Y + B_4 Z,$$

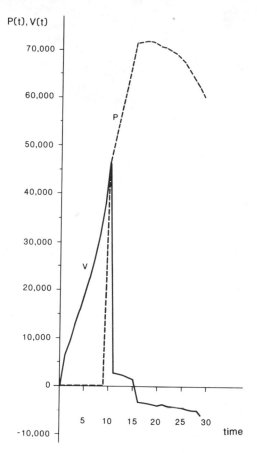

Panel IIIb. Pension Values (P) and Option Values (V) for Hypothetical Worker Hired When "Old" (Plan 3). *Figure 6.2 continues on next page.*

where

$$X \equiv \sum_{i=1}^{t} V_i, \quad Y \equiv \sum_{i=1}^{t} i, \quad Z \equiv \sum_{i=1}^{t} (A_{0+t}).$$

Equation (4) is the basic estimating equation. It allows for estimation of age-tenure specific hazard rates.

Implicit in the derivation of equation (4) is the assumption that all workers are alike in V, once t and A_0 is known. This would be true if there were no variation in salary history and if all workers began employment at the same age, A_0. Of course, in reality, these assumptions

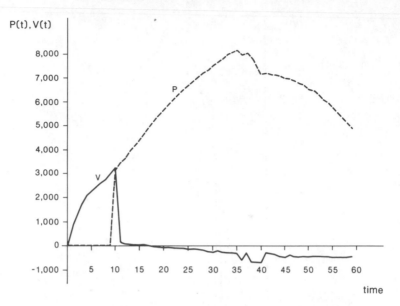

Panel IVa. Pension Values (*P*) and Option Values (*V*) for Hypothetical Worker Hired When "Young" (Plan 4)

cannot be valid. It is conceptually possible to calculate the *V* vector for every worker in the sample; we take an intermediate approach. Workers are separated by plan and by starting age. Thus, there are eighteen groups: for each plan, workers were classified as having started work between ages 20 and 35, 36 and 50, and 51 and older. The results below throw out information on the intermediate groups and focus on workers who started when they were young or old. The $N(t)$ that appears on the left-hand side of equation (4) is the number of individuals in a given plan, within a given starting age category, that have tenure of t years. For the calculation of Z, it was assumed that A_0 was 25 if the workers began when young, and that A_0 was 55 if the workers began when old. Workers were assumed to earn \$40,000 in 1984 and the wage growth rate was set at 3 percent. The discount rate for all purposes was 5 percent. The coefficient on X is then the effect of pensions on the probability of leaving. Note that, for now, nothing having to do with workers' wages is being held constant. Implicitly, it is assumed that $W_t = R_t$ for all t.

There are 366 observations, 61 for each plan. The 61 observations come from 45 tenure categories for workers who started employment at age 25 and 16 tenure categories for workers who started at age 55.

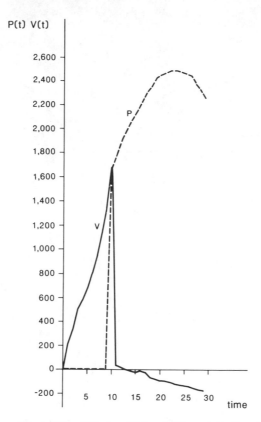

Panel IVb. Pension Values (*P*) and Option Values (*V*) for Hypothetical Worker Hired When "Old" (Plan 4). *Figure 6.2 continues on next page.*

The basic equation is reported in column 1 of table 6.1 (pp. 184–85). The variable of interest, *X,* has a negative coefficient. This is the opposite of what is expected. Higher *V(t)* should be associated with a lower propensity to leave. Comparison with other columns provides the reason for this anomalous result.

First, compare column 1 with column 2. "Old" is a dummy that equals 1 when the observation is associated with the group that started in the 50 and above category. Note that (Old)(*X*) has a positive coefficient that is more than an order of magnitude than the one on *X*. Evidently, *V* is not important for workers who start when young, but is important for those who start when old. For these old hires, *V* has an effect on turnover propensities. This is not a proper rationalization, however, because there should be no difference between old and young

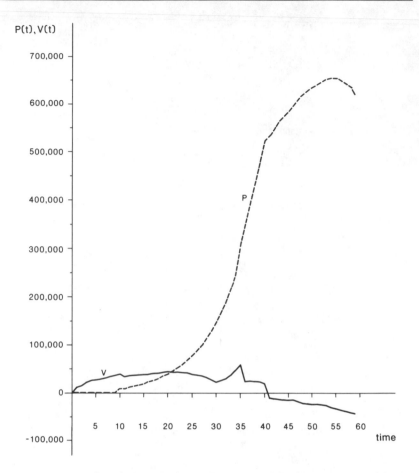

Panel Va. Pension Values (*P*) and Option Values (*V*) for Hypothetical Worker Hired When "Young" (Plan 5)

workers that is not already captured by the calculation of *V*. There are some possible explanations.

The most obvious is the selection of the wrong discount rate. Suppose that 5 percent is too low a discount rate. Then there is a variation in the *V* series for young workers that really should not be there relative to the variation for old. If a higher discount rate were used, *V* would not vary for the young and a larger coefficient on *V* would be the likely result. In fact, there exists some discount rate that would make the coefficient on (Old)(*X*) zero. All differences between old and young in turnover behavior would be captured by *V*. It is conceivable, but at least to our minds totally intractable, to simultaneously estimate the discount rate. (Note that Old by itself is simply a shifter, reflecting that

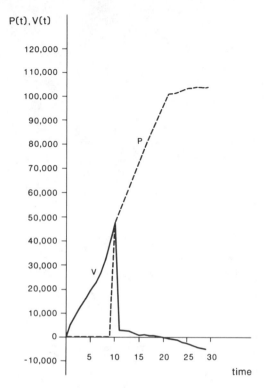

Panel Vb. Pension Values (*P*) and Option Values (*V*) for Hypothetical Worker Hired When "Old" (Plan 5). *Figure 6.2 continues on next page.*

a different number of individuals get hired in when old than when young. That is, N_0 for old hires is not the same as N_0 for young hires.)

A second, and perhaps more important, factor in the explanation of the negative coefficient on *V* is that the equation estimated in column 1 ignores wages altogether. To take account of this, we must allow for wages and wage growth to shift the relationship in two ways. First, firms that pay higher average wages or offer more wage growth may have a different number of new hires, N_0. This may be because of a trade-off of fewer numbers of higher quality workers, or other factors. Second, given that the worker has joined the firm, wage levels and wage growth have an effect on retaining the worker. These shift *G* and are parameterized by adding *W* (wage level) and WG (wage growth) to equation (2). This implies that $(t)(W)$ and $(t)(WG)$ belong in the estimating equation. These terms really relate to the average net difference between W_t and R_t. This is not quite correct, however. A more complete approach would build the parameterization of *R* into *G* directly. Then

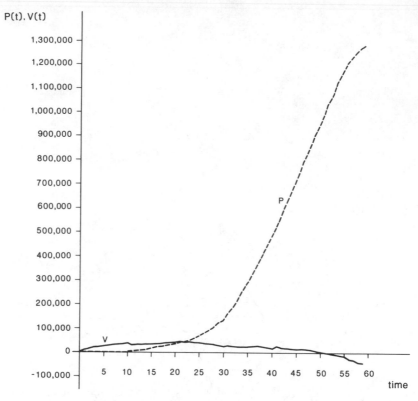

Panel VIa. Pension Values (*P*) and Option Values (*V*) for Hypothetical Worker Hired When "Young" (Plan 6)

the discount rate and all coefficients could be estimated simultaneously. Given the tentative nature of our data, we have chosen not to undertake this difficult estimation.

Because of data problems, the wages for workers in plan 4 (a pattern plan that is independent of salary) are not reported correctly. As a result, all those 61 observations are dropped. The equation estimated in column 2 was reestimated without these 61 observations. These results are contained in column 4 and do not differ substantially from those of column 2. Column 5 reports the results when the wage variables are incorporated. (Wage growth for each plan was estimated in the usual manner.) As can be seen from the coefficient on $(t)(W)$, higher wage firms are less likely to lose their workers. The sign on V for young workers becomes positive, but is still statistically different from that for older workers.

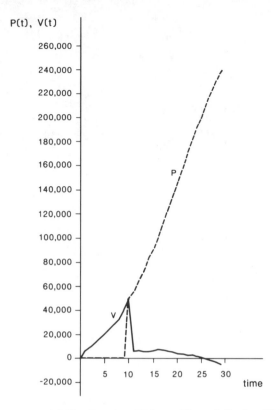

Panel VIb. Pension Values (*P*) and Option Values (*V*) for Hypothetical Worker Hired When "Old" (Plan 6).

To assess the importance of the effect of *V* on turnover, differentiate $(1 - G)$ with the respect to *V*. Estimates from column 5 are used. The elasticity is 2.16 so that a 10 percent increase in *V* reduces the probability of turnover (for old workers) by 22 percent (evaluated at the means). The estimated probability of retention is .96 (at the means). What is perhaps more instructive is to compare what the probability of retention would be if *V* were zero. Under these circumstances, the retention rate would be about .91. This amounts to a doubling of the turnover rate (from 4 percent per year to 9 percent per year) and suggests the possibility of an important effect.

The estimated retention rate seems quite high. There are at least two possible explanations. First, these firms all have pension plans and may have atypical turnover rates as a result. Second, the process may not be stationary. For example, suppose that employment in these firms were declining over time. Then more workers would have been hired

Table 6.1   Estimation of Equation (4) (Dependent Variable = N in 1984)

Independent Variable	(1)	(2)	(3)	(4)	(5)	(6)
					$N = 305$	
Constant $= \ln N_0$	1.96 (.15)	2.87 (.18)	2.92 (.18)	2.94 (.20)	4.27 (.52)	1.96
W = average wage					-7.9×10^{-5} (1.2×10^{-5})	
t (coefficient $= a_0$)	.21 (.02)	.055 (.036)	.043 (.039)	.039 (.041)	.019 (.042)	.204 (.018)
WG (average amount of wage growth)					13.2 (6.9)	
$X \equiv \Sigma\, V_i$ (coefficient $= a_1$)	-1.75×10^{-7} (8.34×10^{-7})	-1.57×10^{-7} (7.78×10^{-7})		-2.47×10^{-7} (9.8×10^{-7})	1.57×10^{-7} (2.4×10^{-7})	
$Y \equiv \Sigma\, i$ (coefficient $= a_2$)	.00033 (.00082)					
$Z \equiv \Sigma(A_{0+i})$ (coefficient $= a_3$)	$-.0056$ (.0004)	$-.0024$ (.0007)	$-.0024$ (.0008)	$-.0019$ (.0008)	$-.0015$ (.0007)	$-.0055$ (.0004)
Old (dummy $= 1$ if observation from 55 year old group)		-1.88 (.25)	-1.64 (.25)	-1.90 (.28)	-1.98 (.25)	

	(1)	(2)	(3)	(4)	(5)	(6)
(Old)(X)	3.34×10^{-6} (1.09×10^{-6})		2.53×10^{-6} (1.34×10^{-6})		2.90×10^{-6} (1.18×10^{-6})	
$P = P(T)$		3.84×10^{-7} (4.9×10^{-7})				
(Old)(P)		8.02×10^{-6} (3.64×10^{-6})				
(t)(W)					4.69×10^{-7} (5.7×10^{-7})	
(t)(WG)					$-.416$ $(.48)$	
ΔP						4.41×10^{-6} (3.01×10^{-6})
R^2	.40	.46	.48	.47	.60	.39
SEE	1.06	1.00	.98	.96	.84	.39

NOTE: Standard errors in parentheses.
Number of observations = 366.

20 years ago than 10 years ago. This makes it appear that turnover rates are low because there is a large number of workers in the $t = 20$ category relative to those in the $t = 10$ category.

There are some other interesting results that come from table 6.1. As expected, the coefficient on Z (age) is negative and statistically significant, but not important in terms of magnitude. There must be some nonlinearity in this relationship that we have not explored. It is likely that, at young ages, increases in age actually reduce the probability of turnover, but at old ages the reverse is true. The effect of tenure on turnover rates cannot be discerned in these data independent of the pension effect. Column 1 reveals that the coefficient on Y is small and unimportant.

It is interesting to compare the "naive" approach, which uses P as the relevant variable, with the more sophisticated approach that uses V. Columns 3 and 6 do that. In column 3, P and $(Old)(P)$ are entered as independent variables and X and $(Old)(X)$ are deleted. They behave in a way similar to that of X and $(Old)(X)$. This is not suprising because the correlation of P with X is .70. However, the interpretation of P is problematic. Do we expect a negative or positive coefficient on P? When P is high, should workers work that year or take the pension?

A better alternative specification enters $P(t) - P(t - 1)$, represented by $\triangle P$ in table 6.1, as the independent variable. This should have a clear positive effect on the number of workers in a given year. More workers should be willing to stay when the change in the pension value associated with working another year is high. (Note that there is no income effect unless the year is worked, so a positive effect is necessary.) Of course, this obscures the fact that there is a greater pension value to working year 9 than in year 1, which is captured by V. Again, V and the change in P, $\triangle P$, are correlated at .4, so even if $P(t) - P(t - 1)$ were totally inappropriate, it would pick up the effect of V. In column 6, the change in P does have an effect in the right direction. (When both $\triangle P$ and X are entered, interacted with Old, $(Old)(X)$ matters whereas $(Old)[P(t) - P(t - 1)]$ does not. Both $\triangle P$ and X enter significantly, but are small. These results are not shown in table 6.1.)

One final problem that should be mentioned is that males and females are mixed in this analysis to obtain a large enough number of observations. Since they have different earnings and experience patterns, future research will separate males from females.

6.3   Conclusions and Summary

We have attempted to investigate the effects of pensions on worker turnover using a newly constructed data set, which contains microdata on actual employees under six different actual pension plans. An important distinction is made between $P(t)$, the *pension value* after t years of service, and the *option value, $V(t)$,* which we argue is the more appropriate value to examine to understand the effects of pensions on turnover.

The paper then calculates and contrasts the profiles of these values for hypothetical employees under the six different plans and some implications are drawn from these profiles. The analysis demonstrates that the effects of vesting are more important for workers who were old at the hiring date than for workers who were young at the hiring date. Although the $P(t)$ profile is flat prior to vesting, the $V(t)$ profile is more continuous. The $V(t)$ profile predicts different turnover behavior than the $P(t)$ profile.

The preliminary results of the actual effect of these (more appropriate) option values on turnover are presented. Assuming a stationary process, these results show that a 10 percent increase in the option value reduces the probability of turnover for old workers by 22 percent. Turnover rates are predicted to be twice as high for workers without pensions as for those with the average pension (a change from 4 percent to 9 percent per year). Finally, we investigate empirically the different implications for turnover of the two measures of pension values.

The results presented here should be regarded as tentative, at best. The data that we currently have do not provide any information on individuals who left the firm. Thus, all inferences about turnover must be drawn from an examination of the tenure distribution of current employees. In future research, after the required data have been obtained, that defect will be remedied. We have also taken a number of shortcuts. A full nonlinear model, which yields the discount factor and hazard function simultaneously, was described, but not estimated. Nevertheless, the fact that such strong effects of pensions on turnover are obtained suggests that this is an area well worth pursuing.

References

Burtless, Gary, and Jerome Hausman. 1980. Individual retirement decisions under an employer provided pension plan and Social Security. Massachusetts Institute of Technology. Mimeo.

Frant, Howard L., and Herman B. Leonard. 1987. State and local government pension plans: Labor economics or political economy? In *Public Sector Payrolls,* edited by David A. Wise. Chicago: University of Chicago Press.

Hausman, J., and David Wise. 1985. Social Security, health status, and retirement. In *Pensions, Labor, and Individual Choice,* edited by David A. Wise. Chicago: University of Chicago Press.

Kotlikoff, Laurence J., and David A. Wise. 1987. The incentive effects of private pension plans. In *Issues in Pension Economics,* edited by Zvi Bodie, John Shoven, and David A. Wise. Chicago: University of Chicago Press.

Lazear, Edward P. 1982. Severance pay, pensions, and efficient mobility, NBER Working Paper no. 854. Cambridge, Mass.: National Bureau of Economic Research.

———. 1983a. Incentive effects of pensions. NBER Working Paper no. 1126. Cambridge, Mass.: National Bureau of Economic Research.

———. 1983b. Pensions as severance pay. In *Financial aspects of the United States pension system,* edited by Zvi Bodie and John Shoven. Chicago: University of Chicago Press.

Mitchell, Olivia S., and Gary S. Fields. 1984. The economics of retirement behavior. *Journal of Labor Economics* 2 (January): 84–105.

Wolf, Doug, and Frank Levy. 1984. Pension coverage, pension vesting, and the distribution of job tenures. In *Retirement and economic behavior,* edited by Henry J. Aaron and Gary Burtless. Washington, D.C.: The Brookings Institution.

Comment   Michael D. Hurd

Defined benefit pension plans typically induce great year-to-year variation in the implicit compensation for a year's work. For example, the value of a pension conditional on separation can jump from zero to a substantial value in the year of vesting. Many previous investigators have viewed this as a spike in compensation and have studied its effect on turnover. The authors perform a useful service by pointing out that the value to a worker of a defined benefit pension plan is not simply the change in the present value conditional on separation. The value will depend on the shape of the pension plan over all possible retirement years. For example, even though a worker may not be vested, the plan becomes more valuable each year until vesting because the worker is a year closer to the vesting date. The authors attempt to quantify the change in value by what they call the option value of the pension plan. The option value is supposed to represent, as far as pension accrual is concerned, the reward from a year of work. To calculate the option value of work in year t, one first finds the retirement date which maximizes the expected present value in year t dollars under the assumption that the worker works during year t. The option value of the plan is this expected present value less the expected present value of the plan given retirement at $t - 1$. The option value has the desirable feature

Michael D. Hurd is a professor of economics at the State University of New York at Stony Brook and a research associate of the National Bureau of Economic Research.

of imputing a positive value to the plan even before vesting. The authors proceed to use the option value to explain the probability of turnover.

The term "option value" is somewhat unfortunate here. It suggests that the worker would be willing to pay at a maximum the option value to work another year. A simplified example shows that is not the case. Suppose the worker is not vested, and that the inflation and interest rates are zero. Then the option value is just the sum of the pension payments should the worker retire at the date when that sum is maximum. But that sum is not what the worker would be willing to pay to work another year, because the worker must work all the future years until the retirement date. Furthermore, if leisure has value, workers may not choose retirement at the date of maximum pension value; then, variations in maximum pension value will be irrelevant for study of turnover. The problem, as revealed in the authors' figure 6.1, is that the budget constraint is nonlinear, probably with nonconvex regions. Choice of retirement date then depends on the global properties of both the budget constraint and the indifference curves. It is simply not possible to summarize the situation with a single number such as the option value. The only internally consistent estimation method we have was developed in the labor supply literature; examples are cited by Lazear and Moore. The authors argue, however, that those methods, based on a global comparison of utility in a diagram like figure 6.1, are not adequate. Their first objection is that the model cannot allow for uncertainty. I do not see the force of this objection, as one could always specify that the budget constraint is offered with some probability. Their second objection is that the model is static, not allowing for interruptions in work. I believe this objection is rather weak. For example, to analyze retirement one could redefine the arguments of the lifetime utility function to be rest-of-lifetime income and leisure after the last reentry into the labor force. Their last objection is that the worker's decision is not simply whether to work or not, but involves choosing over several jobs. But several job choices can be included by constructing budget sets for each job and allowing the global utility-maximizing choice to be made. In that the option value approach evaluates the budget constraint at just one point, whereas the budget constraint should be evaluated to find the global maximum, I believe the approach of the authors is not the best to understand job quitting.

Even if the option value were the appropriate variable to explain the probability of quitting, the data available to the authors make it almost impossible to estimate the relationship. To understand how quits are affected, one needs observations on the leavers and the stayers, except under special circumstances. In these data, only the stayers are observed. If everything were static, estimation might be possible: essentially the original size and composition of the oldest cohorts are deduced from the size and composition of the younger cohorts. But there are 45 tenure categories, which means that the rates of hiring by age would have had to have been constant for 45 years, from 1939 to 1984; this seems unlikely in a growing economy. Without such stability, the number of people in each tenure category can reflect the growth or decline of the company rather than the reaction of the cohorts to the pension plans. Furthermore, even if the rate of hiring by age were steady over such a long period, the estimation method requires that the structure of the pension program remain the same over those years: such stability is necessary if one is to use the pension structure in 1984 to understand turnover rates over past years. Without information on the stability of the pension structure over past years, I am not sure we can have much confidence in an approach that requires it.

In my view, the data could be used in other ways. It should be possible to construct some simple tables which reveal facts about how tenure varies with provisions of the pension plans. For example, if a plan heavily penalizes work after 30 years of service, a table showing the extent of work past 30 years would give us an idea of the importance of that provision. Such tables would provide guidance in modeling and hypothesis testing which could be carried out on data more suited for turnover studies.

In summary, I think the authors have pointed the way toward a better modeling of the influence of pensions on turnover; yet, the data they have are not detailed enough to quantify the effect. Rather than producing some estimates that are difficult to interpret, I would prefer cross-tabulations and tables that describe the data and, in particular, how the age and tenure distributions vary by pension plan.

List of Contributors

B. Douglas Bernheim
Department of Economics
Stanford University
452 Encina Hall
Stanford, CA 94305

Zvi Bodie
School of Management
Boston University
704 Commonwealth Avenue
Boston, MA 02215

Michael J. Boskin
National Bureau of Economic
    Research
204 Junipero Serra Boulevard
Stanford, CA 94305

Gary Burtless
The Brookings Institution
1775 Massachusetts Avenue, NW
Washington, DC 20036

Benjamin M. Friedman
Department of Economics
Harvard University
127 Littauer Center
Cambridge, MA 02138

Thomas A. Gustafson
U.S. Department of Health and Hu-
    man Services
HCFA/OLP

Hubert Humphrey Building
Room 339H
200 Independence Avenue, SW
Washington, DC 20201

R. Glenn Hubbard
Department of Economics
Northwestern University
Andersen Hall
2003 Sheridan Road
Evanston, IL 60201

Michael D. Hurd
Department of Economics
State University of New York at
    Stony Brook
Stony Brook, NY 11794

Laurence J. Kotlikoff
National Bureau of Economic
    Research
1050 Massachusetts Avenue
Cambridge, MA 02138

Edward P. Lazear
Graduate School of Business
University of Chicago
1101 East 58th Street
Chicago, IL 60637

Alan J. Marcus
School of Management
Boston University

704 Commonwealth Avenue
Boston, MA 02215

Robert C. Merton
Sloan School of Management
Massachusetts Institute of
    Technology
50 Memorial Drive, E52-453
Cambridge, MA 02139

Robert L. Moore
Department of Economics
Occidental College
Los Angeles, CA 90041

John B. Shoven
Department of Economics
Stanford University
Encina Hall, 4th Floor
Stanford, CA 94305

Eugene Steuerle
Deputy Assistant Secretary (Tax
    Analysis)

U.S. Department of the Treasury
1500 Pennsylvania Avenue, N.W.
Room 3108, Main Treasury
Washington, DC 20220

Steven F. Venti
Department of Economics
Dartmouth College
Hanover, NH 03755

Mark Warshawsky
Capital Markets Section
Division of Research and Statistics
Board of Governors
Federal Reserve Bank
Washington, DC 20551

David A. Wise
John F. Kennedy School of
    Government
Harvard University
79 Kennedy Street
Cambridge, MA 02138

Author Index

Subject Index

Age: age-consumption profiles, 66–68; age-tenure specific hazard rates equation, 176–77; annuity pricing and, 64–73, 78–79; pension values and, 143, 163, 169–74, 187; retirement income and, 5, 133; value of working additional years and, 179, 189–90; worker turnover and, 174, 186. *See also* Life expectancies
Aged. *See* Elderly
Ameritech Corporation, 93
Annuities: actuarially fair pricing, 64–74, 78–79; adverse selection problem, 3, 73, 79; average premium, 55; bequests and, 3, 53, 61, 64–73, 81; cost per unit of pay-off, 60; deferred nominal life, 141; demand for, 3, 66; government bonds and, 81; individual life, 55–60; individual savings for, 1–3; inflation and, 3, 82; interest rates and, 55; life-cycle models and, 82; life expectancies and, 54, 57–58; load-factor effects, 3, 59, 64–74, 78–79; lump sum value of, 66; market access value, 66; optimal purchase values, 60–64; premiums charged vs. fair values, 58–59; private market, 64; profit and, 53; saving behavior and, 3, 53–83; short sales of, 54; Social Security and, 68–69, 73, 78 n. 1, 80, 82 n. 7; wealth transferability and, 78

Assets: dominated, 60; leveraged physical, 100; pension contribution ratio, 87; pension plan composition, 99; transferability, 78; valuation vs. interest rates, 99–100; valuation equation, 108

Backloading, 143, 146–47, 159 n. 3
Bequests: annuity purchases and, 3, 53, 61, 64–73, 81; bonds and, 69; current consumption and, 64; family dependency and, 61; joy of giving motive, 76 n. 18; nonaltruistic (manipulative), 74; saving and, 71–72; unintentional, 59; valuation of, 69; wealthy individuals and, 81 n. 6
Best's Key Rating Guide: Property-Casualty, 59
Bonds: annuity yield differentials, 81; bequest motives and, 69; direct placement securities vs., 57; interest rate effect on, 99

Canada: Consumer Price Index, 37; marginal tax rate in, 30, 36; tax deferred savings in, 10–11, 48
Capital gains taxes, 85
Career average earnings: income replacement rates and, 132; retirement income and, 119–27
Carnegie Commission Survey, 10
Cat on a Hot Tin Roof (Williams), 82